# Innovation, Technology, and Knowledge Management

**Series Editor**

Elias G. Carayannis, George Washington University, Washington, WA, USA

This series highlights emerging research and practice at the dynamic intersection of innovation, technology, and knowledge management, where individuals, organizations, industries, regions, and nations are harnessing creativity and invention to achieve and sustain growth. Volumes in the series explore the impact of innovation at the "macro" (economies, markets), "meso" (industries, firms), and "micro" levels (teams, individuals), drawing from such related disciplines as finance, organizational psychology, R&D, science policy, information systems, and strategy, with the underlying theme that in order for innovation to be useful it must involve the sharing and application of knowledge.

This book series is indexed in Scopus.

Yasin Hajizadeh • Alexander Poth • Andreas Riel
Editors

# Building Cloud Software Products

Innovation, Technology, and Product
Management

Springer

*Editors*
Yasin Hajizadeh
Amazon, Austin, TX, USA

Andreas Riel (iD)
G-SCOP Laboratory
Grenoble INP - Université Grenoble Alpes
Grenoble, France

Alexander Poth (iD)
Institute of Computer Science, Software
Systems Engineering
University of Hildesheim
Hildesheim, Germany

ISSN 2197-5698          ISSN 2197-5701    (electronic)
Innovation, Technology, and Knowledge Management
ISBN 978-3-031-92183-4          ISBN 978-3-031-92184-1    (eBook)
https://doi.org/10.1007/978-3-031-92184-1

This Springer imprint is published by the registered company Springer Nature Switzerland AG
The registered company address is: Gewerbestrasse 11, 6330 Cham, Switzerland

If disposing of this product, please recycle the paper.

# Series Preface

The Springer book series *Innovation, Technology, and Knowledge Management* was launched in March 2008 as a forum and intellectual, scholarly "podium" for global/local, transdisciplinary, transsectoral, public–private, and leading/"bleeding"-edge ideas, theories, and perspectives on these topics.

The book series is accompanied by the Springer *Journal of the Knowledge Economy*, which was launched in 2009 with the same editorial leadership.

The series showcases provocative views that diverge from the current "conventional wisdom," that are properly grounded in theory and practice, and that consider the concepts of *robust competitiveness*,[1] *sustainable entrepreneurship*,[2] and *democratic capitalism*,[3] central to its philosophy and objectives. More specifically, the aim of this series is to highlight emerging research and practice at the dynamic intersection of these fields, where individuals, organizations, industries, regions, and nations are harnessing creativity and invention to achieve and sustain growth.

---

[1] We define *sustainable entrepreneurship* as the creation of viable, profitable, and scalable firms. Such firms engender the formation of self-replicating and mutually enhancing innovation networks and knowledge clusters (innovation ecosystems), leading toward robust competitiveness (E.G. Carayannis, *International Journal of Innovation and Regional Development* 1(3), 235–254, 2009).

[2] We understand *robust competitiveness* to be a state of economic being and becoming that avails systematic and defensible "unfair advantages" to the entities that are part of the economy. Such competitiveness is built on mutually complementary and reinforcing low-. medium- and high-technology and public and private sector entities (government agencies. private firms. universities. and nongovernmental organizations) (E.G. Carayannis. *International Journal of Innovation and Regional Development* 1(3), 235–254, 2009).

[3] The concepts of *robust competitiveness* and *sustainable entrepreneurship* are pillars of a regime that we call *"democratic capitalism* (as opposed to "popular or casino capitalism") in which real opportunities for education and economic prosperity are available to all, especially—but not only—younger people. These are the direct derivative of a collection of top-down policies as well as bottom-up initiatives (including strong research and development policies and funding, but going beyond these to include the development of innovation networks and knowledge clusters across regions and sectors) (E.G. Carayannis and A. Kaloudis, *Japan Economic Currents*, p. 6–10 January 2009).

Books that are part of the series explore the impact of innovation at the "macro" (economies, markets), "meso" (industries, firms), and "micro" levels (teams, individuals), drawing from such related disciplines as finance, organizational psychology, research and development, science policy, information systems, and strategy, with the underlying theme that for innovation to be useful it must involve sharing and application of knowledge.

Some of the key anchoring concepts of the series are outlined in the figure below and the definitions that follow (all definitions are from E.G. Carayannis and D.F.J. Campbell, *International Journal of Technology Management*, 46, 3–4, 2009).

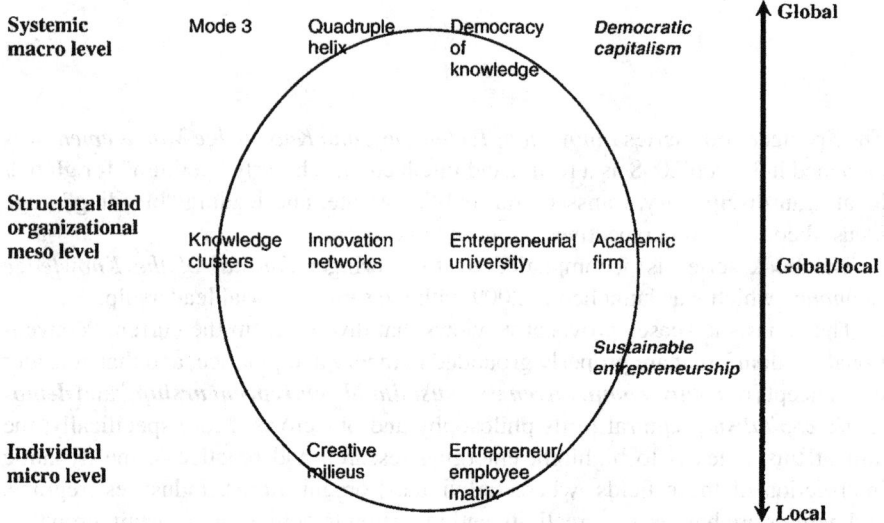

Conceptual profile of the series *Innovation, Technology, and Knowledge Management*

- "Mode 3" Systems Approach for Knowledge Creation, Diffusion, and Use: "Mode 3" is a multilateral, multinodal, multimodal, and multilevel systems approach to the conceptualization, design, and management of real and virtual, "knowledge-stock" and "knowledge-flow," modalities that catalyze, accelerate, and support the creation, diffusion, sharing, absorption, and use of co-specialized knowledge assets. "Mode 3" is based on a system-theoretic perspective of socio-economic, political, technological, and cultural trends and conditions that shape the coevolution of knowledge with the "knowledge-based and knowledge-driven, global/local economy and society."
- Quadruple Helix: Quadruple helix, in this context, means to add to the triple helix of government, university, and industry a "fourth helix" that we identify as the "media-based and culture-based public." This fourth helix associates with "media," "creative industries," "culture," "values," "lifestyles," "art," and perhaps also the notion of the "creative class."

- Innovation Networks: Innovation networks are real and virtual infrastructures and infratechnologies that serve to nurture creativity, trigger invention, and catalyze innovation in a public and/or private domain context (for instance, government–university–industry public–private research and technology development coopetitive partnerships).
- Knowledge Clusters: Knowledge clusters are agglomerations of cospecialized, mutually complementary, and reinforcing knowledge assets in the form of "knowledge stocks" and "knowledge flows" that exhibit self-organizing, learning-driven, dynamically adaptive competences and trends in the context of an open systems perspective.
- Twenty-First Century Innovation Ecosystem: A twenty-first century innovation ecosystem is a multilevel, multimodal, multinodal, and multiagent system of systems. The constituent systems consist of innovation metanetworks (networks of innovation networks and knowledge clusters) and knowledge metaclusters (clusters of innovation networks and knowledge clusters) as building blocks and organized in a self-referential or chaotic fractal knowledge and innovation architecture (Carayannis 2001), which in turn constitute agglomerations of human, social, intellectual, and financial capital stocks and flows as well as cultural and technological artifacts and modalities, continually coevolving, cospecializing, and cooperating. These innovation networks and knowledge clusters also form, reform, and dissolve within diverse institutional, political, technological, and socioeconomic domains, including government, university, industry, and nongovernmental organizations and involving information and communication technologies, biotechnologies, advanced materials, nanotechnologies, and next-generation energy technologies.

*Who is this book series published for?* The book series addresses a diversity of audiences in different settings:

1. *Academic communities:* Academic communities worldwide represent a core group of readers. This follows from the theoretical/conceptual interest of the book series to influence academic discourses in the fields of knowledge, also carried by the claim of a certain saturation of academia with the current concepts and the postulate of a window of opportunity for new or at least additional concepts. Thus, it represents a key challenge for the series to exercise a certain impact on discourses in academia. In principle, all academic communities that are interested in knowledge (knowledge and innovation) could be tackled by the book series. The inter-disciplinary (transdisciplinary) nature of the book series underscores that the scope of the book series is not limited a priori to a specific basket of disciplines. From a radical viewpoint, one could create the hypothesis that there is no discipline where knowledge is of no importance.
2. *Decision makers—private/academic entrepreneurs and public (governmental, subgovernmental) actors:* Two different groups of decision makers are being addressed simultaneously: (1) private entrepreneurs (firms, commercial firms, academic firms) and academic entrepreneurs (universities), interested in optimizing knowledge management and in developing heterogeneously composed

knowledge-based research networks; and (2) public (governmental, subgovern-mental) actors that are interested in optimizing and further developing their poli-cies and policy strategies that target knowledge and innovation. One purpose of public *knowledge and innovation policy* is to enhance the performance and com-petitiveness of advanced economies.

3. *Decision makers in general:* Decision makers are systematically being supplied with crucial information on how to optimize knowledge-referring and knowledge-enhancing decision-making. The nature of this "crucial information" is concep-tual as well as empirical (case-study-based). Empirical information highlights practical examples and points toward practical solutions (perhaps remedies), conceptual information offers the advantage of further-driving and further-carrying tools of understanding. Different groups of addressed decision makers could be decision makers in private firms and multinational corporations, respon-sible for the knowledge portfolio of companies; knowledge and knowledge man-agement consultants; globalization experts, focusing on the internationalization of research and development, science and technology, and innovation; experts in university/business research networks; and political scientists, economists, and business professionals.

4. *Interested global readership.* Finally, the Springer book series addresses a whole global readership, composed of members who are generally interested in knowl-edge and innovation. The global readership could partially coincide with the communities as described above ("academic communities," "decision makers"), but could also refer to other constituencies and groups.

Washington, WA, USA                                                        Elias G. Carayannis

# Overview

- Cloud product development and service delivery in a nutshell
- Holistic view from product management to sustainability engineering
- Explains strategies and presents implementation practices

# About This Book

Cloud-native approaches become essential in IT and OT product development. Cloud-native is more than using the newest cutting-edge services from hyperscalers. Building cloud products benefits from a holistic approach beyond focusing on an isolated cloud paradigm. The book concentrates on a holistic view to empower cloud product and service teams to consider the relevant aspects for their long-term success.

Topics and Features

- build a specific product and service vision and refine it to a roadmap
- establish a life-cycle view: focus the right aspects per life-cycle phase
- elaborate a sustainable set of requirements from UX to energy footprint
- overview of selected key technologies and practical adoption approaches

The book combines advanced research perspectives from academia such as from Universities of Calgary, Grenoble and Lucerne with practical industry learnings for companies such as Amazon, SAP, Villeroy-Boch and Volkswagen.

# Contents

# Contents

# List of Figures

# List of Tables

# Introduction

We, the editors' team, noticed that a lot of cloud products and services are developed. We also think that much more existing IT services are moving to the cloud and new services and products will be built cloud-native in the future. Also, we saw that often cloud products and services are not designed and developed by cloud-natives. Many of these experts often come from other IT areas and also more and more of them coming from outside the IT. A typical non-IT area for example is OT with the objective to cloudify industrial systems with IoT initiatives etc.

We try to offer a holistic view about the cloud product and service topic to empower the reads to adopt presented ideas, concepts and methods for successful cloud products and services with a high-quality to the users.

The focus of the book is to address the different aspects which are relevant to design, build and run cloud products and services. The book starts by reflecting strategic aspects. Considering the user experience as an early design element, also fosters thinking in a product life-cycle to focus on the right aspects at the right time, and presents selected technologies which are often used in cloud setups such as blockchain and AI, too. However, all focus areas are handled on a level that no specific IT or technology knowledge is needed to follow.

The book should help cloud beginners to get a holistic overview about what aspects should be considered during the design and development of cloud products and services. For these readers it can be useful to read the entire book in the presented chapter order. Furthermore, the book also can be helpful for more advanced cloud service and product managers and developers to go deeper into selected topic areas. Therefore, the book is designed to support reading only selected chapters which may have a topic area of interest within the current life-cycle phase of the cloud service.

Introduction

# Chapter 1
# Motivation and Chapter Overview

Yasin Hajizadeh, Alexander Poth ⓘ, and Andreas Riel

**Abstract** Cloud computing has become omnipresent in our daily lives, both in the private and professional domains. In the context of the data age and Industry 4.0 and 5.0, this trend is not going to decline. With increasingly many products and services driven by data and the cloud, there is an evident need to rethink traditional product and service designs, including their underlying processes. At the same time, the environmental footprint of IT, and more particularly data centers, has started becoming a driver for cloud service providers (CSPs) to integrate their IT infrastructure's environmental impact factors such as greenhouse gas emissions in their KPIs. This book covers various topics around these challenges in the form of self-contained chapters. The objective of this introductory chapter is to motivate and summarize each book chapter to help readers navigate and select.

Y. Hajizadeh
Amazon, Austin, TX, USA

A. Poth
Institute of Computer Science, Software Systems Engineering, University of Hildesheim, Hildesheim, Germany
e-mail: poth@uni-hildesheim.de

A. Riel (✉)
G-SCOP Laboratory, Grenoble INP - Université Grenoble Alpes, Grenoble, France
e-mail: andreas.riel@grenoble-inp.fr

© The Author(s), under exclusive license to Springer Nature
Switzerland AG 2025
Y. Hajizadeh et al. (eds.), *Building Cloud Software Products*,
Innovation, Technology, and Knowledge Management,
https://doi.org/10.1007/978-3-031-92184-1_1

## 1.1  The Motivation: Cloud Computing

Cloud computing has become omnipresent in our daily lives, both in the private and professional domains. In the context of the data age and Industry 4.0 and 5.0, this trend is not going to decline. Cloud characteristics such as cost efficiency, flexibility and scalability, maintainability, enhanced security, increased compliance, remote work and digital transformation, big data and analytics, and others are at the origin of this success. The latter does not come without downsides, though. The environmental footprint of IT, and more particularly data centers, has been growing at a tremendous rate and has started becoming a driver for cloud service providers (CSPs) to integrate their IT infrastructure's environmental impact factors such as greenhouse gas emissions in their KPIs. Also, this trend will not cease with the rapidly increasing adoption of artificial intelligence technologies in almost every domain.

With increasingly many products and services driven by data and the cloud, it becomes evident to rethink traditional product and service designs, as well as their underlying process in that they integrate cloud characteristics in a way to maximize added value derived from those. To provide an outstanding example, the data-driven culture of most technology companies necessitates that a product manager must be well-versed in data science. Implementing algorithms and workflows in product management can help speed up repetitive tasks, aid in ideation, and support quick and high-quality decision-making. For example, the newly emerging generative AI field and foundation models (FMs) can be a game-changing tool for product managers. Generative AI has been used to transform businesses and industries by aiding in generating new content, media, code, designs, and ideas. Additionally, traditional data science workflows and techniques such as data manipulation, exploratory analysis, and predictive analysis are often used by product managers to understand and predict product adoption metrics and trends and understand patterns in customer feedback and competitive intelligence.

In this context, the traditional DevOps model has been extended to BizDevOps to combine elements from business, development, and operations to align technology with business objectives in a more integrated and collaborative way. Business leaders, product owners, and other key business roles are increasingly getting involved in planning, feedback, and decision-making, which has become an important success factor in a world of software- and cloud-driven product and service offers.

## 1.2  Summary of Chapters

This book covers various topics around cloud management and selected technologies driven by cloud computing such as machine learning and blockchain. In this book, we aim to balance the academic and industrial views on cloud product management. The following introduction motivates the chapters from an overview perspective. The chapters themselves are self-contained so you can read them separately and independently depending on your specific focus topic on your cloud journey.

## 1.3 Cloud Service Strategy

The setup of a cloud service is a nontrivial topic. It needs expertise and time to design, develop, and deliver a cloud service to customers. To avoid resource-wasting initiatives, building a strategy and refining it to implementation units of delivery increments to serve users is good practice. The refinement is based on the development of a cloud strategy. Cloud product characteristics and market positioning for the specific cloud services refine the cloud strategy. Then the service abstraction level needs to be defined such as platform as a service or software as a service—this defines on which level the own cloud service is built and what is offered. The service offer has to consider the customer and provider views to ensure that technology and market risks are considered adequate. Furthermore, a vision and mission are defined to keep the team around the cloud service aligned, e.g., developers and operating. The specific product strategy is derived. Also, a customer binding approach is selected and integrated into the service design and its market offer. For an attractive offer, a price and value evaluation is needed. This evaluation leads to a pricing policy. The policy is the base to derive price levels for, e.g., free tier or feature packages.

To delve deeper into the topic, read the chapter titled "Cloud Product Strategy, Vision, Market Positioning, and Pricing."

## 1.4 Strategy and Roadmap

As the strategy and roadmap are crucial to ensure shippable increments of a service, these aspects are reflected in more detail. We distinguish between the product and portfolio roadmap to ensure that a specific product fits into the entire portfolio of service offers. The technology roadmap defines which technology is part of the service, namely, the portfolio, to ensure that adequate skills and knowledge are available or components can be used. Then the roadmap focuses on features and use cases to ensure that the increments fit together and deliver value to the users, that is, customers (existing cases in which the user and customer—the person who pays—are different). In cases of different options of feature and use case delivery scenario building can help to identify realistic options. Prioritization can help to select options and build a roadmap for implementation.

To delve deeper into the topic, read the chapter titled "Strategy and Roadmaps."

## 1.5  Technology: Machine Learning Adoption Approach

Machine learning is a technology for handling information in large and complex data. Machine learning is often powered by clouds and becomes itself part of higher cloud services. Currently, cloud providers offer machine learning services to analyze data in workloads or to be embedded into higher-order cloud services. The integration into end-to-end processes needs some reflection and analysis to ensure the expected added value and benefits. Depending on the specific processes' facilitation objective, one or more machine learning approaches should be selected. Furthermore, prerequisites have to be considered before starting implementation of (end-to-end) processes facilitated by any machine learning technology. This includes available data, well-defined predictions, success criteria, and acceptable error thresholds. Based on these prerequisites, different phases of an end-to-end process can be evaluated to initiate machine learning initiatives on "good starting" points such as order management, production planning, or delivery planning. A systematic reflection of an end-to-end process and its potential for machine learning facilitation is a base for success.

To delve deeper into the topic, read the chapter titled "Machine Learning: Get Ready to Measure the Value for Supply Chain Management—Understanding the Value of Machine Learning in the Context of Business Processes."

## 1.6  Technology: Blockchain Technology Selection Approach

Blockchain is a technology that connects stakeholders without establishing trustful relations. The usage of a blockchain and, more generally, distributed ledger technologies can solve many issues for existing use cases or build new use cases of cloud services. However, these digital technologies are not only a chance; they are complex and come with risks. Also, different technology implementations come with their bad sides such as the blockchain implementation comes with a huge energy footprint for the mining. Understanding the basic concepts of different distributed ledger technologies to select the best one for a specific use case is essential. Also, blockchain integration into the service comes with challenges, such as dependencies on the specific technology stack and its constraints and limitations. To build a long-term solution, it is needed to evaluate potential technology options and select the most fitting one for own product or service. A systematic approach is one way to reflect product or service-specific quality risks and helps to identify the needed right technology and feature options, respectively, for the selection of a suitable distributed ledger technology. In the corresponding chapter the BSea approach is presented to address this topic.

To delve deeper into the topic, read the chapter titled "A Quality Assurance Guidance Framework for Blockchain-Based IT Services."

## 1.7  Market Research to Identify and Select Cloud Service Requirements

As cloud services are mass products, namely, mass services, approaches are needed to identify sweet spots in the mass market to serve revenue-generating customers to establish a cloud service. Furthermore, IT services are developed and evolved in iterations and versions; it is vital to prioritize features and capabilities aligned with market chances and revenue considerations, too. This ensures early revenue streams to enable continuous service growth by serving more customer segments. To get the relevant information for market segmentation and an appropriate feature roadmap, a systematic approach is needed to elaborate key requirements early in the cloud service development—before some technology-specific decisions are made for the implementation. Furthermore, a clearer capability and feature roadmap also help product and service owners manage the service evolution with a long-term view and strategy.

To delve deeper into the topic, read the chapter titled "Integrating the Voice of the Customer in Cloud Product Management: The Role and Application of Market Research Techniques."

## 1.8  Systematic User Experience: The User Feedback Is a Key Success Factor

With IT services getting increasingly complex, feedback about user experiences and potential issues has become essential. Different approaches exist to get the user feedback elaborated. It is important that the data is used in a continuous improvement flow to ensure that the product or service gets better over time in the long run. There are active and passive user feedback approaches. Sometimes, the user is "observed" and analyzed, e.g., with tracking frameworks. Sometimes the user is actively involved, e.g., in surveys. Which approach is best suitable depends on the product and service and their users. To ensure a high-quality user experience (UX), users shall be involved early in the development: UX design for the user with early validation loops. UX and usability are a quality characteristic that has to be instantiated for the specific product or service. One aspect that has to be instantiated, for example, is user or customer voice which can be collected in many different ways such as via community forums, and feedback to exposed product or service team members, e.g., product managers. However, UX is much more than user research and usability evaluation. A holistic UX also includes interaction design, visualization, information architecture, and development. Development is technology-centric, while the others are human-centric. The ISO 9241 facilitates the instantiation of UX within a product or service organization.

To delve deeper into the topic, read the chapter titled "User Research and Writer Human Centered Scenarios."

## 1.9    Quality Characteristics in the Context of Cloud Products and Services

ISO standards such as the ISO 25010 define usability and efficiency as quality characteristics. Instantiating these abstract terms for a specific product or service context still requires work. It becomes a unique selling proposition (USP) to balance the quality characteristics smartly. To do this, the product or service requirements must be elaborated, and the generic quality characteristics must be refined for the specific product and service context. This is often not trivial because quality characteristics sometimes can become contrary, e.g., a secure system is an offline system or better a system that is down. However, downtime is a sub-characteristic of availability that should be minimized. Balancing quality characteristics in the context of the requirements can be challenging. An innovative and adequate solution can easily become the USP of the cloud offer. Furthermore, expectations about quality characteristics can change over time. In the past, users accepted limited performance because the technology with static hardware assignments was not elastic. Today, thanks to cloud technology, the acceptance of non-scaling services is significantly lower. Quality management is a continuous job over the entire product and service life cycle to address current life-cycle phases and the changing user expectations or new use cases that are identified over time for the cloud offer or user study groups.

To delve deeper into the topic, read the chapter titled "Make Product and Service Requirements Shippable: From the Cloud service Vision to a Continuous Value Stream Which Satisfies Current and Future User Needs."

## 1.10    Sustainability Becomes a Strategic Asset in a Cloud Product Portfolio

In recent years, cloud computing has grown within an exploding IT market. This has led to an evolution of services based on cloud technology. The service portfolio of large cloud service providers (CSP) has a three-digit service offer today and is continuously growing—especially in the machine learning (ML) context, new services are added currently. This growing service offer finds customers, and each service provision needs resources to run. The huge amount of the service consumption makes it large enough to be considered with a sustainability and ecological footprint view. It has become important to establish a cloud service portfolio that is aligned with sustainability objectives. To reach this the CSP has to build by design sustainability into the services—from the infrastructure that is provisioned to the pricing model of service value units for the customer. Without the corresponding correlation of the price to the resource allocations, customers will always discuss about balancing costs and the sustainability of their workload. This dilemma has to be avoided. What is expected from the CSP is also valid for the customer workload.

The entire service stack has to be aligned with such a policy to ensure rigor and sustainability on end-customer value units. Sustainability becomes a strategic asset in the cloud service portfolio. Systematic sustainable software engineering (SSE) is the key to building sustainable services with the lowest resource allocation for the value units delivered.

To delve deeper into the topic, read the chapter titled "Engineering of Sustainability with Existing Levers in Cloud Services."

## 1.11 Building on Top of Existing Products New Generative Products

With a stack of sustainable and usable services, it is possible to build more sophisticated services and platforms. This requires a design of the service interfaces with the idea to use a service as a building block for other services, e.g., with an API or function library. On this base, generative products and services can become real. However, it demands an active management of the dependencies to the building blocks with their life cycles and strategic planning of the product. A simple example is infrastructure as code (IaC) in which some lines of formal infrastructure description or code specifying an infrastructure setup to run a cloud product or service. This powerful concept can be extended with more complex and abstract "building blocks" or can it be combined, e.g., as a parameterized sequence of descriptions, with other infrastructure descriptions to build more complex setups or variants for different CSPs. This approach to manage complexity by hiding details of the building blocks is useful to automate complex products and their deployments. However, it is not trivial to validate complex setups because often, the included offered methods and tools, respectively, for the verification and validation such as testing are limited. Currently, the area of generative products is evolving fast.

To delve deeper into the topic, read the chapter titled "Managing Generative Products: Different Rules for Software Innovation."

## 1.12 Examples, Facts, and Outlook

An example of the evolution of cloud services and products can be seen in the hyperscaler offers that have grown to more than 100 Google products and over 200 AWS product offers. Also, smaller CSPs offer more than 30 products such as Scaleway from France. For years, the CSPs have launched new products every year. With the growing product portfolios of the CSPs, the usage grows, too. This usage comes with impacts on the environment. The impact of the digital sector comes with growing greenhouse gas emissions. Each digitization project contributes to this fast-growing impact. Each cloud product or service evolves over its life cycle and it is important to manage its sustainability and environmental impact, for example, its energy footprint continuously. With the energy footprint, often a water footprint for cooling is directly related. Digitalization is the chance to rethink established products and services and create better ones during digitalization with holistic modern innovative thinking, designing, implementation, and operating. This book tries to facilitate holistic cloud product thinking to realize the chances coming with digitalization.

# Chapter 2
# Cloud Product Strategy, Vision, Market Positioning, and Pricing

**Andrey Saltan and Hans-Bernd Kittlaus**

**Abstract** Cloud computing has become an integral part of today's IT and business landscapes, providing flexibility and scalable virtual resources for many applications. This chapter discusses important business topics related to managing cloud products, including developing product strategies, positioning products in the market, and choosing appropriate pricing methods. It covers key features and main cloud service models: Infrastructure as a Service (IaaS), Platform as a Service (PaaS), and Software as a Service (SaaS), highlighting their benefits for both customers and providers.

**Keywords** Product strategy · Cloud computing · Cloud pricing

## 2.1 Introduction

Cloud computing has become a critical backbone for modern IT and business environments. In particular, public cloud services have experienced significant year-over-year growth, driven by the increased demand for agile, scalable, and cost-effective solutions. According to the latest update to the IDC Worldwide Software and Public Cloud Services Spending Guide, worldwide spending on public cloud services is forecast to reach $805 billion in 2024 and double in size by

A. Saltan (✉)
LUT University, Lahti, Finland and ISPMA, Stuttgart, Germany
e-mail: andrey.saltan@lut.fi

H.-B. Kittlaus
InnoTivum, Rheinbreitbach, Germany and ISPMA, Stuttgart, Germany
e-mail: hbk@innotivum.de

© The Author(s), under exclusive license to Springer Nature
Switzerland AG 2025
Y. Hajizadeh et al. (eds.), *Building Cloud Software Products*,
Innovation, Technology, and Knowledge Management,
https://doi.org/10.1007/978-3-031-92184-1_2

9

2028, fueled by a 5-year compound annual growth rate of 19.4% [1]. Similarly, Gartner projects that the public cloud services market will expand to \$1.28 trillion by 2028, growing at around 20% from 2023 to 2028 [2]. Notably, this level of sustained growth underscores how cloud now dominates tech spending across infrastructure, platforms, and applications.

Beyond these headline figures, the rapid evolution of data analytics, artificial intelligence (AI), machine learning (ML), and edge computing continues to accelerate cloud adoption. As organizations intensify their investments in AI-driven solutions, they increasingly rely on cloud platforms to build, test, and deploy applications [3, 4]. This environment supports ongoing innovation while also pushing enterprises to modernize their technical and business models. The COVID-19 pandemic gave an additional boost to cloud migrations by amplifying the need for remote work and more elastic infrastructure, contributing to especially high growth rates in 2020 and 2021 [5].

Although public cloud services (i.e., cloud services delivered over the Internet and shared among multiple organizations) garner the most attention, they are only one of three principal deployment models: private cloud (dedicated for single-organization use) and hybrid cloud (combining on-premises or private clouds with public cloud services) also play crucial roles in the broader cloud ecosystem. In this chapter, we will concentrate mainly on public cloud computing services while noting, where relevant, how private and hybrid approaches differ. Furthermore, when we refer to "cloud computing" in this chapter, we are primarily referring to the public cloud model.

From a business standpoint, at least three main categories of cloud providers can be distinguished: (1) traditional enterprise software vendors transitioning to cloud-based deployments, (2) newer "born-in-the-cloud" companies that typically offer a single flagship cloud solution, and (3) large IT vendors seeking to expand into the software or platform-as-a-service (PaaS) space [6]. All of these players are capitalizing on the clear benefits of the cloud model—speed to market, elasticity, and lower entry costs, among others—while confronting new operational challenges, such as reengineering existing business processes, updating pricing strategies, and revising organizational structures around DevOps and continuous delivery [7].

This chapter addresses three essential business aspects of cloud product management: defining cloud product strategy, conducting market research and positioning, and establishing a pricing approach. All these aspects are essential elements of software business strategy, tactics, and operations. Informed decision-making requires the involvement of different stakeholders and comprehensive data analysis. Achieving both appears to be challenging, and processes related to these aspects remain mostly under-managed in the software business. In addition to considering the business aspects mentioned above for cloud computing as a whole, we separately consider their features for main cloud computing models.

To a large extent, our chapter builds on a wealth of existing software product management and business literature, including ISPMA-Compliant[1] Study Guide and Handbook for Software Product Managers by Hans-Bernd Kittlaus [8]. However, product management of cloud computing solutions differs from the way it is performed for software products following the on-premises option. Our analysis emphasizes how cloud computing's distinct characteristics—continuous delivery, rapid market shifts, ongoing service operations—shape the decision-making around product strategy, positioning, and pricing.

To set the stage, we begin with a concise definition and classification of cloud computing, clarifying both customer-facing and production-oriented perspectives. A clear understanding of the technological and operational underpinnings of cloud solutions is critical for recognizing their chief advantages and disadvantages and how these are perceived across the market. Only then can software businesses formulate effective product strategies that capitalize on cloud computing's potential while mitigating its risks.

## 2.2  Cloud Product Definition

Cloud computing has had numerous definitions since its advent at the turn of the twenty-first century [9]. The National Institute of Standards and Technology (NIST) has provided a widely known definition of cloud computing, defining it as "a model for enabling convenient, on-demand network access to a shared pool of configurable computing resources (e.g., networks, servers, storage, applications, and services) that can be rapidly provisioned and released with minimal management effort or service provider interaction" [10]. Below, we highlight four definitions offered by four leading cloud computing providers (HP, Microsoft, IBM, and Amazon Web Services) that additionally reveal the economic essence of cloud computing, complementing the definition provided by NIST:

- **HP:** "The cloud" is not a place, but a method of managing IT resources that replaces local machines and private data centers with virtual infrastructure. In the cloud computing model, users access virtual computer, network, and storage resources made available online by a remote provider. These resources can be provisioned instantly, which is particularly useful for companies that need to scale their infrastructure up or down quickly in response to fluctuating demand [11].
- **Microsoft:** Simply put, cloud computing is the delivery of computing services— including servers, storage, databases, networking, software, analytics, and intelligence—over the Internet ("the cloud") to offer faster innovation, flexible

---

[1]The International Software Product Management Association (ISPMA) is an independent and not-for-profit association dedicated to advancing the discipline of software product management. Both authors of this chapter are associated with ISPMA.

resources, and economies of scale. You typically pay only for cloud services you use, helping you lower your operating costs, run your infrastructure more efficiently, and scale as your business needs change [12].

- **IBM**: Cloud computing is the on-demand access, via the Internet, to computing resources—applications, servers (physical servers and virtual servers), data storage, development tools, networking capabilities, and more—hosted at a remote data center managed by a cloud service provider [13].
- **Amazon Web Services (AWS)**: Cloud computing is the on-demand delivery of IT resources over the Internet with pay-as-you-go pricing. Instead of buying, owning, and maintaining physical data centers and servers, you can access technology services, such as computing power, storage, and databases, on an as-needed basis from a cloud provider [11].

### 2.2.1   Cloud Product Characteristics and Typology

Cloud computing definitions provided by the leading players in the market show how cloud computing is conceived today: clouds are a large pool of easily usable and accessible virtualized resources. These resources can be dynamically reconfigured to adjust to a variable load (scale), also allowing for optimum resource utilization. Looking for the minimum common denominator leads us to understanding that cloud computing works as an umbrella term, and a lot depends on the type of cloud service. However, the following aspects can often be identified:

- **On-Demand Measured Self-Service**: cloud services such as CPU time, storage, network access, and web applications can be allocated automatically as required by customers without any human interaction. Cloud resources and services are monitored, controlled, and optimized by cloud service providers.
- **Broad Network Access**: customers can access cloud resources over the Internet all the time and from anywhere through different types of devices. Customers can fulfill all their needs through a net service using a laptop or a mobile phone.
- **Resource Pooling**: physical and virtual computing resources are pooled into the cloud. These resources are not dependent on location in the sense that customers have no control over or knowledge about their location.
- **Elasticity and Scalability**: computing resources can be rapidly and elastically provisioned and released based on the demand of the customer. Cloud providers can add new nodes and servers with minor modifications to the cloud infrastructure and software. Customers view these resources as if they are infinite and can be purchased in any quantity at any time.
- **Multitenancy**: a cloud offering is usually intended to provide services to multiple customers at the same time. Those customers share cloud resources at the network, host, and application levels. When multiple customers run on the same instance of software solution in the runtime environment without influencing each other or having access to each other's data, it is called multitenancy.

- **Customization:** a cloud is a reconfigurable environment that can be customized and adjusted in terms of infrastructure and applications based on customer demand.

All characteristics are given in the maximum ideal scenario where the provider has unlimited computing resources and the ability to ensure the lack of any unavailability of the service. In a real-life context, all terms and conditions of the offering for each cloud service are documented in the service-level agreement (SLA). This agreement between customers and cloud service provider clarifies and specifies all aspects of the service (e.g., availability of the cloud service 99.95% of the time or data storage in a specific country or region) and defines responsibilities for their violation.

Most cloud computing services fall into three broad categories:

- Infrastructure as a Service (IaaS): The cloud service provider offers a set of virtualized computing resources, such as CPU and memory. IaaS uses virtualization technology to convert physical resources into logical resources that can be dynamically provisioned and released to customers as needed. Some of the major companies offering IaaS include Microsoft Azure, Amazon Web Services (AWS), IBM, and Verizon.
- Platform as a Service (PaaS): With PaaS, a cloud service provider offers, runs, and maintains both system software (i.e., the operating system) and middleware on top of IaaS. PaaS usually provides a software development environment and hosting of applications developed using this platform. Other services may include collaboration, database integration, security, web service integration, and scaling. Customers do not need to worry about having their own hardware and software resources or hire experts to manage these resources. Customers purchase access to platforms, enabling them to deploy their own software and applications in the cloud. Examples of PaaS solutions include Windows Azure, Heroku, Google App Engine, and Apache Stratos.
- Software as a Service (SaaS). With SaaS, cloud service providers often run and maintain application software on top of PaaS. Customers can access the application software through an application interface over the Internet. Unlike traditional software, SaaS has the advantage that customers do not need to buy licenses, install, upgrade, maintain, or run software on their own computer. Examples of companies offering SaaS are Google Documents, Dropbox, Salesforce, HubSpot, and Zendesk.

These three types of cloud computing are sometimes called the cloud computing "stack" because they build on top of one another. Figure 2.1 illustrates the difference between these three main types in comparison to traditional on-premises IT solutions and pure data hosting and colocation [14].

As more cloud-based models are continuously introduced in the markets, the acronym XaaS (anything-as-a-service) has been coined to cover this variety of services [15]. Such services include database-as-a-service (DBaaS), desktop-as-a-service (DaaS), communications-as-a-service (CaaS), and monitoring-as-a-service

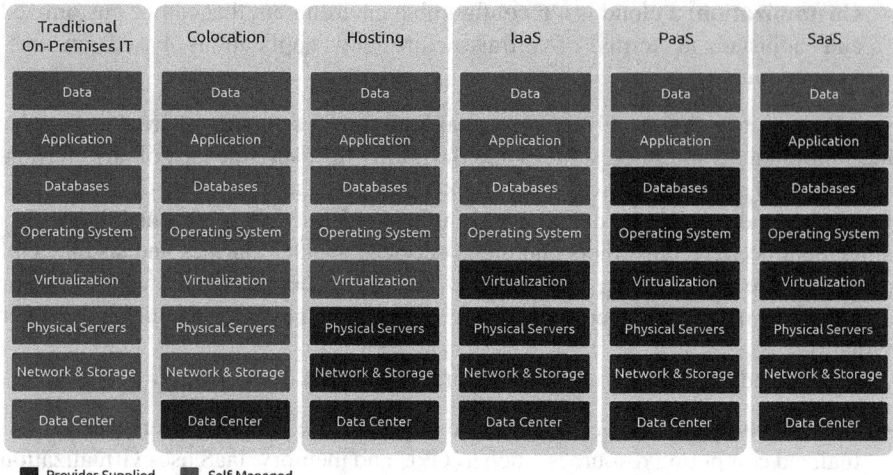

| Traditional On-Premises IT | Colocation | Hosting | IaaS | PaaS | SaaS |
| --- | --- | --- | --- | --- | --- |
| Data | Data | Data | Data | Data | Data |
| Application | Application | Application | Application | Application | Application |
| Databases | Databases | Databases | Databases | Databases | Databases |
| Operating System | Operating System | Operating System | Operating System | Operating System | Operating System |
| Virtualization | Virtualization | Virtualization | Virtualization | Virtualization | Virtualization |
| Physical Servers | Physical Servers | Physical Servers | Physical Servers | Physical Servers | Physical Servers |
| Network & Storage | Network & Storage | Network & Storage | Network & Storage | Network & Storage | Network & Storage |
| Data Center | Data Center | Data Center | Data Center | Data Center | Data Center |

■ Provider-Supplied    ■ Self-Managed

**Fig. 2.1** Cloud computing stack

(MaaS). While all these models are currently available, we focus on the three canonic types introduced by NIST within this chapter.

The transition to the cloud model is revolutionizing the software market, sending shockwaves through the IT market, significantly impacting both cloud providers and customers. Such a shift would not be possible without the significant benefits that this model brings to both sides of the market. Along with the key features and types of cloud computing services, understanding these key benefits is important when talking about the business and marketing aspects of cloud computing.

### 2.2.2 Cloud Products from the Customer Perspective

Below, we list the main benefits that drive further adoption of cloud from the customer perspective:

- Cost efficiency
- Payment flexibility as customers pay for the services they use
- Access to enterprise-level IT resources and infrastructure
- Rapid global scale up and scale down of the resources based on the requirements at any time
- Accessibility from any location
- Ease of use and maintenance managed by cloud provider
- Security as cloud providers offer a broad set of policies, technologies, and controls that strengthen overall security, protecting from potential threats.

One of the biggest advantages of cloud computing is the ability to reduce IT and software costs. It starts with minimal initial investments for the IT infrastructure and the opportunity to run software without upfront purchase of licenses. Multiple case studies and research investigations assure that in the long term, cloud services are more financially beneficial than traditional legacy solutions. The widely accepted approach for the determination and estimation of long-term direct and indirect costs for IT and software products and services is total cost of ownership (TCO) [16].

There is no single formula for calculating TCO. It should be calculated by each company individually taking into account multiple factors. The simplest calculation considers the following factors:

- Initial investments / Acquisition costs
- Installation and customization costs
- Operation costs
- Maintenance costs
- Downtime costs
- Remaining value
- Personnel Costs

However, this list can be significantly expanded. In the calculation, the formula itself takes into account the evaluation of a number of risk factors. Many cloud providers have their own TCO calculation services (e.g., offered by AWS [17]) that they use to show basic value, and they use this tool to convince customers to purchase their cloud services.

## 2.2.3 Cloud Products from the Provider Perspective

From the provider perspective, benefits of transition to a cloud computing model are the following:

- Obtain long-term higher profit margin and revenue.
- Reduce opportunity costs and utilize economies of scale.
- Expand the range of services provided.
- Obtain market leadership and change "the rules of the game."
- Increase the reliability of customer relationships.
- Facilitate geographical expansion.
- Facilitate upgrading, modification, and customization processes.
- Obtain agility and scalability of development and deployment.
- Obtain better quality of business analytics for decision-making.
- Avoid software piracy.

Cloud transition challenges:

- Redesign the business model and strategy to address such issues as the economy of scale, servitization, and shift from on-premises to on-demand.
- Ensure that the pricing scheme provides a sufficient level of flexibility and total cost reduction for customers.
- Provide customers with tangible arguments for cloud solution benefits, including cost reduction and performance increase.
- Design new pricing strategies and policies.
- Redefine the customer segments to address geographical expansion and customization.
- Provide customers with strong arguments against prejudices concerning the high risks of security and privacy while using cloud solutions.
- Focus on using direct Internet-related channels as major communication and sales channels.
- Reconsider partners' networks to address the new structure of distribution channels, including other cloud providers.
- Design reliable SLA ensuring its compliance with the cloud model.
- Ensure compliance with regulations across countries and industries.

## 2.3   Cloud Product Mission and Vision

Mission and vision statements have guided organizations for decades, initially on a company-wide level [18]. A **mission statement** typically defines a company's fundamental purpose—its business, objectives, and approach—while a **vision statement** describes the desired future position or overarching aspiration. In practice, these concepts can blend: some organizations present a single statement that combines their purpose, goals, and values. We can define them more briefly:

- The mission statement is the definition of the purpose of existence.
- The vision statement is the description of the desired future position.

Over time, these foundational concepts have been increasingly applied at the product level. This holds especially true for cloud products, where the pace of innovation and customer expectations require a clear articulation of purpose and direction. A cloud product vision, for instance, outlines what the product will become over a strategic time horizon—usually between 1 and 5 years—depending on the product's nature and market dynamics.

### 2.3.1   Mission Statement for Cloud Products

A product mission is directly linked to how a product is positioned in its target market. Positioning itself is about ensuring the product occupies "a clear, distinctive, and desirable place relative to competing products in the minds of target customers"

[19]. In other words, the mission statement and the positioning are deeply inter-twined: the mission offers the essence of what the product does and why, while positioning provides the context and uniqueness in the marketplace [20].

Below are some examples of mission statements in the cloud (or cloud-related) domain [21, 22]. Notice how each is short, memorable, and abstract, yet effectively conveys what the product or service is designed to accomplish:

– Facebook: "To give people the power to build community and bring the world closer together."
– LinkedIn: "To connect the world's professionals to make them more productive and successful."
– Uber: "To bring transportation—for everyone, everywhere."
– Amazon (retail platform): "We strive to offer our customers the lowest possible prices, the best available selection, and the utmost convenience."
– Amazon Web Services: "The AWS mission is to enable developers and busi-nesses to use web services to easily build and be paid for sophisticated, scalable applications."
– Slack: "Slack brings all your team's communication together, giving everyone a shared workspace where conversations are organized and accessible."
– Mailchimp: "Send better e-mail. We help millions of customers to find their audience, engage their clients, and build their brand."

These examples illustrate how a concise mission statement underpins everything from marketing messages to product development choices. The product mission is also the basis for positioning the product in its target market, or it is the condensed summary of the positioning of the product. What is a product mission statement good for? In combination with the positioning, it serves as the foundation of all marketing messages. It is also the linchpin for decisions regarding product changes and extensions answering the question "Is this still in line with our mission?"

## 2.3.2 Vision Statement for Cloud Products

While a mission statement explains "why we exist," a vision statement describes "where we are headed." Vision statements for cloud products point to an ambitious, yet achievable future. Here are a few examples drawn from cloud-centric or digital businesses [22]:

– Facebook: "People use Facebook to stay connected with friends and family, to discover what's going on in the world, and to share and express what matters to them."
– LinkedIn: "To create economic opportunity for every member of the global workforce."

- Uber: "Smarter transportation with fewer cars and greater access. Transportation that's safer, cheaper, and more reliable; transportation that creates more job opportunities and higher incomes for drivers."
- Amazon (retail platform): "To be Earth's most customer-centric company, where customers can find and discover anything they might want to buy online."

Some of these statements resemble mission statements more than "future state" descriptions. Others (particularly Uber and Amazon) emphasize a clear vision of what the future could look like. A truly effective cloud product vision can also include details on customer value, technology aspirations, and the unique role the product will play in its market.

All of the examples above are quite brief. However, vision statements can be more comprehensive such as this vision for a CRM SaaS product [23]:

> For a mid-sized company's marketing and sales departments who need basic CRM functionality, the CRM-Innovator is a Web-based service that provides sales tracking, lead generation, and sales representative support features that improve customer relationships at critical touch points. Unlike other services or package software products, our product provides very capable services at a moderate cost.

A strong product vision is often essential to engage and convince all stakeholders inside and outside of the company of the worth of a product. A vision describes what the future product will be, why it is needed, and why it will be successful [24]. The elements of the product strategy provide the details that turn the vision into a manageable and executable path to the future. In bigger companies, a product vision needs to be aligned with the corporate vision.

The first version of the product vision is needed when work on the development of the product's first version starts. Over time, the product vision continues to evolve so that it always looks ahead, at least within the limits of the proposed strategic timeframe vision.

A compelling product vision can energize stakeholders—both internal teams and external audiences—and serve as a "guiding star" for strategic decisions. It typically addresses:

- **Conceptual Image:** What the future product will be.
- **Customer Value Proposition:** Why the product is needed and how it uniquely solves pain points.
- **Business Value:** How it will generate success for the vendor (e.g., revenue, market share, brand leadership).

A product vision always focuses on a point in the future and is presented as a relatively short statement, usually no more than one page. The vision needs to be phrased from a marketing perspective, in a style that has a motivating effect on external and internal stakeholders by painting a desirable, ambitious, but achievable future. The product vision is especially important throughout the start phase when the first version of the product is conceived and developed.

The term "product vision" is also used in connection with agile methodologies, in particular Scrum. While it is not mentioned in the Scrum Guide [25], most Scrum consultants consider it an important element of the Scrum approach. Originally, this agile product vision was focused on a given development task. It was supposed to describe in a condensed way what the Scrum Team was asked to develop within a couple of weeks or months. Over time, some Scrum consultants, e.g., Pichler [26], have broadened the scope and use product vision in the sense defined here.

### 2.3.3   Development of a Product Vision

A convincing product vision looks very straightforward, logical, and easy. However, developing it is a more difficult and time consuming task than most people expect. We suggest the template used in a number of software companies [8]. It can support the development of a vision by focusing on the problem space and the solution space. The problem is described in a solution-neutral manner and explains the pain points addressed by the solution as well as the criteria used for evaluating product success from the customer perspective. The solution is described in terms of use scenarios, features, benchmarks, and the unique value proposition. A combination of the product manager's draft as a synthesis of ideas and contributions solicited internally [27] and a workshop approach [28] can be recommended.

Figure 2.2 illustrates the template. The example is drawn from a product that tracks consumables in an operating theatre. This template ensures that relevant information is collected but does not automatically result in a wording that is marketing oriented. The second step turns it into a marketing statement. This transformation can be made by re-ordering the presentation of the vision statement:

> In order to significantly decrease clinics' effort and increase the availability of operating theatres, the Consumables Tracking Solution (CTS) reduces the nurses' and analysts' manual work by tracking the use of consumables in an operation, enabling its analysis, and

| **Problem statement** | |
| --- | --- |
| the problem of | immense effort for reporting consumables |
| affects | nurses, and the clinic overall |
| the impact of which is | inefficient use of operating theatres |
| a successful solution | increases the availability of the operating theatres. |
| | |
| **Position statement** | |
| for | nurses and analysts |
| who | administrate, assist in, and improve operations |
| the | **Consumables Tracking Solution (CTS)** |
| that | tracks the use of consumables in an operation, enables its analysis, and automates reporting |
| unlike | the current labor-intensive manual approach |
| our product | increases the efficiency of operations and delivers decision-support for consumable planning and improvement. |

**Fig. 2.2**  Example of a problem and position statement [29]

automating reporting. It enables clinics to increase the efficiency of the operation work and deliver decision-support for consumable planning and improvement.

Often companies want shorter vision statements like the following:

The Consumables Tracking Solution (CTS) increases clinics' efficiency and reduces cost by automating the tracking, analysis and reporting of consumables in operating theatres.

In order to achieve the buy-in of the product team members, it can help to develop and evolve the product vision in workshops with the key team members. In later stages of the product life cycle, when vendors usually want to reduce their investment level, it becomes more difficult to come up with a convincing vision statement.

A compelling product vision can be a powerful instrument to keep the product team aligned and on track, especially during the development of the initial version of the product. It can also be a good marketing tool during initial product launch and during later phases of the life cycle communicating the core direction of the product development.

Research underscores the significance of a clear vision in new product development projects. In high-tech industries, Lynn et al. [30] found that product success correlates most strongly with having a robust vision alongside a well-defined development process. Further analysis by Lynn and Akgün [31] considered factors such as vision clarity, vision stability, and how strongly team members support and share the vision:

- **Vision Clarity:** Correlates with success in both evolutionary market/technical innovation and revolutionary innovation (but not as strongly in incremental innovation)
- **Vision Stability:** Correlates with success in incremental and evolutionary market innovations
- **Vision Support:** Correlates with success in incremental and evolutionary technical innovations

In other words, the right balance of a clear, stable, and widely shared vision can drive a project's success—especially in cloud-based solutions, which often undergo rapid evolutionary or even revolutionary changes.

Mission and vision statements—once purely the domain of overall corporate strategy—are now equally vital for individual products, particularly in cloud computing. The mission concisely states the product's reason for being, setting the context for positioning and guiding core decisions. The vision presents a compelling snapshot of the future, inspiring stakeholders to rally behind a shared goal.

In dynamic, fast-paced cloud markets, a clearly articulated mission and vision not only drive internal focus and motivation but also resonate with external audiences—customers, partners, and investors—who want to see purpose, innovation, and staying power. In subsequent explorations of product strategy, market positioning, and pricing, it is essential to remember that mission and vision statements are the cornerstones that shape each decision, feature priority, and market message. These statements keep the product both grounded and aspirational, ensuring it remains relevant, differentiated, and enduring in an ever-changing landscape.

## 2.4   Market Positioning

Formally, positioning is the process of defining a product's identity and communicating this identity to target audiences. Less formally, it can be described as a technique for presenting products in the most favorable light to potential customers. An efficient market positioning allows companies (cloud providers in our case) to create a strong competitive position, define a clearer target market, connect its products to consumer needs, and, as a result, improve acquisition, monetization, and the retention of customers [8]. Ultimately, good positioning facilitates both external communications (sales and marketing) and internal decision-making, providing a framework against which to evaluate new features, pricing models, and market opportunities.

### 2.4.1   Market Positioning Contents

According to Kotler and Armstrong, a product's objective is "to occupy a clear, distinctive, and desirable place relative to competing products in the minds of target customers" [19]. This clarity of focus makes it easier for sales and marketing teams to tailor messages to specific groups and ensures that product development remains aligned with strategic goals.

Dunford identifies four major options to frame and position product on a strategic level, which are fully consistent with the case of cloud services [20]:

– Dominate an existing product category.
– Dominate a segment of an existing product category.
– Reframe an existing product category.
– Create a new product category.

The choice largely determines the entire scope of subsequent decisions required for market positioning. Since market competition is inevitable, one of the important aspects of positioning is the question of how a product differentiates itself in the market. This question is related to the concept of unique value proposition which describes value elements that none of the available alternatives can provide. For proprietary products including cloud solutions, the typical differentiating arguments are better functionality, higher level of integration, and performance.

Once the market for the product has been defined, the positioning must focus on describing the value delivered by the product. This has to be updated over time as the value of the product will hopefully increase with each new version or release. The value must be considered from the customer's perspective; for example, which business outcomes does the product enable, and how does it solve real-world problems? Market segmentation, i.e., building customer segments as subsets of the total market of the product, may be needed when various segments experience different business values from using the product [32]. Customer usage analytics, easily implementable for cloud providers, offer significantly more opportunities for real-time analysis and tracking of how cloud solutions are used and what value customers gain from it. When processed properly, such analytics can not only help to increase the quality of the product, but also to better position it.

Cloud providers need to be specific about the customer segment(s) they are targeting so that they can develop a thorough understanding of customer needs. This understanding is key to developing compelling value propositions that help sell the product. Here, methods like the Value Proposition Canvas can help [33, 34]. However, this does not mean that customer segments always have to be narrowly focused; according to Moore [23, 35] how broad or narrow the target segment can be depends on the maturity of the respective market. For example, when bringing to market a completely new type of B2B product (what Moore and Dunford call a new product category), it is often useful to kick-start mainstream adoption by focusing on a small, well-defined market niche (the beachhead segment). The strategy is to expand into adjacent market niches later one after the other (bowling alley strategy). Once the new product category is better understood in the market and broad adoption sets in at a fast pace (tornado phase), the vendor's next top priority is capturing a market share. At this stage, an undifferentiated strategy is suitable.

Customer understanding is translated into the value propositions that (hopefully) strongly resonate with the customer segments and help sell the products [36]:

- Pain relievers "eliminate or reduce negative emotions, undesired costs and situations, and risks your customer experiences or could experience before, during, and after getting the job done."
- Gain creators "create benefits your customer expects desires or would be surprised by, including functional utility, social gains, positive emotions, and cost savings."

Delivering a compelling value proposition in the cloud often requires more than a standalone product. Additional services, integrations, or partner solutions are typically necessary to create what Moore [23] refers to as the concept of the whole product. In other words, providers must identify and secure all the complementary components—analytics tools, support services, or third-party apps—that help customers derive full value. By ensuring these components are readily accessible, cloud providers can strengthen their positioning and better address the complete needs of their user base.

## 2.4.2 Market Positioning Processes

Positioning is not a one-time exercise but rather an iterative process involving product management, marketing, sales, and executive leadership. This alignment is especially crucial for cloud solutions, which tend to evolve more rapidly than traditional software. Several interdependent factors come into play—market segments, product definitions, pricing, and competitive context—which must be revisited regularly [8].

1. **Determine Customer Value.** It begins with analyzing how and why customers use your product. Alternatives might be a competitor's offering, a custom in-house solution, or simply doing nothing. Pinpointing the drivers of customer value (e.g., reduced costs, operational efficiencies, compliance benefits) sets the foundation for more precise marketing messages and pricing models.
2. **Identify Differentiating Features.** Some features will hold greater importance for certain segments. A single standout capability that resonates strongly with one segment can become the central theme of your positioning. Highlight how that feature outperforms alternatives, providing qualitative (and if possible, quantitative) evidence to support marketing efforts.
3. **Define Value Parameters.** Understand the parameters that determine product value—for example, CPU usage or storage for an IaaS and number of active users for a SaaS productivity tool. These parameters may later inform a value-based pricing model, where the perceived benefits align with the cost.
4. **Testing, Experimentation, and Feedback.** Cloud providers often have unparalleled access to real-time usage data, enabling continuous experimentation with different positioning statements or messages. More conventional research methods—surveys, focus groups, in-depth interviews—can supplement usage analytics. Over time, refine your positioning based on how customers respond.
5. **Adjust and Evolve.** As the product matures, new releases may shift your positioning emphasis. For instance, a performance upgrade might suddenly become a prime differentiator, or a newly added compliance feature might open doors to a heavily regulated industry. Regularly revisiting your positioning statement ensures it stays aligned with your latest offerings and emerging market needs.

Market positioning is the strategic link between a cloud product's core offerings and its target audience's expectations. By clearly defining how the product meets specific needs, articulating distinct advantages, and continuously refining the message to reflect the product's growth, cloud providers can secure a robust foothold in a competitive environment.

In an industry defined by constant innovation, an agile yet well-structured positioning strategy can make the difference between a product that thrives and one that struggles to find its place. By investing time in understanding market segments, orchestrating the whole product experience, and consistently monitoring customer feedback, cloud providers can build and maintain a compelling, lasting position in their chosen market.

## 2.5   Product Strategy

A product strategy describes how a product should evolve over a strategic timeframe—typically 1 to 5 years—depending on the product's nature and market context [8]. For cloud-based products, the strategy must remain dynamic to keep pace with rapidly changing technologies and evolving customer demands. It is the product manager's responsibility to define and continuously refine this strategy, ensuring it aligns with the organization's overall mission, vision, and market positioning.

When effectively articulated, a product strategy serves as a blueprint, linking the product's vision to the specific activities, resources, and decisions that will guide it into the future. In large companies, each product's strategy must also align with the broader corporate strategy and the strategies of any related products in the portfolio.

The product vision acts as the starting point for developing a detailed product strategy. A strong vision statement conveys the aspirational end state for the product, while the strategy provides the roadmap to get there. Similarly, the strategy should reflect the market positioning by clarifying how the product meets specific customer needs and stands out from competitors. By continually verifying that each strategic decision supports the mission, vision, and positioning, product managers maintain consistency across all initiatives.

### 2.5.1   Product Strategy Contents

Building from that foundation, a comprehensive product strategy should address several interdependent elements [8]. These elements not only provide structure but also ensure that all functional areas (such as engineering, marketing, sales, operations) work cohesively:

- **Positioning:** What is the target market? What is the value that customers in the target market get from using the product? Is segmentation required because of different value propositions for different customer groups? Which partnerships and alliances are needed?
- **Product Definition:** What is the scope of the product in terms of functionality, quality, and UX design? What is the suggested architecture? For SaaS, what is the business architecture?
- **Delivery Model:** How is the product delivered to customers? For cloud products, this is SaaS, PaaS, or IaaS. What degree of customer-specific tailorability is needed/shall be provided?
- **Service Strategy:** Which product-related services are needed/can be offered? Who can offer them?
- **Sourcing:** Where do we find the people needed for developing the product? Shall we make or buy the components of the product?
- **Pricing:** What is the right pricing approach (value- vs. cost-based pricing)? What is the price structure and the price level?
- **Financial Management:** How will revenues and costs develop over the strategic timeframe? Which actions need to be taken based on actual vs. planned numbers?
- **Ecosystem Management:** In which ecosystems are we represented with our product? Do we want our product to be the foundation of an ecosystem of its own? Which roles do we want to play in the relevant ecosystems? Do we establish a partner program, and in which areas?

- **Legal and IPR Management:** How can we protect our product/our company against potential legal risks, including contracts, the protection of intellectual property, open source, and compliance?
- **Performance and Risk Management:** What are the relevant measures for business performance? Which actions need to be taken based on actual vs. planned numbers? Which product-related risks are we facing? How can we mitigate these risks?

These elements often appear in a single, cohesive product strategy document. The need for internal consistency is high because changes in one area (e.g., adjusting the pricing model) typically impact others (e.g., financial forecasts or positioning).

## 2.5.2  Product Strategy Processes

Responsibility for the strategy lies primarily with the product manager, who must collaborate with stakeholders across the organization. This inclusive, iterative process ensures the strategy reflects diverse perspectives and achieves buy-in:

- **Initial Development:** Often begins with a hypothesis about product-market fit, validated through testing and feedback.
- **Ongoing Updates:** As the product evolves, the strategy must be revisited and refined to reflect actual market conditions and organizational changes.

In startup contexts, this process is especially iterative. Teams commonly follow the cycle of hypothesis → minimum viable product (MVP) → test → conclusion. Ries defines an MVP as the "version of a new product which allows a team to collect the maximum amount of validated learning about customers with the least effort" [37]. The development and implementation of a product strategy are intertwined through this iterative process.

When a product (and company) is successful and mature, the product strategy tends to be more stable. An update of the product strategy is a more evolutionary process. The implementation of the product strategy is more separated. Since the elements of the product strategy cover all the product-related functional areas of the software organization, all of them need to be involved in and contribute to its implementation. That is shown in ISPMA's SPM Framework [8] as depicted in Fig. 2.3.

Continuous measurement is key to validating product strategy. Potential metrics include:

- **Adoption and Engagement:** Monthly active users (MAUs), session length, or usage frequency
- **Revenue and Growth:** Monthly recurring revenue (MRR), customer acquisition cost (CAC), or lifetime value (LTV)
- **Operational Metrics:** Uptime, mean time to recovery (MTTR), or cost-efficiency
- **Customer Satisfaction:** Surveys, Net Promoter Score (NPS), and churn analysis

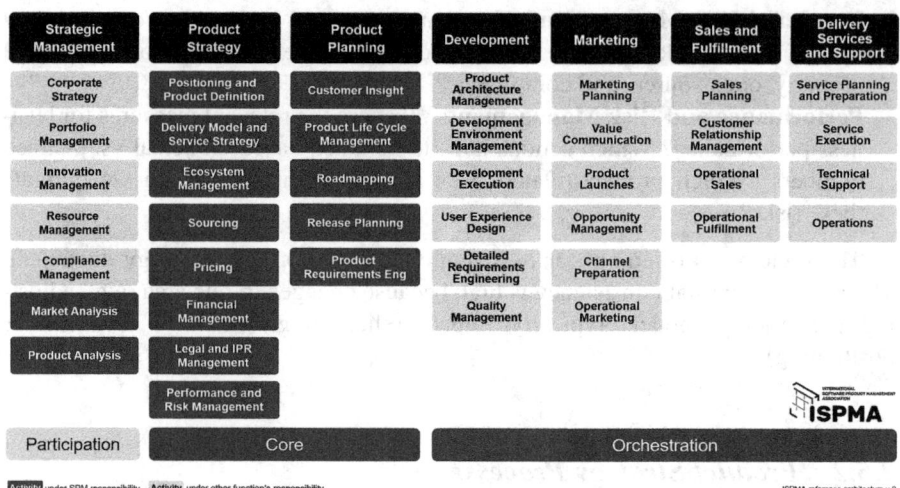

**Fig. 2.3** ISPMA software product management framework

Comparing actual performance with targets helps stakeholders decide whether to adjust tactics or pivot strategically. In stable companies, updates to the product strategy are more gradual, but they still benefit from periodic reviews to handle shifts in market conditions or emerging technology trends.

### 2.5.3   Strategic Considerations in the Current Cloud Markets

#### 2.5.3.1   IaaS Vendors

At its simplest form, infrastructure as a service (IaaS) is highly commoditized: offering storage and processing power alone provides limited differentiation. This leads to intense price-based competition—"a race to the bottom" that generally favors volume leaders like AWS [38]. Consequently, many IaaS vendors layer software and specialized services on top of basic compute and storage, effectively moving up the stack toward SaaS-like offerings.

Dropbox exemplifies this transition. Founded in 2007, it grew rapidly via a freemium model. By 2017, it introduced Dropbox Paper, a collaborative document-editing service delivered via a web application [39]. This shift from simple file storage (IaaS-like utility) to a richer SaaS solution highlights how vendors can move beyond commodity infrastructure.

#### 2.5.3.2   SaaS Vendors

In the software as a service (SaaS) domain, early expectations predicted that usage-based pricing would dominate. Yet a quick survey reveals that fixed-price subscriptions often prevail. Reasons include:

- **Customer Budgeting:** Fixed subscriptions are simpler for B2B budgeting.
- **Vendor Simplicity:** Implementing usage-based billing can be complex and costly.
- **Trust Issues:** Customers may distrust metered measurements they cannot independently verify.

Despite the notion of "on demand," many providers effectively bundle services into subscription tiers—like Dropbox's fixed storage tiers—ensuring more predictable revenue and stronger customer stickiness.

### 2.5.3.3   Approaches to Customer Binding

Platform as a service (PaaS) and certain advanced SaaS offerings can foster deep customer binding. When a platform includes a proprietary development environment or complex integrations, switching costs rise. Organizations often embed significant effort customizing apps and workflows, making them reluctant to move to a competitor's platform. With PaaS and SaaS offerings, there is more inherent differentiation and customer binding. In particular with PaaS, customer binding can become really strong when the platform includes a proprietary development environment that customers use for developing their own application software and/or customizations.

Whether you are offering IaaS, PaaS, or SaaS, your product strategy anchors all development and go-to-market efforts in a coherent framework. By integrating short-term actions with a long-term vision, you can effectively deliver value, capture market share, and foster lasting customer loyalty in a constantly evolving landscape.

## 2.6   Pricing of Cloud Products

We define pricing as the process of decision-making to determine the monetary compensation and related conditions for the goods and services the customer is offered. The entire scope of these decisions, practices, underlying conditions, and processes in respect to cloud products is referred to as cloud pricing. With value-based pricing, the value propositions are the basis for price considerations. In addition, a software vendor must consider factors such as costs, business goals, market segment, and the ability of customers to pay.

Pricing is an essential, crucial, and challenging element of cloud product management and product strategy. Even a small change in the cloud solution price may significantly impact a vendor's financial performance. Defining the price for a solution is part of the comprehensive pricing management strategy that companies have to manage. An efficient pricing management requires sophisticated decision-making and analytics, as well as coordination and finding compromises between the many business functions involved [40].

Pricing serves as an essential bridge between different business functions (e.g., product management, revenue management, cost management, retention management) and business units (e.g., R&D, production, sales, marketing). The decision-making in pricing is based on an integrated analysis of different perspectives and streams of information. All of this also applies to cloud solutions. We summarize the concept of pricing and its application to the software industry in general before exploring existing knowledge on the role of pricing for cloud providers.

While the commercial success of software companies is very dependent on appropriate pricing, decisions on designing and implementing pricing have always been challenging. If there is a lack of focus in pricing at strategic, tactical, or operational levels, the product and the company are likely to fail. The transition toward the cloud-based business model enables new options for software companies in software development, delivery, and operation. These options have implications for pricing by creating and magnifying the number of pricing design, experiment, and control methods available. These methods include recurring subscription fees, new methods to ensure efficient price discrimination, and real-time usage tracking [40]. However, these new options can also cause obstacles for companies when old pricing principles and practices become obsolete, and the companies' vision of how the new ones should be designed is unclear.

### 2.6.1  Cloud Product Pricing Strategies, Structures, and Models

We start with an overview of cloud pricing practices with pricing strategies. It is commonly agreed to distinguish three main pricing strategies: value-based pricing, market-based pricing, and cost-based pricing [41, 42]. However, cloud service providers have adopted a variety of pricing strategies besides the three main pricing strategies discussed below.

**Value-Based Pricing Strategy:** This pricing strategy is grounded in the value perceived by the customer. Perception value is based on the customers' perceptions of what is expected compared with what is delivered. The necessity to evaluate this value and associated challenges make this strategy much more subjective in comparison with other pricing strategies. The common term of perceptive value is value for money, i.e., the ratio between the customer value of a cloud service and the price. The main advantage of value-based pricing is its subjective fairness for consumers that can compare their expenses with the benefits gained. However, it is challenging to construct, because the perceived value is primarily measured by the satisfaction of the individual customer, i.e., there can be strong heterogeneity among customers which may require additional segmentation.

**Market-Based Pricing Strategy:** This pricing strategy is grounded in the analysis of the market equilibrium of all customers and cloud service providers. The market-based pricing takes into consideration two kinds of impacts on pricing: price sensitivity and market competitiveness for similar services.

**Cost-Based Pricing Strategy:** This pricing strategy is grounded in the analysis of a cloud service provider's cost structure. One of the primary reasons to adopt this strategy is that it is clear-cut and tangible. It can also be considered as the "fact"-based pricing. Cost-based pricing can articulate a unit cost and provide a measurement for benchmark comparison. It is one of the managerial tools for many decision-makers to drive business performance. However, since the variable cost for self-developed software products is low, cost-based pricing is usually not directly applicable to SaaS offerings.

All three pricing strategies exist in practice; however, it is very difficult to talk about the frequency of their usage in the cloud context. Even though many pricing experts emphasize advantages and importance of value-based pricing, cost-based and market-based pricing are still common. On the one hand, the cost-based approach helps decision-makers set a baseline to charge customers for the minimum price so that they can at least cover their expenditures. On the other hand, market-based pricing allows companies to rely on market forces and consider the current situation as an equilibrium.

There are many approaches to further structure and systematize pricing. We will pursue the most common and comprehensive one, called the strategic pricing pyramid [43, 44] (see Fig. 2.4), and adapt it to the cloud context.

Strategic pricing starts with a clear understanding of customer segments and value delivered to the customers (the bottom layer of the pyramid).

- **Value Creation** is the manner in which value is generated in a customer organization from using the cloud solution, including the metrics that show the impact of certain parameters on the value. Segmentation may be needed if value creation

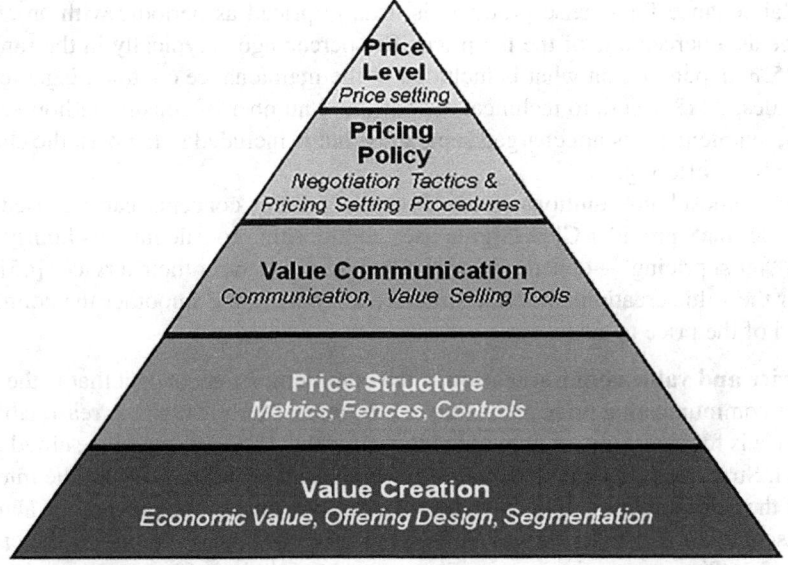

**Fig. 2.4** Strategic pricing pyramid

varies across different segments. For example, SaaS providers may distinguish between two market segments: B2B and B2C.

- **Price Structure** is the manner in which the prices for a given cloud solution are offered, including the metric by which those prices may vary depending on the customer's specific parameters (e.g., single price, price based on a number of users, capacity, usage, or the volume of licenses acquired).

The metrics used in the price structure can be determined using value analysis performed at the previous step. Metrics should mirror the generation of customer value which allows cloud providers to justify the price in relation to that customer value. For example, IaaS provider Amazon Web Services: Elastic Compute Cloud (EC2) structures its pricing based on the number of processing unit hours and the amount of storage space. Marketing automation SaaS provider MailChimp structures its pricing based on the number of active subscribers and features used. More options are available to define a price structure including the following:

- One time vs. periodic, also known as subscription-based pricing
- Fixed price (one time or periodic)
- Usage-based pricing (periodic), e.g., based on number of transactions, users, or usage hours
- Free, i.e., no charges, but revenue is generated through advertising

The resulting price structure may be quite complex, in particular with usage-based pricing when the actual price is calculated anew every month based on the customer's usage metrics from the previous month. In that case, it is important to ensure that back-office systems can reliably handle the complexity and issue correct invoices.

Maintenance for license products is usually priced as periodic with an annual charge as a percentage of the list price. The percentage is typically in the range of 12–25%, depending on what is included in the maintenance contract, e.g., version upgrades, 24x7 access to technical support, and number of consulting hours. With SaaS, maintenance is not charged separately, but is included in the periodic charges of the SaaS offering.

For some cloud solutions, more dynamic pricing concepts can be used. For example, IaaS provider CloudSigma uses an algorithm to calculate its hourly pricing—"burst pricing"—depending on the current demand for their services [45]. The better the value creation and price structure alignment, the smoother the communication of the price to customers.

- **Price and value communication** is the communication concept that is the basis for communicating price and value to customers by showing how reasonable the price is for a customer compared to the value they get from using the cloud product. Strategic pricing also includes processes and policies to ensure the integrity of the price structure in the market, for example, fences that prevent the abuse of discounts (e.g., student discounts require proof of student status) or the criteria for handling "exception requests" in price negotiations (discounting criteria as part of the pricing policy layer in the pyramid).

- **Pricing policy** is a formal definition of the manner in which prices may be altered, e.g., price level or price structure, who can alter it, under what circumstances, and to what degree. The policy sets governance criteria for the whole company regarding price. If the company has a separate pricing unit, that unit can usually veto any transactions that do not adhere to the policy.
- **Price level** is the actual amount of charge within the price structure. Competitive analysis can help to determine the price level. At what price are competitors offering their cloud solutions? Does the solution have competitive advantages/disadvantages that justify price differences? The price level at which we want to offer the product can be set by carefully analyzing these aspects.

The combination of price structure and price level is turned into a price list. Then, a sanity check needs to be performed by calculating the overall revenue from the forecast of the number of customers in different categories and the price list and comparing it to the cost forecast.

## 2.6.2   Decision-Making in Cloud Product Pricing

It is imperative to keep in mind that price does not sell a product. The product must fit the customers' needs. Then, price can become the differentiator between doing nothing, buying a competitor's equally useful product, and buying your product. Pricing too low or discounting too deeply will lead to leaving a lot of "money on the table," particularly when this becomes predictable. Pricing too high will lead to a weak market share.

There is no silver bullet for pricing of cloud solutions and a lot of factors should be taken into account. The first factor affecting pricing is the type of cloud service. The difference in the types of cloud services is elucidated the most when looking at the economic characteristics of these types (PaaS, SaaS, IaaS) and their associated pricing practices. IaaS pricing is similar to the pricing of commodity goods like water or electricity, while SaaS pricing has more in common with pricing for gym membership. In a similar way to a gym membership, the customer acquires access to the service, most often through a subscription model. Just like gyms, providers often have several subscription options which, in the case of services, differ in terms of features, number of available transactions, and/or the amount of memory provided. Finally, additional services can be purchased separately.

With this variety of options, the situation is quite complicated. The solution here is continuous experimentation on all levels of the pricing pyramid based on the analysis of customers, competitors, and internal resources. The last important thing to remember is that pricing and in particular the governance rules related to pricing are an ongoing source of conflict among various business units. Sales has different, short-term objectives than business units responsible for pricing.

## 2.7 Conclusions

Public cloud computing has rapidly evolved into a cornerstone of modern IT and business operations, with forecasts projecting continued, unprecedented growth well into the next decade. As noted, worldwide spending on public cloud services is rapidly growing and demonstrates that the strategic significance of the cloud is only increasing. The COVID-19 pandemic accelerated this momentum, driving organizations of all sizes—across diverse industries—to prioritize cloud adoption. As a result, many enterprises have overcome initial skepticism in favor of the cloud's compelling value proposition: flexibility, scalability, and cost efficiency unmatched by traditional on-premises architectures.

This surge in demand has facilitated the rise of new service-oriented business models, radically transforming sectors such as finance, healthcare, retail, and telecommunications. Consequently, the cloud computing landscape is characterized by intense competition among both established and "born-in-the-cloud" vendors. Yet, technological excellence alone does not guarantee success. To capitalize on the extraordinary market opportunities, companies must carefully craft clear product visions, robust market positioning, and competitive pricing strategies that align with the fast-paced dynamics of cloud adoption.

This chapter aimed to serve as an essential guide for those involved in designing and executing cloud product strategies. By synthesizing the state-of-the-art research and professional best practices, we have introduced relevant concepts, frameworks, and models, adapted specifically to address the realities of cloud environments. These practices draw upon well-established product management techniques from the broader software industry while acknowledging the unique demands of continuous delivery, evolving customer expectations, and pricing models intrinsic to the public cloud.

Finally, it is important to underscore that cloud product management is far from static. As the cloud paradigm continues to mature and expand, new methodologies and practices will inevitably emerge. Therefore, any product strategy must be treated as a living instrument—it should be regularly assessed, refined, and updated in response to shifting market conditions, technological innovations, and organizational changes. In this rapidly evolving landscape, success will favor those who combine strong foundational knowledge with the agility to continually adapt and innovate.

## References

1. Da Rold, S., Smith, E., Minonne, A., Clement, M. A., & Rawool, K. (2024) Worldwide software and public cloud services spending guide.
2. Singh, H., Graham, C., Schumacher, R., Cheparthi, A., Mehta, V., & Upadhyay, S. (2021). *Forecast: Public cloud services, worldwide, 2022–2028, 2Q24 update.* Gartner, Inc.

3. Gill, S. S., Tuli, S., Xu, M., Singh, I., Singh, K. V., Lindsay, D., Tuli, S., Smirnova, D., Singh, M., Jain, U., Pervaiz, H., Sehgal, B., Kaila, S. S., Misra, S., Aslanpour, M. S., Mehta, H., Stankovski, V., & Garraghan, P. (2019). Transformative effects of IoT, Blockchain and artificial intelligence on cloud computing: Evolution, vision, trends and open challenges. *Internet of Things, 8*, 100118. https://doi.org/10.1016/j.iot.2019.100118

4. Gill, S. S., Xu, M., Ottaviani, C., Patros, P., Bahsoon, R., Shaghaghi, A., Golec, M., Stankovski, V., Wu, H., Abraham, A., Singh, M., Mehta, H., Ghosh, S. K., Baker, T., Parlikad, A. K., Lutfiyya, H., Kanhere, S. S., Sakellariou, R., Dustdar, S., Rana, O., Brandic, I., & Uhlig, S. (2022). AI for next generation computing: Emerging trends and future directions. *Internet of Things, 19*, 100514. https://doi.org/10.1016/j.iot.2022.100514

5. Aggarwal, G. (2025). How the pandemic has accelerated cloud adoption.

6. SaaS Spending Hits $100 billion Annual Run Rate; Microsoft Extends its Leadership. In: Synergy Research Group. https://www.srgresearch.com/articles/saas-spending-hits-100-billion-annual-run-rate-microsoft-extends-its-leadership. Accessed September 19, 2021.

7. Saltan, A., & Seffah, A. (2018). Engineering and business aspects of SaaS model adoption: Insights from a mapping study. (p. 13).

8. Kittlaus, H.-B. (2022). *Software product management: The ISPMA®-compliant study guide and handbook*. Springer.

9. Regalado, A. (2011). *Who coined "Cloud Computing"?* MIT Technology Review.

10. Mell, P., & Grance, T. (2011). *The NIST Definition of Cloud Computing*, 7.

11. What is Cloud Computing? In: HP, Inc. https://www.hpe.com/us/en/what-is/cloud-computing.html. Accessed September 19, 2021.

12. What Is Cloud Computing? A Beginner's Guide | Microsoft Azure. In: Microsoft, Inc. https://azure.microsoft.com/en-us/overview/what-is-cloud-computing/. Accessed September 19, 2021.

13. What is Cloud Computing? | IBM. In: IBM, Inc. https://www.ibm.com/cloud/learn/cloud-computing. Accessed September 19, 2021.

14. Rumale, A. S., & Chaudhari, D. N. (2017). Cloud computing: Software as a service. In *2017 second international conference on electrical, computer and communication technologies (ICECCT)* (pp. 1–6).

15. What Is XaaS (Anything as a Service)? | NetApp. https://www.netapp.com/knowledge-center/what-is-anything-as-a-service-xaas/. Accessed September 19, 2021.

16. Martens, B., Walterbusch, M., & Teuteberg, F. (2012). Costing of cloud computing services: A total cost of ownership approach. In *2012 45th Hawaii international conference on system sciences* (pp. 1563–1572). IEEE.

17. AWS Pricing Calculator. https://calculator.aws/#/. Accessed September 19, 2021.

18. Bain & Company. (2018). Mission and Vision Statements. https://www.bain.com/insights/management-tools-mission-and-vision-statements/. Accessed September 19, 2021.

19. Kotler, P., Armstrong, G., & Harris, L. C. (2019). *Principles of marketing* (8th ed.). Pearson.

20. Dunford, A. (2019). *Obviously awesome: How to nail product positioning so customers get it, buy it, love it*. Ambient Press.

21. Miteva, A. (2020). 101 Incredible mission statement examples (in 2021) - mktoolboxsuite.com. https://mktoolboxsuite.com/mission-statement-examples/. Accessed September 19, 2021.

22. Difference Between Vision & Mission Statements: 25 Examples. https://www.clearvoice.com/blog/difference-between-mission-vision-statement-examples/. Accessed September 19, 2021.

23. Moore, G. A. (2014). *Crossing the chasm: Marketing and selling disruptive products to mainstream customers* (3rd ed.). HarperBusiness, an imprint of HarperCollins Publishers.

24. McGrath, M. E. (2001). *Product strategy for high technology companies: Accelerating your business to web speed* (2nd ed.). McGraw-Hill.

25. Sutherland J, & Schwaber K. (2020). The scrum guide. The Definitive Guide to Scrum: The Rules of the Game.

26. Pichler, R. (2010). *Agile product management with scrum: Creating products that customers love*. Addison-Wesley.

27. Gorschek, T., Fricker, S., Palm, K., & Kunsman, S. (2010). A lightweight innovation process for software-intensive product development. *IEEE Software, 27*, 37–45. https://doi.org/10.1109/MS.2009.164
28. Chesbrough, H. W. (2011). *Open innovation: The new imperative for creating and profiting from technology, Nachdr*. Harvard Business School Press.
29. Future Internet Social and Technological Alignment Research | FI-STAR Project. https://cordis.europa.eu/project/id/604691. Accessed September 19, 2021.
30. Lynn, G. S., Abel, K. D., Valentine, W. S., & Wright, R. C. (1999). Key factors in increasing speed to market and improving new product success rates. *Industrial Marketing Management, 28*, 319–326. https://doi.org/10.1016/S0019-8501(98)00008-X
31. Lynn, G. S., & Akgün, A. E. (2001). Project visioning: Its components and impact on new product success. *Journal of Product Innovation Management, 18*, 374–387. https://doi.org/10.1111/1540-5885.1860374
32. Weinstein, A., & Weinstein, A. (2004). *Handbook of market segmentation: Strategic targeting for business and technology firms* (3rd ed.). Haworth Press.
33. Osterwalder, A., Pigneur, Y., Bernarda, G., & Smith, A. (2014). *Value proposition design: How to create products and services customers want*. Wiley.
34. Osterwalder, A., Pigneur, Y., & Tucci, C. L. (2005). Clarifying business models: Origins, present, and future of the concept. *CAIS, 16*. https://doi.org/10.17705/1CAIS.01601
35. Moore, G. A. (2004). *Inside the tornado: Strategies for developing, leveraging, and surviving hypergrowth markets*. HarperBusiness Essentials.
36. Osterwalder, A., Pigneur, Y., & Clark, T. (2010). *Business model generation: A handbook for visionaries, game changers, and challengers*. Wiley.
37. Ries, E. (2019). *The lean startup: How constant innovation creates radically successful businesses*. Penguin Business.
38. Dolan, R. J., & Easwar, K. C. N. S. Worldwide.
39. Lattin, J., Levine, P., & Randolph, J. Dropbox.
40. Saltan, A., & Smolander, K. (2021). Bridging the state-of-the-art and the state-of-the-practice of SaaS pricing: A multivocal literature review. *Information and Software Technology, 133*, 106510.
41. Campbell, P. (2017). The anatomy of SaaS pricing strategy.
42. Saltan, A., & Smolander, K. (2021). How SaaS companies price their products: Insights from an industry study. In E. Klotins & K. Wnuk (Eds.), *11th international conference, ICSOB 2020* (pp. 1–13). Springer Nature Switzerland AG.
43. Hogan, J, & Nagle, T. (2005). What is strategic pricing? SPG Insights 7.
44. Nagle, T. T., Hogan, J. E., & Zale, J. (2016). *The strategy and tactics of pricing: A guide to growing more profitably* (5th ed.). New International Edition.
45. Cloud Utilisation Management is Key to Performance. https://www.cloudsigma.com/cloud-utilisation-management-is-key-to-performance/. Accessed September 19, 2021.

# Chapter 3
# Understanding Product Strategy and Roadmaps

**Saeed Khan**

**Abstract** Refining a product strategy into a roadmap is neither a simple nor straightforward task. Initially, a strategy must be defined for a specific product, addressing aspects such as the scoped time frame, solving a specific problem, or fitting into a portfolio strategy. While a strategy delineates what should and should not be done, the roadmap focuses on balancing short-term objectives, such as sales targets, with long-term goals to ensure future readiness. To achieve this balance, scenarios and use cases can be developed and prioritized for the roadmap. For instance, the BRICE framework can be applied for prioritization. However, strategies often resemble hypotheses, and the roadmap serves as a means to validate these hypotheses—acknowledging that not all hypotheses will be correct, making them akin to bets. The process of defining and refining a product strategy and roadmap is illustrated with examples from well-known companies, highlighting both successful and less successful bets.

**Keywords** Product strategy · Product roadmap · Cloud roadmap

## 3.1 Introduction

If you ask a dozen product managers what a roadmap is, you'll likely get a dozen different answers. Some will talk about a detailed plan, some will talk about strategy and vision, some will define it in short-term timelines, others in longer time

S. Khan (✉)
MaRS Discovery District, MaRS Centre, Toronto, ON, Canada
e-mail: skhan@transformationlabs.io

Y. Hajizadeh et al. (eds.), *Building Cloud Software Products*,
Innovation, Technology, and Knowledge Management,
https://doi.org/10.1007/978-3-031-92184-1_3

35

horizons. The answers will vary and in all likelihood, most will be incorrect. The word roadmap means different things to different people.

If a product manager tells a salesperson that some particular functionality is "on the roadmap," the salesperson will likely assume it is committed to be built and they'll want to know when, so they can decide if it is something they can sell. In contrast, if a product manager tells an engineer something is "on the roadmap," the engineer will likely ignore the news, because it's not something that needs to be analyzed, designed, and built in the near future.

So what exactly is a product roadmap? A product roadmap is a time-based representation of product strategy.[1] In other words, it shows the product-related components of your key strategies and **roughly** when they will be delivered over time. A roadmap is *not* a detailed plan, nor is it a delivery commitment. A roadmap is not a list of features to be built. It shows the key product-related elements that derive from your strategies and helps define a more detailed plan, ensuring important product goals have focus prioritization.

## 3.2   Types of Roadmaps

There is no single type or format for a roadmap. There can be different types of product roadmaps depending on the need.

There can be internal and external roadmaps. Internal roadmaps are internal to the company, business unit, or even team. They will be more detailed and may contain elements that are either confidential or not important to other groups. For example, an internal roadmap may include technology investments, infrastructure changes, security improvements, and changes that a company wouldn't want to share publicly.

An external roadmap may be less detailed than an internal roadmap and may also include timeframes that are less aggressive than an internal roadmap. That is, a company may not want to reveal their strategic goals and timeframes in a public fashion and tip off their competitors.

There can be product and portfolio roadmaps. A product roadmap only represents a single product, whereas a portfolio roadmap would include several (related) products that are part of a larger portfolio.

There can also be technology roadmaps that show the underlying technology changes that will occur to support the strategies in play. Depending on the audience (external, internal, partner, customer, analyst, etc.) and the need (a sales deal, an analyst briefing, an internal technical discussion, an executive briefing, etc.), a roadmap can take many forms with varying levels of detail, timeframes, and confidence.

---

[1] https://www.sciencedirect.com/science/article/pii/S0007681321000161.

## 3.3   Roadmaps, Strategy, and Objectives

Roadmaps don't exist in a vacuum, but in a context of other critical business planning entities They are an integral part of business and strategic planning.

The following hierarchy—which I call the Vision Stack[2] shows the relationship between key business elements such as vision, objectives, strategy, etc. Each layer provides context and focus for the layers below it.

# The Vision Stack

**Alignment from Vision down through to Plans**

For any business, there should be a clear business vision, objectives, and strategy. The vision is a timeless aspirational goal of that business. For example, for Tesla, that vision is:

> To create the most compelling car company of the twenty-first century by driving the world's transition to electric vehicles.

It's a statement of purpose. It doesn't talk about **how** or have specific target dates or metrics. And it's not an objective. That is, it doesn't say something like "to be the leading company accelerating the transition to renewable energy."

A good vision answers the question "Why do we exist and why are we doing what we are doing?". To fulfill a vision, a company defines objectives and strategies (choices) to support and achieve those objectives. The objectives are typically business focused but can also include technical, financial, or other types, depending on the context. For any product in a company, there should also be a vision, objectives, and strategies. These would follow a similar model as above. For example, a product vision is a timeless, aspirational goal for a product. The product objectives will be

---

[2] https://swkhan.medium.com/the-vision-stack-part-1-dd9a3a771985.

defined within the context of that vision and the strategies created to support those objectives.

The roadmap sits below the product strategy and above product plans. That is, it is defined in the context of the overall vision, objectives, and strategies and in turn constrains and helps focus the specific product plans that will be implemented.

### 3.3.1 Objectives

As stated earlier, objectives are typically business objectives—e.g., a revenue target, customer acquisition goal, product usage target, etc.—that will drive adoption, growth, profitability, etc. depending on the lifecycle stage of the product. There could also be technical, production, market share, expansion or other objectives defined for a product.[3]

For example, in 2020, Tesla had a production goal of 500,000 vehicles. Given that there was clear demand for their cars, the production goal not only helped them deliver on their backlog of orders but also forced them to figure out how to continue to scale up their manufacturing capability, which of course is a key business objective.

### 3.3.2 Strategy

Strategy can be a nebulous concept. Just like the term roadmap, ask 10 people to define strategy and you'll likely get 10 different answers, with many of them incorrect. Sometimes people say something like: "our strategy is to be a leader in our market." That's not a strategy, that's an objective.

A strategy can be thought of as a specific, coordinated approach to solving a problem or reaching a goal. For example, when solving a crossword puzzle, one can have a strategy, such as solving the short words first and then using those to solve the longer ones.

In sports, teams and coaches have strategies for defeating their opponents. For example, a football team may have a strategy to run the ball as much as possible instead of passing it because they know the opposing team has a weak defense.

In essence, a strategy is a hypothesis, choice or a bet that a team or organization makes based on knowledge and evidence, to help fulfill its objectives, i.e., what must a company do or where should it focus, in addition to regular operations to achieve its objectives.

For example, a company that provides disaster recovery software and services may decide that in order to grow and outpace their competition, they need to expand geographically, i.e., the hypothesis (or bet) is that this is the best way to grow.

---

[3] https://swkhan.medium.com/driving-clarity-and-alignment-via-business-and-product-objectives-6d2c9cca2046.

If the company has been focused on North American markets, then the next question is where to expand into. Based on market trends or other research, they believe (i.e., another hypothesis) the best place to expand into is the UK and Western Europe. They will need to consider the business, organizational, go-to-market, and product implications of this strategy.

For example:

- Do they open up new offices and staff them with sales and marketing teams or work with channel partners?
- Do they need a unified go-to-market plan in the UK and Europe or does it need to be regional or country specific?
- What product changes are needed to support this strategy?
- How should they price the product?
- Are there data privacy and security requirements that must be addressed?
- How will they measure the success of this initiative?
- Etc.

The strategy affects many parts of the company, with the product needs being only a part of the overall actions to support the strategy.

Good strategies help companies focus on both what they will do and what they won't do. This is very important to understand. If a strategy is a key component in achieving an objective, then it must have focus and effort behind it, and that alone will reduce (if not eliminate) other activities that aren't tied to a given strategy. In that sense, strategy helps prioritize work to be done and feeds into a roadmap that will be developed.

Strategies must incorporate and account for company capabilities—what the company does well and what it doesn't—market and competitor realities and ability to execute within a timeframe aligned with objectives.

Continuing with the Tesla example, in 2019, they produced about 370,000 vehicles. Their goal was 500,000 vehicles in 2020 (a 50% increase over 2019). They simply couldn't do what they did in 2019 to hit that number, and simple incremental improvements wouldn't be enough either.

Tesla needed to try some new strategies to get to their target. Tesla focused on improving production times at their existing plant in Fremont, California, increasing capacity by opening up a new plant in China and launching the Model Y SUV to increase sales.[4] Opening a new plant and launching the Model Y were not guarantees, especially during the pandemic. But as it turned out, they were successful, as Tesla manufactured almost 510,000 vehicles in 2020.

Not all strategies are tied to annual business objectives like we just explained. Often a strategy, particularly a core product strategy, has a much longer timeframe. If you've heard of the Tesla Master Plan,[5] it can be summarized as:

- Build sports car.
- Use that money to build an affordable car.

---

[4] https://techcrunch.com/2021/01/02/tesla-delivers-nearly-500000-vehicles-in-2020/.

[5] https://www.tesla.com/blog/secret-tesla-motors-master-plan-just-between-you-and-me.

- Use *that* money to build an even more affordable car.
- While doing above, also provide zero-emission electric power generation options.

This was effectively their product strategy. The ultimate goal was to get a mass market vehicle that most people could afford—the Model 3—to market. But in order to do that, they needed to learn how to design, manufacture, deliver, and support their vehicles. It wasn't just about making money. This strategy helped them achieve those goals over a period of about 10 years, with a clear product roadmap—the sports car (Model S), the more affordable SUV (Model X), and the truly affordable Model 3.

Note that the roadmap didn't specify the exact timelines and deliverables but it gave them clear direction and priority, with the year to year, model to model details to be worked out in more detailed design, manufacturing, and delivery plans.

### 3.3.3 Portfolio Strategy

For companies with multiple products, there can also be portfolio objectives and strategies. These define how multiple products can be integrated, bundled, marketed, and/or sold together to better compete in the market than each of the products could individually.

Probably the best example of a successful product portfolio strategy is Microsoft Office.[6] Originally, Microsoft Word, Excel, and PowerPoint were sold individually and competed directly against other standalone products. Word competed against WordPerfect and WordStar, Excel against Lotus 123 and Borland Quattro Pro, and PowerPoint against Aldus Persuasion and Harvard Graphics, amongst others.

While each competitive product had its strengths and weaknesses, only Microsoft sold all three types of products (word processing, spreadsheet, and presentations). Both Excel and Word were functionally strong, while PowerPoint (an acquisition) was not a leader in its category.

But by creating Office that included all three—something no other company could do—and selling Office at a discounted price compared to multiple standalone products, Microsoft dominated the market for desktop office productivity tools. And over time, Microsoft added other products such as Outlook, Publisher, etc. to further depend against competitors and maintain its market dominance.

Microsoft made it easy for companies to buy Office, and once it was in widespread use, it was difficult for competitors to make inroads on corporate desktops. Standalone competitors to individual products (e.g., WordPerfect,[7] Aldus Persuasion[8]) were virtually shut out of the market, and other suites created in

---

[6] https://en.wikipedia.org/wiki/Microsoft_Office.

[7] https://en.wikipedia.org/wiki/WordPerfect.

[8] https://en.wikipedia.org/wiki/Adobe_Persuasion.

response to Office, such as Borland's Office[9] (WordPerfect, Quattro Pro, Corel Presentation), failed to achieve traction. Even free alternatives such as StarOffice[10] and LibreOffice[11] couldn't overcome Microsoft's grip because of functional gaps, document compatibility, or other reasons.

Microsoft Office has been one of the most profitable software products ever. In 2016 alone, Microsoft Office generated $24B in revenue, with $12.4B of operating income (i.e., gross profit). Compare that to $8.1B of TOTAL revenue for Windows in that same year.[12]

Microsoft Office shows the power of a great portfolio strategy and the lasting impact it can have on a company and an industry.

### 3.3.4   Roadmaps Without Strategy

Is it possible to have a roadmap without strategy? Technically the answer is yes, because many companies do exactly that. But the question is whether those companies have good roadmaps that have a firm basis in business and that help them accelerate towards their vision. The answer to that is probably not.

Good roadmaps derive from strategies that support objectives. If you don't have strategies, then how can you have a roadmap? You may have something that you call a roadmap—a set of product goals and deliverables over time, but where did those deliverables come from?

This is a common pattern within companies. They have objectives, often a revenue target, and their "strategy" is to close deals, sign up customers, etc. But without actual business strategies (that tie back up to objectives and vision), what connects their objectives to their roadmap? And how can that roadmap be described because it's no longer an articulation of product strategy.

## 3.4   Strategies and Prioritization

As mentioned earlier, strategies help define what will be done and also what won't, where to focus and where not to focus. Strategies also help with prioritizing work by providing a context to compare and evaluate what is and isn't important.

Here's a common scenario that occurs in many software companies. The company has set forth with product objectives, such as a revenue target for the year, and asks product management to create a roadmap. The first question is, what product strategy (or strategies) should the company follow?

---

[9] https://en.wikipedia.org/wiki/Borland.

[10] https://en.wikipedia.org/wiki/StarOffice.

[11] https://en.wikipedia.org/wiki/LibreOffice.

[12] https://office-watch.com/2017/office-profitable-part-microsoft/.

The answer is often: whatever generates revenue or moves them closer to the target they set. The first problem is that this is not strategy. The second problem is that it's the deal (size) that drives the product work and functionality and not a clear vision and prioritization that aligns with what the broader market demands.

A large deal with a few riders attached, to build some functionality that is particular to that one customer is actually worse for the company than a smaller deal that helps fund and accelerate product functionality that supports the vision and broader market needs.

This is a pattern repeated many times over in companies. Strategies help you say no to work that doesn't align with your objectives. The roadmap is a product-focused articulation of those strategies. And when there aren't any strategies, there really isn't a roadmap.

What is there instead are a lot of plans and work driven by short-term, deal-driven priorities. The "roadmap" and plans merge, and the explicit connection back up to the objectives (aside from revenue) and the vision are broken. This results in what is often called a "feature factory."[13]

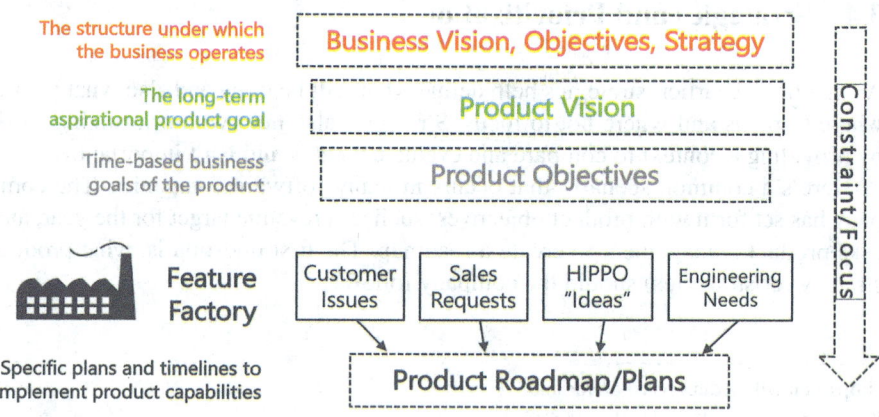

---

[13] https://cutle.fish/blog/12-signs-youre-working-in-a-feature-factory.

The challenge here is that while there can be success in the short term—i.e., hitting revenue targets—there is little investment in longer-term success and truly addressing changing market needs. If a company hits their sales targets this year, they are not well positioned to accelerate their growth the next year because their focus has been short term and deal driven.

And just to be clear, it's not that these customer issues, sales requests, HIPPO ideas, etc. disappear when a company has defined strategies; no, they still exist. But the difference is that those strategies define a clear context of what is important to the business and why.

So when these issues, requests, ideas, needs, etc. are raised, they can be evaluated in that context, and decisions can be made about what takes priority. Without that strategic context, the prioritization will likely end up being tied to the biggest deals, or the loudest voices or the HIPPO's choice.

The cascading focus, from vision to objectives to strategies to roadmap, etc., helps connect plans and actions directly back up to objectives and vision. Prioritization is built into the process. This doesn't mean that more tactical or deal-driven work is blocked. What it means is that that work must be prioritized intentionally within the context of the strategies. It also means that sometimes tough decisions must be made to walk away from a deal or negotiate with customers to ensure strategies aren't derailed in pursuit of short-term revenue.

## 3.4.1  Scenarios and Use Cases

Once a roadmap is defined, and product plans are being developed, a common question is "What features are we building?". In all honesty, this is a problematic question. Building "features" should not be the goal of any software company. What people should be asking is "What customer problems are we solving?", or "How will we enable our customers to achieve their goals?"

Focus on solving customer problems[14] (vs. building features) is the best way to ensure that what is provided to customers is actually valuable to them. It's never been easier to build software, and thus it's never been more important to understand what is meaningful, useful and valuable to the market. Why? Because developing software is not an exercise in writing code or building features. It's an exercise in enabling customers to achieve better outcomes in the work that they need to do. And if it is easy for you to build software, it's also easy for your competitors.

Where a company can gain real competitive advantage is in truly understanding what customers need and what will enable them to achieve better outcomes, and then focusing on delivering that. The deeper the understanding of the problems and needs, the better the potential value of the solutions that are delivered.

Understanding user scenarios—i.e., the context and flow of the work they need to do—is the first step in developing and delivering valued solutions. It's not simply

---

[14] https://www.upwardspiralgroup.com/blog/the-importance-of-focusing-on-customer-pain-points-solving-problems-vs-selling-solutions.

understanding *what* they want to do, but also *who* needs to do what, *how that work needs to be performed, when i*t must be done, and most importantly *why.*

Each of those questions—who, what, when, how, and why—provides detail and context to what the real user scenarios and use cases are. The knowledge enables product teams to build valuable and lasting solutions that will be used and not relegated to "shelfware."

### 3.4.2   Scenarios Describe the Real World

For example, in an HR application, the concept of booking holiday time may sound very simple. An employee goes into the application, identifies the dates they want to book their holiday, and then blocks them off and (if necessary) a message is sent to a manager requesting approval.

For the manager, getting these requests is not as simple as just approving them. The manager needs to make sure that staffing levels for their team—e.g., a customer support team—are maintained to provide proper levels of service to their customers. If there are specific SLAs for certain accounts for certain tiers of customers, the manager needs to ensure the staff with the knowledge and skills to meet those SLAs are always available. And what about planning for availability around holidays? The manager may need help with that, again to ensure staff availability as well as both fairness to employees and accommodation of their needs.

The manager needs a completely different interface with very different scenarios supported than an individual employee simply booking time off. Different departments in the same company may have different policies related to holidays. For example, a sales operations department may have policies against booking time off at the end of a quarter, to ensure staff are available to process and close end-of-quarter deals. But the same policy may not be needed for an engineering team as their responsibilities are not tied to calendar quarters.

Each of these scenarios must be understood, documented, prioritized, analyzed, and deconstructed into requirements for a product team to implement.

It is only by understanding the real-world objectives and constraints of people's jobs that a company can build a product that meets those needs. Without this context, a company focusing on building "features," without a clear connection to the real world, will deliver little value to customers and ultimately is a source of waste and missed opportunity for the vendor.

## 3.5   Prioritization

As described earlier, when thinking about a roadmap, prioritization is driven by objectives—i.e., what are the most important product goals (and the strategies to support those objectives)? There is a clear connection to what is important and why.

This doesn't mean that sales requests, customer escalations, HIPPO ideas, etc., cannot be considered, but they must be considered in the context of those strategies. Do they support the strategies? Do they help achieve the objectives those strategies support? Do they help the company achieve its longer-term goals?

If the answer to these questions is "No," then it should be an easy decision not to pursue them. But that is often not the case. Short-term revenue, "the potential" of a significant deal, an "opportunity" identified by an executive, etc., all too often derail plans and strategies. The cost can be significant, as resources and focus are diverted to support these tactical and often risky initiatives. And, if or when the deals don't close, or ideas don't pan out, is there an accounting of what was lost, not just with respect to the deal or idea, but also in the strategies and efforts that were deprioritized to accommodate them?

An approach to solving this problem is to acknowledge that these escalations and deals will appear and have a set of decision filters that are applied to each one, e.g., alignment with strategy, alternative of NOT pursuing the opportunity, applicability to other customers, etc.[15]

There is no predefined set of filters that can be applied in all cases. Companies think this through and decide how they want to prioritize work, opportunities and decisions. The value of decision filters is that they bring a standard, open, and consistent approach to making prioritization decisions. The trick though is not in defining them but in sticking with them, especially when the decisions are difficult. Otherwise, their value disappears and there is only the appearance of a standard, open, consistent process.

### 3.5.1 The Problems of Prioritization Frameworks

In business, prioritization can be both a complex and imprecise activity. One approach people have taken is to use prioritization frameworks to address both the complexity and ambiguity. There are *many* prioritization frameworks that have been defined and can be used. Some of the more popular or well-known ones include but not limited to MoSCoW,[16] Opportunity Scoring,[17] RICE/BRICE,[18] Impact vs. Effort,[19] WSJF,[20] etc. While they all have their differences, they also have some similarities, and those similarities also reveal their weaknesses.

---

[15] https://swkhan.medium.com/how-to-deal-with-b2b-sales-driven-feature-requests-5199ec308a38.

[16] https://en.wikipedia.org/wiki/MoSCoW_method.

[17] https://www.productplan.com/glossary/opportunity-scoring/.

[18] https://medium.com/swlh/use-brice-not-rice-scoring-for-product-prioritization-8e2fa3546748.

[19] https://openpracticelibrary.com/practice/impact-effort-prioritization-matrix/.

[20] https://www.scaledagileframework.com/wsjf/.

The first similarity/weakness is that they are based on estimates, which often have significant margins of error and those are not included in the calculations.

The second is that they promote a bottom-up approach when prioritizing, i.e., a focus on individual tasks and "features" as opposed to objectives and strategies. A third problem with the formula based frameworks—e.g. RICE/BRICE, WSJF—is that as formulas, they are not mathematically valid, and thus provide values that are non-sensical.

## 3.6    Estimates and Margins of Error

Let's drill down into the first issue.

BRICE is a prioritization framework and is defined as:

Priority Value = (Business Importance * Reach * Impact * Confidence) / Effort.

Thus, the higher the priority value, the more important or valuable the task or problem is to the company, or at least that's what the model claims.

Now each of those elements—Business Importance, Reach, Impact, Confidence and Effort—seems reasonable to consider, and having some way to relate them all seems like a good approach. And yet, this approach is almost certain to lead people down a false path of confidence.

First, note that each of these elements is a subjective assessment. There are no absolute measures here—e.g., impact, confidence, etc. —and even effort, which may appear analytic is not. Why? Because we know that, with the exception of the smallest tasks, even when people perform very detailed analyses of effort, those analyses are at best estimates because they cannot account for unknowns that will arise during the course of the work.

Often these elements are scored on a very subjective scale of 1–5 or 1–10 where 1 is lowest and 5 (or 10) is highest.

Thus, each of the elements is at best an estimate with a margin of error (MoE) built into it. But the BRICE equation has no way of accounting for those MoEs.

A simple mathematical rule when dealing with MoE is that for each element in a formula that has an MoE, the MoE should be expressed as a percentage of the value of the element, and that the total MoE of the result of the formula is the SUM of the MoEs of each element.

$$\text{Total MoE} = \text{Sum}\left(\text{MoE}_1 + \text{MoE}_2 + \text{MoE}_3 \ldots\ldots \text{MoE}_n\right)$$

As an example, if the MoE of each element in the BRICE formula is 15% (a conservative MoE by any measure), then given there are five elements in the calculation, the total MoE of the calculation is 75%, i.e., 15% × 5 elements.

Now let's think about that. A number/value with a + or −75% MoE is almost useless when comparing against other numbers. If I told you the temperature tomorrow would be 20°C, ±75%, that would be a range of 5° to 35°. Or if a sales rep forecast their expected target for the year as $1,000,000 ± 75%, that would be anywhere between $250,000 and $1,750,000. Both of these are utterly useless to anyone who cares about them.

Now if we apply this to work that needs to be prioritized, we get the same useless result.

For example, if we have 2 initiatives, Init1 and Init2, and they have BRICE values of 45 and 65 (where higher is "better"), then it would appear that Init2 with a score of 65 is the preferred one.

But if we include the MoE of each (let's assume it's the same 75% value we described earlier), then their values are 45 ± 75% and 65 ±75%. Converting those to values they become:

| Initiative | Value | Low MoE (−75%) | High MoE (+75%) |
| --- | --- | --- | --- |
| Init1 | 45 | 11 | 79 |
| Init2 | 65 | 16 | 114 |

Now, looking at these ranges—11 to 79 and 16 to 114—and knowing that there is such a large overlap when the MoE is included, can anyone say with certainty that Init2 is absolutely preferred to Init1? No.

The MoEs are a necessary part of the calculation. If they are not included, then while the exercise looks analytic and definitive, it is actually just a form of prioritization theater.

Now whether one uses BRICE or Impact vs. Effort (which only has two factors), the MoE issue remains. You cannot turn estimates into absolutes simply by ignoring the MoE.

## 3.7   Bottom-Up Prioritization

The second major problem with prioritization frameworks is that they involve, if not encourage, a bottom-up prioritization mindset. Think about what would be prioritized via these frameworks. It's not strategies or important business objectives. The items that are evaluated via these frameworks are features or smaller tactical initiatives. Are these aligned with higher-level strategies and objectives? If so, they should be prioritized using those. If they are not, then why not? Why are they important?

Prioritization frameworks often are applied to orphan tasks or initiatives, i.e., those not attached to a strategy or those that arise in a feature factory. Another place where prioritization frameworks are used is in prioritizing backlog items, i.e., prioritizing a long list of "features" that have accumulated over time. In both of these cases, the bottom-up prioritization gives the false belief that important things are being prioritized because they bubble up to the top of the framework. If there isn't a clear tie back up to agreed-upon objectives and strategic priorities, then there is no way to know if something is or isn't important aside from "gut feel" or "the prioritization framework said so." I'm sure the problem with both of those reasons is self-evident.

In short, these prioritization frameworks lead back to a feature-factory mindset or process with an analytic appearance that is likely to work against a company's longer-term goals.

## 3.8   Conclusion

Strategy is a difficult activity to do well. In fact, one could say that there's a fine line between strategy and fantasy.[21] If strategy was easy, everyone would not only be successful at it, but also everyone would agree on exactly what it is. The fact that neither of these is true indicates that there is still a lot of work to be done by executives in this area.

Even experienced executives fail impressively in this. A notable strategic failure in tech was in 2011 when HP CEO Leo Apotheker proclaimed that:

WebOS (the OS in their HP TouchPad tablet) was key to their overall market strategy "**for at least the next TWO YEARS**."

Remember that Apple had introduced the iPad a year earlier in 2010 and the tablet market was hot, hot, hot. HP had also acquired Palm Computing in 2010[22] for over $1B to aid in this tablet strategy. And yet, only a few months after making that proclamation, Apotheker talked about the tablet "disaster" that HP was facing.[23]

This is why people should look at strategies as hypotheses or bets. They are beliefs of the right way forward, but market conditions and the realities of business are never static nor guarantees for success. We should expect some strategies to succeed, while some will not. And so, the roadmaps, plans and priorities that fall out from those strategies must be viewed with that uncertainty in mind. A product roadmap is a product-centric articulation of strategy. A product plan includes work driven by the roadmap but will also include tasks from more tactical sources, such as sales opportunities or other customer or technical commitments.

In the end, the goal is to align the work the company does back up to the vision and objectives of the business, and set a path for future success. Vision, objectives, strategy, roadmaps and plans all need to be aligned and work together to move the product and company forward. When any of them are missing or out of alignment, friction and disruption occur. This causes loss of potential and momentum to company plans and success.

---

[21] https://medium.com/swlh/theres-a-fine-line-between-strategy-and-fantasy-982431e83b94.

[22] https://www.hp.com/us-en/hp-news/press-release.html?id=416441#.YV9XrKBE2F0.

[23] https://www.zdnet.com/article/hps-apotheker-recounts-touchpad-disaster-in-post-mortem/.

# Chapter 4
# The Challenges of User Research in Product Management

Saeed Khan

**Abstract** User research is a broad field that encompasses understanding market dynamics, customer needs, and user problems. It involves creating human-centered scenarios to identify opportunities for defining, developing, delivering, and selling products that meet user needs. The primary challenge is to comprehend the users' problems and pain points, rather than merely addressing interesting issues. To tackle this challenge, various types of user research can be utilized. This chapter presents both generative and evaluative user research, as well as approaches such as attitudinal and behavioral, and quantitative and qualitative research. It outlines research methods and techniques for conducting user research effectively. Additionally, it discusses the reasons why user research is often not conducted with sufficient time to gather profound insights.

**Keywords** User research · Generative user research · Evaluative user research · Cloud services

## 4.1 Introduction

User research and discovery is a broad topic related to customer, user, market and product research.

It is about understanding market, customer, and user problems and identifying opportunities so that you can define, develop, deliver, market, operate, sell, and improve products that completely meet those market and customer needs.[1]

---

[1] https://www.nngroup.com/articles/discovery-phase/.

---

S. Khan (✉)
MaRS Discovery District, MaRS Centre, Toronto, ON, Canada
e-mail: skhan@transformationlabs.io

© The Author(s), under exclusive license to Springer Nature Switzerland AG 2025
Y. Hajizadeh et al. (eds.), *Building Cloud Software Products*, Innovation, Technology, and Knowledge Management, https://doi.org/10.1007/978-3-031-92184-1_4

49

We live in a complex and dynamic world that needs specific solutions and products to address specific problems and leverage new and valuable opportunities.

How can anyone build successful products that people will use and benefit from without really understanding needs, problems, and opportunities?

Einstein is attributed as saying[2]:

> If I had an hour to solve a problem I'd spend 55 minutes thinking about the problem and five minutes thinking about solutions.

And who are we to argue with Einstein?

Seriously though, understanding problems, both broadly and deeply, is fundamental to product success.

> The quality of your solution (not just the product, but the entire go-to-market, including pricing, messaging, positioning etc.) all depend on the depth of your understanding of the problem.

The challenge with discovery is not just about understanding problems so you can build something people need. It's also about understanding the people themselves, the environments they work in, the ways they'll acquire the product, how they perceive the value of the solution, etc. so that you can also optimize marketing, sales, services, support, etc. and align the company to maximize success.

It's really strange, but there are so many products brought to market that fail, and the number one reason for failure is no market need. CB Insights[3] in their analysis of reasons why startups fail describes it this way:

> Tackling problems that are interesting to solve rather than those that serve a market need was cited as the number one reason for failure in a notable 42% of cases. As Patient Communicator wrote, "I realized, essentially, that we had no customers because no one was really interested in the model we were pitching. Doctors want more patients, not an efficient office."
>
> Treehouse Logic applied the concept more broadly in their post-mortem, writing, "Startups fail when they are not solving a market problem. We were not solving a large enough problem that we could universally serve with a scalable solution. We had great technology, great data on shopping behavior, great reputation as a thought leader, great expertise, great advisors, etc., but what we didn't have was technology or business model that solved a pain point in a scalable way.

Market and customer discovery and research are an antidote to this problem. Sadly, a lot of companies feel they can iterate their way to success, and mantras like Build, Measure, Learn[4] are misapplied and lead people astray. It's akin to a Ready, Fire, Aim[5] approach.

Instead people should focus on a Learn, Analyse, Build (LAB) cycle. It won't guarantee success, but it will help you understand what you're doing and why, *before* investing significant time and resources into building the wrong products.

---

[2] https://conversational-leadership.net/quotation/hour-to-solve-a-problem/.

[3] The Top 20 Reasons Startups Fail.

[4] https://theleanstartup.com/principles.

[5] https://i-lead.com/ila-articles/ready-fire-aim/.

This is akin to the OODA[6] loop—Observe, Orient, Decide, Act, i.e., understand the situation and *then* act based on that understanding.

## 4.2  Types of User Research

There are many types of user research. If we ask people to name them, the most common ones that are cited are surveys, interviews, focus groups, A/B tests, and possibly card sorting exercises. These are all examples of research *techniques*, and there are many more. Some other research techniques include:

- Usability testing.[7]
- Ethnographic (observational) studies.[8]
- Eye-tracking studies.[9]
- User feedback capture.[10]
- Intercept surveys.[11]

These are all research techniques, used in specific contexts and with specific goals. But there are higher levels of research that can be considered when thinking about discovery. One way to break out research is generative (or exploratory) research and evaluative (or validation) research.

### 4.2.1  Generative Versus Evaluative Research

Generative research is usually applied when you are exploring a new product area or market or looking for new problems to address. It's difficult work because there are so many unknowns. It's a bit of a treasure hunt in that you don't know where the treasure is, and you have to look for clues and signals that may or may not be accurate. And you might even overlook the treasure if you don't interpret the clues correctly.

Evaluative research is typically done once you've identified a problem or have a specific objective and you want to learn more about that, e.g., you've heard from many customers that your product has security issues and you want to identify them and then decide how to address them.

---

[6] https://en.wikipedia.org/wiki/OODA_loop.

[7] https://en.wikipedia.org/wiki/Usability_testing.

[8] https://en.wikipedia.org/wiki/Ethnography.

[9] https://en.wikipedia.org/wiki/Eye_tracking.

[10] https://hpi-epic.github.io/dt-at-it-toolbox/methods/09%20-%20Feedback%20Capture%20 Grid.pdf.

[11] https://rmsresults.com/2021/04/15/what-is-an-intercept-survey/.

Generative and evaluative research can be used together. The "classic" Double Diamond[12] diagram incorporates both generative and evaluative research into it, with generative in the first diamond and evaluative in the second.

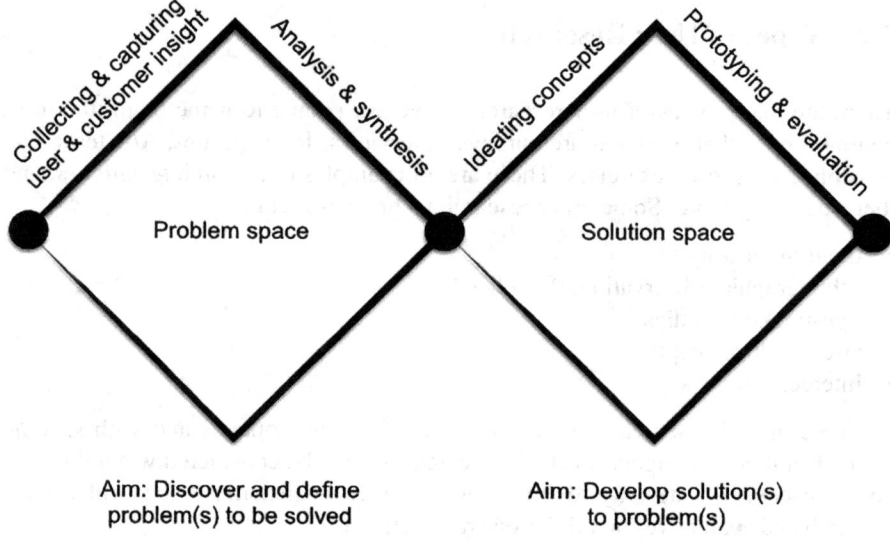

Source: http://stopandfix.blogspot.com/2015/07/the-double-diamond-process.html

But there are other ways to think about types of research. One could look at attitudinal vs. behavioral research, or qualitative vs. quantitative research.

### 4.2.2   Attitudinal Versus Behavioral Research

Attitudinal[13] research focuses on asking people about their views or opinions. Interviews and surveys are classic techniques for attitudinal research. Behavioral research is research through observation. A/B tests, usability studies, and eye-tracking studies are all classic examples of behavioral research because they require the participants to actively perform tasks in order to conduct the research. Each approach has its strengths and it's important to understand them. For example, asking people what they will do in a certain situation (attitudinal) vs. what they actually do in that same situation (behavioral) are often very different. There's a great line by advertising industry legend David Ogilvy[14] that speaks to this directly.

---

[12] https://www.designcouncil.org.uk/our-resources/the-double-diamond/.

[13] https://www.nngroup.com/articles/attitudinal-behavioral/.

[14] https://en.wikipedia.org/wiki/David_Ogilvy_(businessman).

The trouble with market research is that people don't think what they feel, they don't say what they think and they don't do what they say. - David Ogilvy

## 4.2.3   *Quantitative Versus Qualitative Research*

A third way to think about research is to break it down into quantitative (numerical) research and qualitative (non-numerical) research. We are generally familiar with quantitative research.[15] A/B tests, eye-tracking studies, and numerical survey questions all fall under the quantitative category. Quantitative research is generally performed on large numbers of people to collect "statistically significant" amounts of data, i.e., to draw conclusions from the data, we want to ensure it is large enough not to have a significant amount of noise or outlier data in it. Quantitative data helps us understand the "what" about a situation. For example, in A/B tests, we can learn what choices or preferences people have in a given situation.

Qualitative research (non-numerical) is any research that focuses on opinions or other subjective data. Qualitative research is done on smaller sets of participants than quantitative. The main reasons are that it is much harder to conduct than quantitative research, and interpreting the data is more difficult as well. For example, conducting a survey or an A/B test with 1000 participants is not much more difficult than with 100 people.

But conducting interviews with 1000 people is 10 times more effort than with 100 people. And quite honestly, with qualitative data, the focus is on identifying common signals or data in smaller data sets. A qualitative study with 50 people is a significant study in many cases and often far fewer participants can yield excellent results.

So the question arises as to how to make sense of all these research types and techniques.

First, generative and evaluative research are distinguished by their aims. Generative focuses on learning and exploring to find out about new concepts and ideas, whereas evaluative focuses on getting more clarity and understanding about specific known concepts. But there is no restriction on the specific techniques that are used, i.e., interviews can be used in both, surveys in both, etc.

Another way to think about these research types and techniques is to see the research types as characteristics of the techniques, i.e., can we map those types to those techniques in any way? And the answer is yes. Here's one way to think about them.

---

[15] https://www.fullstory.com/blog/qualitative-vs-quantitative-data/.

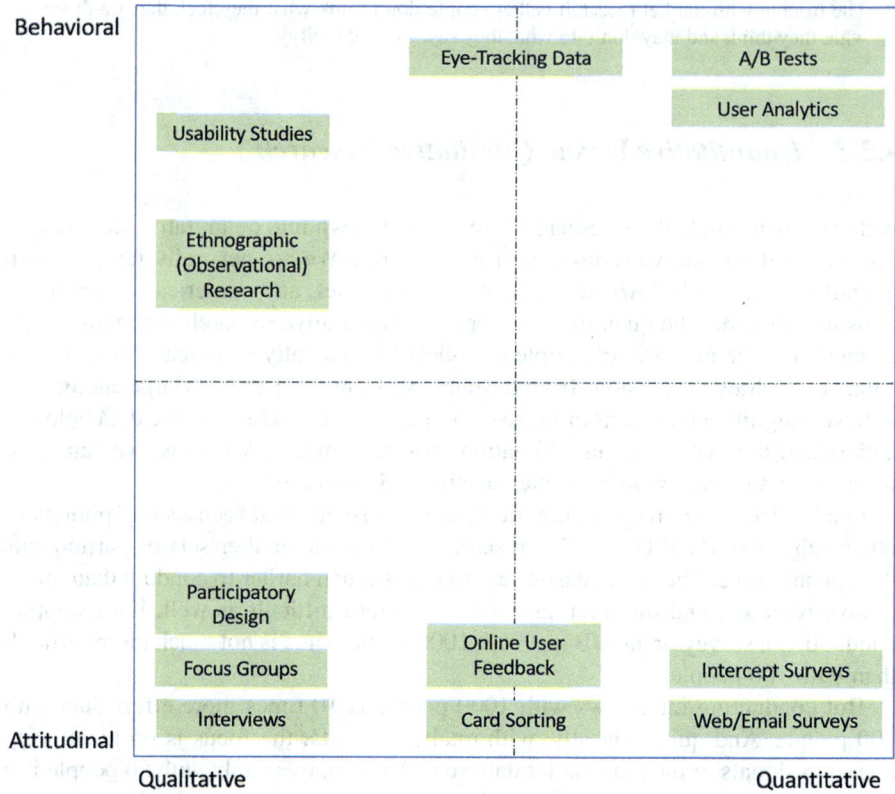

This is NOT a comprehensive list of all research techniques. A more detailed diagram can be found here.[16] There are others that could be mapped in this way, but there is a clear pattern of techniques being either heavily attitudinal or behavioral and being generally quantitative or qualitative.

It is up to the researcher to understand which type of research is most appropriate for their needs and to understand that a mix of types is often the best way to get a clear understanding of the customer, user, or other research topics being investigated.

### 4.2.4   Who Should Conduct the Research?

In modern technology companies, discovery should be a team sport. The goal of discovery is to gain market understanding, to understand customer and market needs, workflows, problems, objectives, etc. and to convert that into actionable

---

[16] https://www.nngroup.com/articles/which-ux-research-methods/.

insights[17] for the company to use in product design, development, marketing, and sales. It's a complex and multidimensional job and should not be taken on by a single individual—i.e., a product manager typically—to complete. It's best to get a small team representing key participants in the product development and delivery process.

For generative research, where the goal is to learn about new problems or markets, the team should consist of product management, product marketing, and user experience (UX) at minimum. Engineering can be part of the team where needed. The decision whether to include them or not really depends on the company, domain, and research focus. Engineering could include development, but also include data science or representatives of other technical teams.

For evaluative research, where there is a specific product focus, the key members should be product management, UX, and engineering. This is often called the product trio.[18]

Product marketing is not a required participant in evaluative research, but could participate if it was meaningful to them. The goal is to include those who can benefit the most from firsthand participation in the research. Additionally, depending on the company and type of product, team members from data science, customer success, or even professional services may benefit from participation.

It's important to note that firsthand participation gives the participants a very rich and nuanced understanding of the research that was performed. When conducting research, there is nothing better than to hear people speak firsthand, ask questions as they arise, and internalize the findings with that rich context.

Reading a report or having the findings presented to you (i.e., second or third hand) will never provide the same depth of understanding as firsthand participation. The report or presentation itself will be a summarization of the research. Most people cannot or will not be able to spend as much time thinking about the research and internalizing it the way the primary researchers have done. And if the bulk of the research is qualitative, the findings—essentially insights and conclusions arrived at from the research—will always be short of nuance and detail.

This is an important point to remember. The best research projects can go to waste if the research and findings cannot be understood or accepted by other stakeholders. They will bring their own personal biases, beliefs, and knowledge gaps to the research. This is not to imply any malice—though that is possible—but simply a statement of fact for how we consume and internalize new information. Often the most challenging part of any research, especially projects that have findings counter to existing internal beliefs, is to have those findings adopted and utilized by internal teams. They are not as attached to the findings as the research team, so they will not always keep it top of mind in their actions and decisions.

---

[17] https://aguayo.co/en/blog-aguayo-user-experience/insights-vs-findings-smart-research/.
[18] https://www.producttalk.org/2021/05/product-trio/.

## 4.2.5 Remote/Distributed Teams

One of the challenges in discovery is the fact that people are working remotely or in distributed teams. In many industries, it is rare to find everyone colocated in a single office all working together face to face. This is true for both the companies doing the research—e.g., product vendors—and their customers.

This makes research more difficult and, especially for observational studies, almost impossible in some cases. It also requires investment in interactive tools and better interview skills. It's very different to have a group of people sitting around a table and conducting a focus group or panel interview or even a card sorting exercise, and doing the same online via conferencing tools.

There is a change in the way people respond to questions, the way they react to other people's comments, and the way they interact with cards, Post-it notes, or other props when in person vs. when online. It's important to understand this because it can impact the data that is collected from the research that is done.

Having said that, given the nature of the world we live in, it's also a reality that we have to deal with. Intuit, makers of Quicken, had a very famous Follow Me Home[19] program to better understand how their users use their product in their home environments, i.e., an Intuit representative actually goes to a customer's home and observes the customer using the product in their home office or environment.

They get to see what their office or desk setup is like, what other tools they use, how they actually use the product, what challenges they face, etc. This program, essentially ethnographic research, has helped Intuit better understand their users in ways that couldn't be done otherwise.

The pandemic has impacted that for obvious reasons, but Intuit has created a remote Follow Me Home program because of how important it is to them to truly understand customer needs.

So it is possible, in fact necessary, for remote and distributed teams to continue to perform discovery work. And whether through process changes and/or new tool adoption, insights can still be uncovered and utilized.

### 4.2.5.1 Identifying and Evaluating User Problems

While the topic of discovery is wide (generative, evaluative, behavioral, attitudinal, qualitative, quantitative etc.), one of the core goals of discovery is to identify and understand problems—and more specifically user problems. Let's define the term "users" first.

Users are the specific set of people who you believe will use and benefit from your product. Users is a very generic term, and it's better to describe them in some meaningful way. For example, in an application that identifies patterns and problems in enterprise data, such as a data profiling tool, the target user would likely be a data analyst, data steward, or data engineer.

---

[19] https://blogs.intuit.com/2021/01/21/why-every-company-should-be-doing-a-follow-me-home/.

It's best to be specific when thinking about users by identifying the specific groups or roles that you are targeting, as opposed to referencing them as "users." This is because specificity begets focus. If we think of specific roles—e.g., data engineers—we can describe them in terms of the goals of their job, their general duties, and who they interact with and do it in a way to distinguish them from data stewards and data analysts. The challenges they face—their user problems—may be similar to, but likely won't be identical to, those faced by stewards and analysts, because they have different goals in their job, different skills, different tasks and workflows, and different people they interact with.

Often the term persona[20] comes up. While it is beyond the scope of the article to dig into this topic, it's important to understand the term as it is often misunderstood. A persona is an archetype, based on research, that describes a role or type of individual—e.g., a data analyst—their objectives, challenges, goals, and jobs in sufficient detail so that engineers, product managers, designers, etc. can make better decisions when designing and building products for them. Personas don't replace ongoing interaction with real people, but help create a better understanding of them for product teams.

### 4.2.5.2    Identifying and Evaluating User Problems

User problems are problems users face in their jobs that can potentially be addressed by your company and/or products. Understanding these problems really comes down to understanding all the relevant aspects of their jobs and often inferring how you can help. Users are experts in their problems. They are not experts in how a vendor might solve them. In user interviews, focus on user issues and the life of the user. The more you can understand about their world, the better you can identify how to solve their problems with your products and services.

To understand user problems, it is important to understand and describe the objectives and scenarios (workflows) that apply to the roles we are interested in addressing with our product.

But one should first have a clear understanding of what types of companies or organizations the product is targeting, i.e., the target market.

For example, a data engineer in a small company, working on small datasets, often from a single source, will likely have very different objectives and workflows than a data engineer in a large enterprise, working on a team and with many systems of different sizes. For example, that enterprise data engineer may have to access both cloud and on-premise databases, data lakes, and other data stores. Although their job titles are similar, their duties, required knowledge, objectives, workflows, technical environments and skillsets will be very different.

---

[20] https://www.interaction-design.org/literature/article/personas-why-and-how-you-should-use-them.

Aside from company size, a target market can also focus on industry (e.g., finance, manufacturing, pharmaceuticals, etc.), geography, company type (private, public, non-profit, etc.), and/or other factors that are relevant.

Once the target market is identified, then focus on the roles or personas that are important to understand. At the highest level, in B2B software, it's important to understand buyers, users, and influencers. Buyers are people who are instrumental in the buying and decision-making process. Users are people who will directly use an application. Influencers are involved in the decision-making process and like their name implies, will influence the buying decisions, but are not the ones ultimately responsible for making it. We'll focus on users for now.

As stated earlier, it's important not to think of users in a generic way. Most non-trivial B2B software products have more than one type of user. For example, in a CRM system, there will likely be one or more administrators and different types of users from sales, marketing, services, etc.

How a sales rep uses the system will be different than how a sales leader (e.g., VP of sales) uses it. And certainly how a marketing manager uses it will be different from how a sales leader uses the CRM system.

The following diagram summarizes this breakout of market segments and user types.

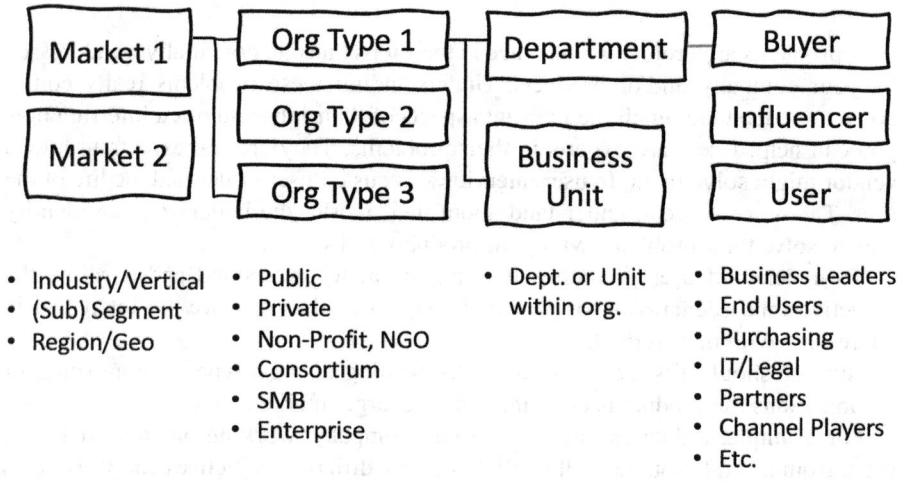

For any given market or market segment, there may be one or more types of distinct organizations. In any given organization, you may be focusing on one or more departments or business units. And within those, you'll likely find your buyers, influencers and users. This is obviously a simplified diagram, but the breakout of Market—Org Type—Department/BU-Buyer/User etc. is important to understand and map out. Once you reach this level of specificity, it becomes much easier to define who those users are and then get focused on their work, their objectives, their challenges, their workflows, etc.

## 4.3   Challenges to Overcome

Customer discovery and research work is critical to product success and yet very few product managers spend much time on it. In their 2024 State of Product Management and Marketing report[21] (n = 881), Pragmatic Institute asked respondents to indicate how many **hours per month** they spend engaging with customers and evaluators. This included three activities:

- Interviewing customers
- Interviewing untapped potential customers
- Conducting win/loss analysis of recent evaluators

The numbers are quite stunning.

| Activities | Ave. Hours per month |
|---|---|
| Interviewing customers | 4.8 hours |
| Interviewing untapped potential customers | 2.4 hours |
| Conducting win/loss analysis of recent evaluators | 2.2 hours |

So, on average respondents spent just over 1 hour per week interviewing customers, and just over 30 minutes per week in the other two activities. This represents about 7% (or less) of their total time on critical activities to gain market insight. The majority of their time - And from the same survey, respondents indicated they spent over 40 hours per month prioritizing requirement for development, creating roadmaps, product demos and sales collateral, and planning for launch. i.e. all activities that require market and customer knowledge. And yet, they spent scant time acquiring that important knowledge.

Clearly there is significant room for improvement, but it's important to understand why there is so little discovery work done and ways to address it. The major reasons can be summarized as follows:

- Culture
- Time
- Access
- Skill and Ability
- Implementing Findings

---

[21] https://www.pragmaticinstitute.com/resources/state-of-product-management-marketing.

### 4.3.1  Culture

Most product managers and product teams are very busy focusing on tasks they've planned or putting out fires that arise, i.e., responding to customer issues, bugs, sales requests, etc. The culture in many companies is focused on outputs and delivery, i.e., working with engineering, prioritizing the work that is needed, and attending meetings with cross-functional stakeholders. This is also supported by data in the Pragmatic survey.

Culture plays a big role in the work that is deemed important and "getting out of the office" is difficult in these environments. Product leadership needs to make discovery a priority, help product managers, and place a real focus on this work. It's a culture shift that must happen as markets get more competitive.

Amazon is an example of a very successful company that has built a culture around being "customer obsessed."[22] Their "working backwards"[23] approach— starting with the potential customer perspective and benefits and working backward to the products/services to achieve those benefits—is an example of that.

### 4.3.2  Time

A lack of time, or at least a perceived lack of time is another barrier to product discovery. Planning and executing discovery work takes time and effort, and product teams are already overloaded with day-to-day tasks. This often ties into the culture issue as well. When time is a commodity, the urgent and immediate tasks get priority, not the ones that will pay dividends weeks or months later.

### 4.3.3  Access to Customers

Another barrier that confronts many product managers is access to customers to perform research. Sales teams often don't trust product managers (or others) to speak with *their* customers, or they want to be involved in any customer interactions.

This is both a culture problem and problematic. Whether it is a trust issue, a control issue, or some other reason, without the freedom to speak with customers *without* the presence of a sales representative, research will always be skewed. Customers will not speak as openly in the presence of a sales representative as they will without their presence because the nature of the sales relationship is very different than the product relationship.

---

[22] https://www.amazon.jobs/content/en/our-workplace/leadership-principles.

[23] https://www.aboutamazon.com/news/workplace/an-insider-look-at-amazons-culture-and-processes.

Without clear and unfettered access to customers, discovery is weakened and its outputs are less valuable to the company.

### 4.3.4 Skills and Ability

Even with a supportive culture, time to research, and access to customers, not having the ability and skills to do effective discovery work can be a barrier. Discovery requires both quantitative and qualitative research and the ability to interview and analyze data and assimilate it to identify meaningful insights. These are not skills that are often taught in school or in companies. While some people seem to be adept at this, many are not.

Like any other complex task, discovery can be done well or done poorly. Those who've done it for years or have been formally trained will be better at it than those new to it. Companies should understand this and help those without formal discovery training get that, either through working with and shadowing more experienced people or by having them trained in workshops or with consultants.

Discovery is an investment in the future of the company and discovery training is an investment in the people who will help define that future.

### 4.3.5 Implementing Findings

The value of discovery work is not simply to learn and gain new insights. The real value comes from using those insights within the company to change behaviors, plans, decisions, and actions, i.e., implementing new product initiatives tied to messaging, positioning, pricing, strategy, roadmaps, etc.

This can be a challenge because all of those items mentioned above require change by others. And that change requires them to buy into and believe in the research findings. And that requires them—people who likely weren't involved in the research process—to displace their existing beliefs and motivations with the new information uncovered and change their plans to accommodate.

This is far more difficult than most people understand. People have goals, plans, and incentives in motion and new data may disrupt that. And it's not that they don't necessarily believe the findings, but they may not put the weight on those findings that is needed to change their views, decisions and actions.

It's a complex problem, but understand that research findings often have to be sold internally; they will not always be readily accepted with open minds.

The best executed discovery projects can wind up sitting on a shelf, so to speak, because the people who conducted it didn't do the socialization and sales work to get the findings adopted.

## 4.4   Conclusion

Discovery is a core competency in product management. It's the fuel that feeds innovation and business success. It is complex and difficult to execute well, and given the various barriers that may hinder the people doing the work, it is well worth the effort and, in fact, is the only way, outside of luck, to create sustainable business value for any company.

# Chapter 5
# Integrating the Voice of the Customer in Cloud Product Management: The Role and Application of Market Research Techniques

**Dana Naous and Christine Legner**

**Abstract** The cloud paradigm fundamentally changes the way software is developed, deployed, and priced. For cloud providers, this shift demands well-defined services with clearly specified features, delivery methods, and pricing models. Yet, traditional requirements engineering methods, which rely on close interactions with users, are difficult to apply for mass-market cloud services. Therefore, market research techniques can effectively support the design of high-utility cloud services through the incorporation of user preference measurements. For instance, conjoint analysis (CA), a widely used consumer research technique, allows for the estimation of user utilities, market segmentation, and analysis of willingness to pay. In this article, we present a method component that extends existing requirements elicitation techniques for cloud services through CA. We document this method component through a meta-model and procedure and demonstrate its application in a study on secure cloud storage services. Additionally, we evaluate its feasibility, usefulness, and ease of use of method component with experts. This research advances cloud product management by adapting and refining CA techniques for the specific context of cloud services.

**Keywords** Software product management · Cloud services · Conjoint analysis · User preferences · Requirements engineering · Requirements elicitation

This chapter is based on material from the first author's dissertation: "Understanding User Perceptions and Preferences for Mass-Market Information Systems – Leveraging Market Research Techniques and Examples in Privacy-Aware Design," submitted to the University of Lausanne in 2020. The dissertation is available at https://serval.unil.ch/resource/serval:BIB_A59913C24BC1.P001/REF.pdf

D. Naous (✉) · C. Legner
Faculty of Business and Economics (HEC), University of Lausanne, Lausanne, Switzerland

## 5.1   Introduction

Cloud computing has introduced a paradigm shift in which software and IT resources are delivered as a service over the Internet. For the IT industry, this shift marks a transition from selling software and IT resources as standalone products to offering them as integrated services, which include delivery, technical support, and maintenance. However, designing cloud services presents unique challenges due to the cloud market dynamics and unknown requirements of heterogeneous and distributed end users [1, 2]. As global competition and the number of offerings grow, cloud service providers must become more responsive and attuned to customer preferences. This entails not only delivering functional services but also emphasizing non-functional attributes and developing suitable business models.

Cloud product managers are emerging as critical gatekeepers, responsible for gathering product requirements, making decisions on product features and release planning, and preparing and implementing the business case [3]. Despite the central role of product management in modern software development, it receives relatively little focus within the cloud domain [4]. Product managers oversee requirements throughout various stages starting from elicitation and prioritization to selection and defining product releases (spanning pre-development to post-development). Obtaining customer feedback is crucial at every step to capture the needs as well as user expectations for the product [5]. Traditional requirements engineering methods and tools available to product managers are predominantly qualitative, relying on close interaction with selected users, account executives, and sales teams to better understand end users' needs. Additionally, they gather requirements from online forums where users share reviews and feedbacks on both the vendor's and competitor's products. For cloud services, product managers lack methodological support for systematically eliciting and quantifying user requirements across a diverse and distributed user base. Consequently, they tend to overhear the "voice of the customer" while focusing on technology and schedule [6].

In commercial settings, consumer research has demonstrated a strong link between user's preferences and a product's success. Accordingly, market research techniques are employed to evaluate product features by consumers, allowing estimation of user preferences and analysis of trade-offs in the selection of products and services. These techniques have proven to provide valuable input for designing commercial products that align with users' needs and can similarly be applied in the development of cloud services. One of these techniques is conjoint analysis (CA) [7], a widely used method in market research for understanding consumer preferences and predicting purchasing behavior. CA is gaining traction in information systems (IS) research [8–11] where it has been applied to explore design choices for mobile applications and online and cloud services. A review of CA studies in IS [12] highlights its potential as a robust approach for designing and evaluating mass-market IS. CA facilitates the assessment of requirements along multiple dimensions by a large sample of users, thereby incorporating functional, non-functional, and business model aspects and providing reliable insights into user's preferences.

In this paper, we seek to support product managers in designing cloud services by leveraging CA techniques from market research. We introduce a method component adapted to the cloud context that addresses the concrete challenges that product managers face in requirements-related activities for mass-market systems. The method component was designed based on method engineering guidelines [13] and complements existing requirements management approaches with a reliable understanding of user preferences. It is documented by means of a (1) meta-model describing the conceptual elements of this method component and their relationships and (2) a procedure model outlining the different phases, along with methodological guidance. We illustrate this method component with examples from a study on cloud storage services and provide an expert evaluation of its usefulness, ease of use, and feasibility as a preference-based approach. Our results demonstrate that CA fosters a deeper understanding of different user segments and their preferences, and that the empirical insights can effectively inform design refinement and requirements prioritization.

The remainder of this chapter is structured as follows: We begin with a review of the literature on requirements management for cloud services and applications of CA. Then, we present the research approach for constructing the method. Following this, we present the method component and illustrate it with a CA study on cloud storage services. Finally, we discuss the expert evaluation of the method component.

## 5.2 Prior Research

### 5.2.1 Requirements Management for Cloud Services

For the software industry, the shift from customer-specific to market-driven systems with cloud computing necessitates more thoroughly defined products. In addition to core functional features, cloud service design must also address delivery and pricing models as well as non-functional attributes, such as privacy options, high availability, or scalability. Thus, product management plays an important role and is an essential area to guarantee market success and the largest business value [3]. At the core of software product management [14] is requirements management, i.e., gathering, identifying, and organizing requirements. Requirements management links portfolio management and product roadmapping to release planning (see Fig. 5.1). By translating product roadmaps into detailed product requirements lists, requirements management informs prioritization and selection of requirements in the release planning.

Requirements management is given little attention in the cloud domain [4]. As a consequence, release planning for cloud services is often done ad hoc with informal selection of requirement [6]. Product managers lack methodological guidance for systematically eliciting and quantifying user requirements in order to avoid biases and ensure customer acceptance. Market-driven RE methods were suggested to deal with mass-market software [15] and thus should be also applicable for cloud

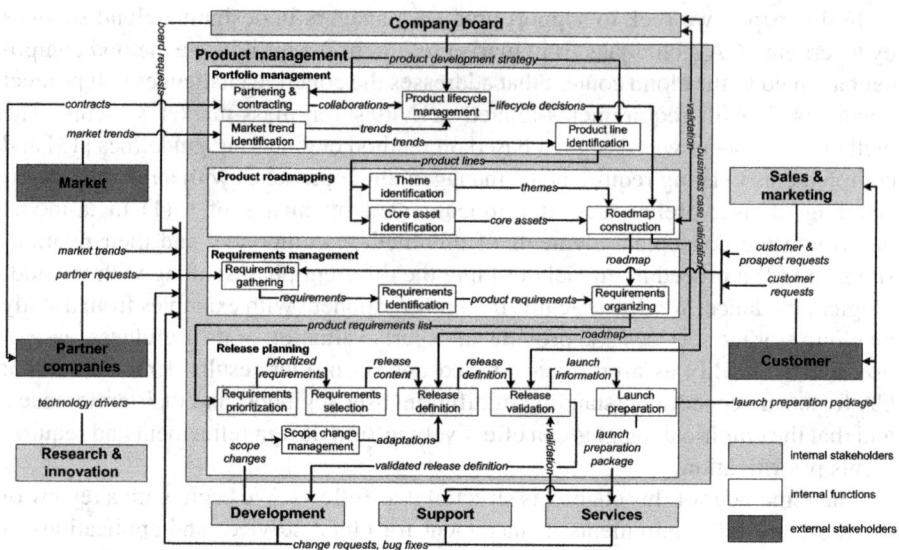

**Fig. 5.1** Reference framework for software product management (based on [14])

services. However, the suggested methods rely on developers' knowledge or on classical elicitation approaches with user representatives for a new design. After the first release, requirements are mostly collected by current user experience and feedback. In the pre-development stage, customer feedback is commonly captured through traditional methods involving interviews and questionnaires or via prototyping and A/B testing, and in post-development through reviews, usage data, and support tickets [5]. The monitoring of usage data is commonly referred to as product telemetry, which relies on performance, log management, and analytics tools for cloud development [16]. To further engage users, crowd-based approaches [17] introduce automated ways of deriving requirements through collecting and analyzing user feedback from large user groups on various channels such as app stores, forums, or social media.

Customer feedback serves as an input to plan further incremental releases where an additional set of requirements is implemented. The main activity is to manage new and changing requirements [18] which creates a challenge for release planning. To prioritize requirements, users and designers have to compare requirements to determine their relative weights of importance in the implementation of a software product [19, 20]. However, with the increasing number of requirements and stakeholders this process becomes more and more complex.

In the cloud context, these approaches are not sufficient and face challenges with user reach to integrate the heterogeneous needs as well as the prioritization of requirements. On the one hand, the traditional approaches do not scale with the increasing number of requirements and a heterogeneous and distributed user base. On the other hand, handling a large set of requirements creates a burden and becomes tedious for the customers and engineers performing it. Therefore, the need to integrate the "voice of the customer" calls for new approaches (that target the crowds) to ensure widest customer reach and acceptance as well as the representation of users' preferences in product designs.

## 5.2.2   Understanding User's Preferences

Economic research on the choice theory [21] explains that market behavior is generated by maximizing consumer preferences. Thus, modeling the decision-making process and the cognitive mechanism that govern behavior enables understanding and predicting use. As such, measuring the preference structure can help predict the mostly accepted product combinations based on inputs of product attributes, personal experiences, and social and economic factors that shape perceptions and attitudes. A very promising approach in understanding user preferences is the use of techniques from consumer-oriented marketing research, such as conjoint analysis. CA allows producing a reliable understanding of consumer's preferences based on quantitative empirical data. While market research techniques are widely used for developing commercial products, to date, they have not been fully embraced for software product development.

As a concept from mathematical psychology established by Luce and Tukey [22], conjoint measurement is used to measure "the joint effects of a set of independent variables on the ordering of a dependent variable" [23]. In a CA study, a product is defined in terms of attributes and attribute levels. Based on a consumer evaluation in a survey setting, a utility function is estimated and translated into a preference structure that reflects the most accepted characteristics in a product.

Applying the CA can be challenging due to the many steps and methodological choices required to achieve the preference structure. It also involves selection from different alternatives. Green and Srinivasan [7] highlight some differences between the alternatives suggested for each step in a CA study:

1. The selection of a preference model determines the preference function based on the defined attributes' influence over the respondents' utility. It forms the basis for determining partial benefit values for the respective attributes. The three main models of preference suggested are the vector (1), ideal-point (2), and part-worth (3) models. With a set of $T$ attributes and $J$ stimuli in a study, $y_{jp}$ denotes a respondent's preference level for the $p$th attribute of the $j$th stimulus. The vector model depicts the respondent's preference $s_j$ for the $j$th stimulus as:

$$s_j = \sum_{p=1}^{T} w_p y_{jp} \qquad (5.1)$$

where $w_p$ denotes the individual's importance weight for $T$ attributes.

The ideal-point model depicts preference $s_j$ as inversely related to the weighted squared distance $d_j^2$ of the location $y_{jp}$ of the $j$th stimulus from the individual's ideal point $x_p$, where $d_j^2$ is defined as:

$$d_j^2 = \sum_{p=1}^{T} w_p \left( y_{jp} - x_p \right)^2 \tag{5.2}$$

The part-worth model depicts preference $sj$ as:

$$s_j = \sum_{p=1}^{T} f_p \left( y_{jp} \right) \tag{5.3}$$

where $f_p$ is a function denoting the part-worth for the levels of $y_{jp}$ of the $p$th attribute.

2. A part-worth function is mainly used in CA because of its flexibility in designing the attribute evaluation function. The part-worth function model is compatible with different shapes of preference functions, and it allows for better estimation when evaluating categorical attributes. In addition, a mixed model combining the three alternative models (vector model, ideal-point model, part-worth function model) was suggested; it introduces a dummy variable and is similar to a multiple regression approach.
3. The data collection method involves selecting the conjoint method for evaluation. Traditional approaches involve the full-profile or pairwise evaluation. The original approach in CA, also called concept evaluation or full-profile, is based on rank orders of consumers' preferences regarding product profiles (also called stimuli), which comprise several attributes and levels associated with the product characteristics. As such, CA provides insights into user preferences for the different attributes based on a complete product evaluation. Besides concept evaluation, Johnson [24] suggests an alternative approach called the trade-off matrix or pairwise approach. In this approach, respondents evaluate a pair of attributes providing information about the trade-offs among all product features. Its strength is its ability to support a large number of attributes since it can provide predictions based on the evaluation of subsets of attribute pairs [24]. The full-profile approach is the most frequently used one since it provides a more realistic description of the stimuli. With the extensions of the adaptive and choice-based CA methods (see Sect. 5.2.3), the variety of choice for evaluating the full profiles increases.
4. For full profile, the next step is stimulus set construction, which is mainly based on fractional factorial orthogonal design, which reduces the number of stimuli and facilitates evaluation. This method assumes no interaction effects between the selected attributes. For adaptive methods, partial profiles and self-explicated tasks are used to reduce complexity of the conjoint evaluation.
5. For the stimulus presentation, there are several variations based on verbal description, paragraph description, or graphical representation. The choice of the presentation depends on the subject of the study and can be a combination of

methods. Furthermore, the application of conjoint analysis to some product categories could use other stimulus types as prototypes or actual products.

6. The measurement scale depends on the study purpose and the data collection method. Both the full-profile and the pairwise approach can use ranking to capture the order of preferences or purchasing intentions. The full-profile approach can also use ratings, which requires respondents to grade (subjectively) the perceived benefit on a numbered scale. As an alternative, choice-based methods introduced another measurement scale that can then be treated as a choice-probability model.

7. Finally, the estimation method for the partial benefit values is selected based on the dependent variable type resulting from the measurement scale. While an ordinal-scaled variable could use multivariate analysis of variance (MONANOVA) [25], an interval-scaled variable can use an ordinary least squares (OLS) regression, for example. In addition, LOGIT or PROBIT models can be used when the data collection method is choice-based [26]. In that case, individual-level utility function is estimated using Hierarchical Bayes.

CA is a well-suited to problems in marketing as an approach to quantify judgmental data as quantifiable preferences. Green and Rao [23] have paved the way for leveraging CA in the context of product design, by making different suggestions: (1) relative importance of attributes and levels, price–value relationship measurement by analyzing the consumer trade-off for price and quality of products, and attitude measurement to analyze the trade-offs between several product attributes. This involves analyzing the utility for collections of items to facilitate the combination packaging of certain product types, (2) cost–benefit analysis to study the willingness to pay (WTP) for certain attributes and design products accordingly, and (3) clustering or segmenting customers based on their utility functions. Furthermore, Johnson [24] referred to another application using (4) market simulation, which is used to estimate the market shares of currently available or new products based on the study sample's predicted consumer preferences.

## 5.2.3 Conjoint Analysis in Mass-Market Software Product Design

A comprehensive literature review of CA studies in the IS domain [12] highlights a growing number of CA studies targeting mass-market software design in multiple domains. These include mobile (M) applications, online (O) services covering social networks, website design and online banking services, and more recently cloud (C) services and Internet of things (IoT) (see Table 5.1). As conjoint surveys facilitate collecting feedback on product features and their combinations from larger numbers of users, they address a critical concern in the design of mass-market services [1, 2]. By prioritizing product features based on user choices, CA is most commonly used to elicit user requirements and thereby guides the design of

**Table 5.1** An overview of CA studies on mass-market software

| Conjoint study | Domain | Study purpose | Attributes type | | Analysis techniques | | | | |
|---|---|---|---|---|---|---|---|---|---|
| | | | Functional | Non-functional | Economic | Relative importance | Segmentation | Willingness to pay | Market simulation |
| Zubey et al. [27] | M | Design | | x | x | x | | | |
| Baek et al. [28] | O | Pricing | x | x | | x | x | x | |
| Brodt and Heitmann [29] | M | Design | x | x | | x | x | | |
| Kim [30] | M | Design | x | x | x | x | | x | |
| Mueller-Lankenau and Wehmeyer [31] | M | Design | x | x | | x | | | |
| Haaker et al. [32] | M | Pricing | x | x | x | x | x | x | |
| Bouwman et al. [9] | M | Design,adoption | x | x | | x | | | |
| Mann et al. [33] | O | Pricing | x | x | x | x | | x | |
| Krasnova et al. [34] | O | Design | x | x | x | x | x | x | |
| Song et al. [35] | M | Design | x | | x | x | x | | x |
| Doerr et al. [36] | C | Pricing | x | x | x | x | | x | |
| Ho et al. [37] | O | Design | x | x | | x | x | | |
| Koehler et al. [10] | C | Pricing | x | x | x | x | x | | |
| Fritz et al. [38] | M | Pricing | x | | x | | | x | x |
| Choi et al. [39] | M | Design | | x | x | x | | | x |
| Daas et al. [40] | C | Pricing | x | | x | x | | x | x |
| See-To and Ho [41] | O | Design | x | | x | x | | | |
| Abramova et al. [42] | O | Design, pricing | x | | x | x | | | x |
| Mihale-Wilson et al. [11] | IoT | Design,pricing | | x | x | x | | x | |
| Mikusz and Herter [43] | IoT | Design | x | x | | x | | | |
| Baum et al. [8] | O | Design,pricing | x | | x | x | | | x |
| Schomakers et al. [44] | O | Design | x | x | x | x | | | |
| Wessels et al. [45] | O | Design | x | x | x | x | | x | |
| Zibuschka et al. [46] | IoT | Design,pricing | x | x | x | | x | x | |

Legend: *M* mobile, *O* online, *C* cloud, *IoT* Internet of things software products. It is also applied to inform pricing strategies and analyze users' preferences and behavior in adopting new technologies. The existing CA studies typically analyze user preferences for sets of 5 to 12 attributes, covering mostly combinations of functional and non-functional aspects, but also addressing economic aspects including pricing or business model elements, as well as security and privacy considerations. CA enables the analysis of individual and group preferences by determining the relative importance of features and the application of market segmentations and simulation techniques.

In terms of analysis techniques, the relative importance of attributes has been widely used in the majority of studies, such as those by Bouwman et al. [9], Brodt and Heitmann [29], and Zubey et al. [27], to develop optimal application designs. In the context of cloud services, Burda and Teuteberg [47] and Koehler et al. [10] utilize CA to explore user preferences for cloud features, aiding the enhancement of existing services or pricing decisions. Other studies cover economic features and apply WTP techniques to study the tradeoffs among different attributes through variations in a price attribute [28, 32, 40]. Moreover, Koehler et al. [10] applied segmentation to define different configurations of software as a service based on users' estimated preference structure. In addition, CA is used to understand privacy tradeoffs for designing personal assistants in the IoT domain [11]. To conclude, existing CA studies in the IS domain reveal that market research techniques offer valuable insights into mass-market system design including cloud services. However, these studies remain one-time efforts, and further reflections and adaptations are needed to fully leverage CA from market research in software product management.

## 5.3    Research Objectives and Approach

Our research aims at assisting cloud product managers by leveraging market research techniques. More specifically, we build on our previous research on market research techniques for mass-market systems' design [48] to introduce and assess a method component for eliciting and analyzing user preferences in the context of cloud service design. This method component (in line with Karlsson and Wistrand [49]) adapts advanced CA techniques to address the unique specificities of cloud services and provides methodological guidance for their application. A method component, as defined by Karlsson and Wistrand [49], is "a self-contained part of a systems development method expressing the transformation of one or several artifacts into a defined target artifact and the rationale for such a transformation." Accordingly, the suggested method component is meant to complement existing software product management and requirements management frameworks, such as the one presented in Sect. 5.2.1 (Fig. 5.1). The method component is documented through a meta-model and a procedure model. The meta-model specifies a conceptual model with main constructs and relationships, while the procedure model outlines phases, along with methodological guidance.

For developing the method component, we follow method engineering, i.e., "the engineering discipline to design, construct and adapt methods, techniques and tools for the development of information systems" [13]. We combine an inductive approach building on field research and a deductive approach based on literature [50]. This allows us to integrate practical insights from adapting CA into mass-market software design with theoretical foundations from market research and software product management literature. The inductive approach is based on a field study on cloud platforms that employed CA to identify the relative importance of cloud service attributes, segment users based on their preferences, and simulate design choices [51]. This study and the discussion of the results with practitioners, including cloud product managers, provided insights on how different CA techniques may inform requirements management and release planning. As part of the deductive procedure, we refined the methodological guidelines based on insights from a systematic literature review. From 70 IS publications utilizing CA to analyze product design, pricing, and user adoption, we identified 24 CA studies focusing on online, cloud, and mobile services and addressing challenges related to mass-market software product management (see Sect. 5.2.3). From our thorough review of these studies, we derived adaptations specific for cloud services and methodological recommendations for applying CA in this context (Table 5.2).

For demonstrating the method component, we apply it to a scenario for cloud product management, here: the design of cloud storage services with a focus on security and privacy aspects. This corresponds to a situation where user requirements are gathered as a response to the users' increasing privacy awareness and as input for the incremental release planning of cloud storage solutions. Based on a survey of 144 users of personal cloud storage, we use adaptive choice-based CA to identify the relative importance of secure and privacy-preserving features and segment users. The results demonstrate the feasibility and utility of the method component. For evaluating the method component, we conduct a workshop as practice-oriented evaluation [52, 53]. The method was demonstrated for multiple implementation scenarios to a group of six experts with experience in software product management and who are exposed to the cloud industry. Based on the presented implementation scenarios, experts assessed the usefulness, ease of use, and feasibility of applying the preference-based approach for product management.

## 5.4 CA in Cloud Product Management: A Method Component

The proposed method component aims at supporting product managers in developing cloud services by suggesting methodological guidelines for applying CA: (1) how requirements should be specified and presented, to serve as input for CA, and (2) how CA can inform requirements elicitation and analysis. The method component can be integrated in various phases of the cloud service life cycle and is supported by a meta-model and a procedure model, with clearly defined activities and outcomes.

**Table 5.2**  Research process following method engineering

| I. Method construction | | | |
|---|---|---|---|
| **Ia. Deductive approach** | | **Ib. Inductive approach** | |
| Structured literature review of existing CA studies in IS to adapt CA techniques for mass-market software product design and derive methodological recommendations | | Explorative study employing CA techniques for cloud platform design to refine the method component based on insights from its practical application | |
| **Publication type** | Journal | 36 | **Purpose and domain** | Design and simulate business models for PaaS |
| | Conference | 34 | | |
| **Domain** | Mobile and IoT | 29 | **CA type** | Adaptive choice-based CA |
| | Cloud | 7 | | |
| | Online | 24 | **Sample** | 103 developers (target PaaS users) |
| | Other IS | 10 | | |
| **CA techniques** | Relative importance | 70 | | |
| | Segmentation | 30 | **CA techniques** | • Relative importance • Segmentation • Market simulation |
| | Willingness to pay | 21 | | |
| | Market simulation | 7 | | |
| **II. Demonstration** | | | |
| Demonstration of the method component in incremental release planning (example: secure cloud storage services) | | | |
| **CA type** | Adaptive choice-based CA | | |
| **Sample** | 144 cloud storage service users | | |
| **CA techniques** | • Relative importance • Willingness to pay • Segmentation | | |
| **II. Evaluation** | | | |
| Expert evaluation of the method component with three product managers, one product analyst, and two business analysts | | | |
| **Evaluation criteria** | • Usefulness • Ease of use • Feasibility | | |

## 5.4.1  Integration in the Cloud Service Life Cycle

The method component can be integrated in different phases of the life cycle, starting from the initial concept to the iterative design and evaluation of cloud services, as illustrated in Fig. 5.2. In the initial phases of the life cycle, CA provides insights into how core features of cloud services align with individual and group preferences, providing input for defining product concepts and roadmaps. By measuring trade-offs between functional, non-functional, and economic features, CA complements traditional requirements engineering techniques and can guide the definition

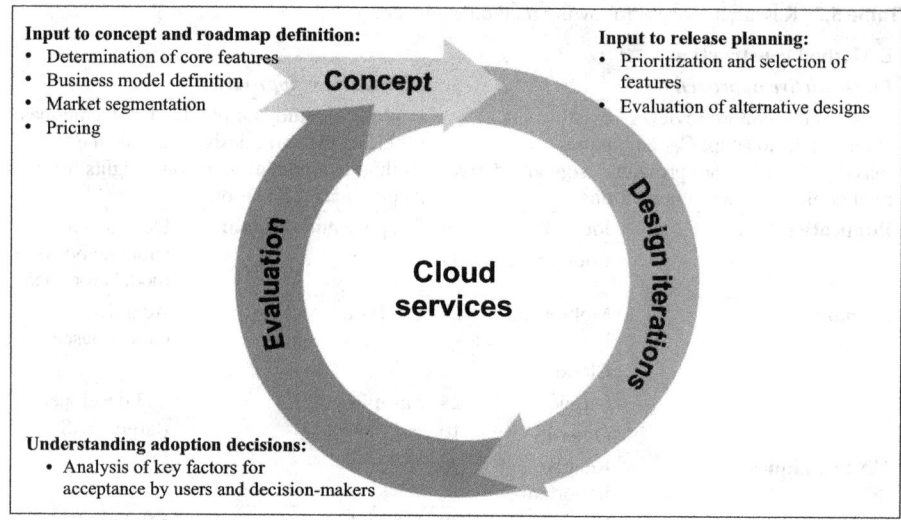

**Fig. 5.2** Framework for CA in cloud product management based on Naous and Legner [12]

of business models, target market segments, and pricing strategies. For subsequent design iterations, CA can support the prioritization and selection of features and the evaluation of alternative design variations by engaging a large number of customers and potential users. This data-driven approach complements existing techniques, providing valuable input to release planning.

### 5.4.2 Meta-Model

The method component is built around two primary constructs—*requirements* and *stakeholders*—which are linked to the main *CA constructs* supporting the requirements-related activities in product management.

*Requirements*, as a fundamental concept, can be viewed from two converging perspectives: the objectives or challenges of stakeholders and the solutions to these challenges [54]. Ideally, these perspectives translate into product requirements (or features). Originally, two types of requirements are distinguished for software systems [55]: (1) functional corresponding to what the system should do and (2) non-functional corresponding to how the system functions related to performance, quality, design constraints, and external interface. For cloud services and other mass-market software products, these categories of requirements are insufficient, as additional economic and operational aspects (i.e., business-model elements) determine users' choices [12]. This distinction extends the categorization of requirements into three types: *functional, non-functional,* and *economic.*

*Stakeholders* are the source of these requirements, but have different roles: they can be the *requestors* who buy or pay for the system (individual or organization), the

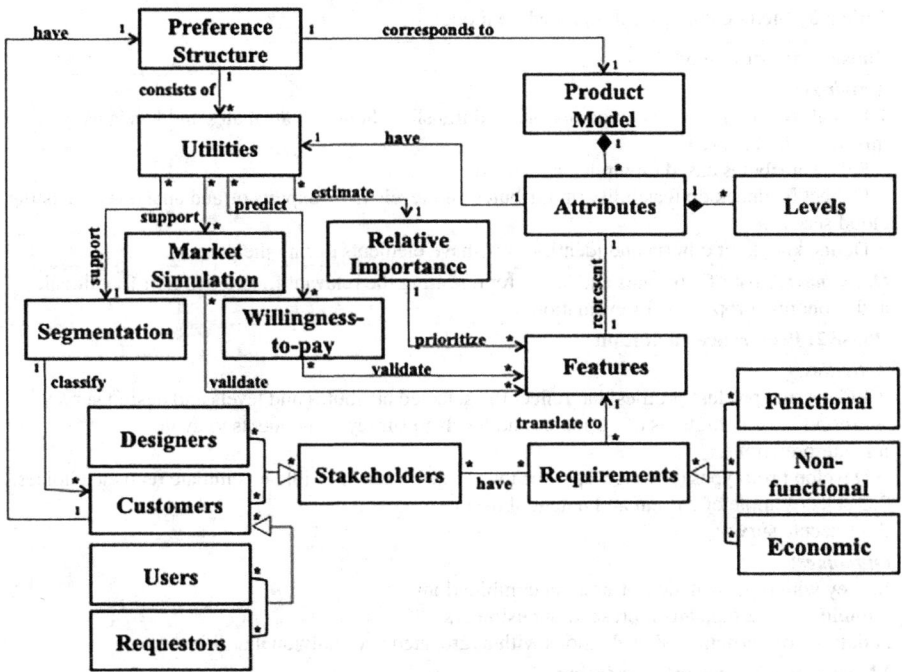

**Fig. 5.3** A meta-model of the method component

*users* who practically interact with the software product (often distinguished based on their expertise in novice and expert users [56], or the *designers* who develop the system. In the meta-model, we represent them as two categories of stakeholders providing input in RE: (1) *customers* who determine system requirements, including requestors and users, and (2) *designers* who validate requirements. Each group has specific views and interests in the software product.

Additionally, the meta-model (Fig. 5.3) represents main *CA constructs* that support RE comprising: (1) the *product model* with attributes and levels corresponding to product requirements; (2) *utilities* as a result of customers' preference structure that governs their product choices; and (3) *CA techniques* for processing the utilities including *relative importance, willingness to pay, market simulation* that help in validating and prioritizing requirements, and *segmentation* for classifying customers based on different preferences.

## 5.4.3   Procedure Model

The step-by-step procedure for applying CA in cloud service design consists of three main phases: product modeling, preference elicitation, and preference implementation. For each phase, we document the main activities, provide recommendations on methodological choices, and outline the outcomes derived from our

**Table 5.3** Method component—procedure model

| Phase 1: Product modeling |
| --- |
| *Activities:* |
| 1.1 Analyze cloud service design options and translate them into attributes and levels using a mixed-method approach: |
| • Select attributes based on inputs from users. |
| • Collect feedback on feasibility of attributes and levels from experts or/and analysis of existing cloud services. |
| • Define knockout criteria and identify must-have elements during the process. |
| *Outcomes:* A list of attributes and levels representing the relevant functional, non-functional, and economic properties for evaluation |
| **Phase 2: Preference elicitation** |
| *Activities:* |
| 2.1 Construct product profiles that reflect the selected attributes and levels and design survey |
| • Present clear definitions of attributes and levels to survey respondents to avoid misinterpretations. |
| • Develop prototypes (or mock-ups) for feature sets when possible to simulate realistic choices. |
| 2.2 Select sample of current and potential users |
| 2.3 Execute survey |
| *Outcomes:* |
| Survey with representation of product combinations |
| Sample with participants representing customers |
| A data set of participants' evaluations with aggregated and individual utilities |
| **Phase 3: Preference interpretation** |
| *Activities:* |
| Analyze utilities to answer specific questions in requirements management and prioritization: |
| 3.1 Use relative importance of attributes for getting weights |
| 3.2 Use willingness to pay (WTP) for measuring tradeoffs among attributes and attribute levels |
| 3.3 Use segmentation to define user groups with similar preferences for bundling options |
| 3.4 Use market simulation to facilitate attributes variations for competitive analysis |
| *Outcomes (depending on the applied technique):* |
| • Preference structure for attributes and tradeoffs (3.1) |
| • Price premium for specific attributes/levels (3.2) |
| • User segments and their preference structure (3.3) |
| • Expected market shares for attributes combinations (3.4) |

inductive-deductive approach, which includes the review of CA studies and our insights from CA applications (see Table 5.3).

### 5.4.3.1 Product Modeling

The objective of this phase is to analyze the design options for the cloud service and translate them into an attribute list with attribute levels to represent relevant characteristics. A key methodological concern in this phase is selecting suitable attributes and attribute levels that align with core design properties or features. For cloud services, attributes may cover any of the identified requirements categories: (1) functional properties; (2) non-functional properties such as accessibility, privacy,

**Table 5.4** Attributes based on previous conjoint studies on cloud service design

| Requirements | Attributes | | |
|---|---|---|---|
| **Functional** | • Specific functionality<br>• Customization<br>• Community features | • Storage space<br>• Dev./test environment | • Monitoring. |
| **Non-functional** | **Accessibility (e.g., supported devices and platforms)** | | |
| | • Offline access<br>• Mobile access | • Distribution channel<br>• Accessibility | |
| | **Privacy and security (e.g., supported devices and platforms)** | | |
| | • Security and reliability<br>• Information use | • Privacy control<br>• Encryption | • 1 |
| **Economic** | • Pricing model (subscription, pay per use, etc.)<br>• Contract duration | | |

and security features; and (3) economic and business model features such as pricing models. As reference and source of inspiration, Table 5.4 summarizes attributes along these three categories that were used in prior conjoint studies on cloud service design.

It is recommended to use a mixed-method, multi-stage approach to attribute and level selection. This ensures representation of different stakeholders and capturing different types of requirements. A common approach in CA studies is to evaluate attributes from similar existing products or gather input from product experts on potential and feasible characteristics. Most academic studies also analyze literature for the initial selection of the attribute list. User insights are equally essential at this stage to determine the set of features for evaluation, employing traditional approaches for requirements elicitation such as questionnaires and interviews [39] or group elicitation techniques like focus groups [29]. To finalize the attribute list, it is crucial at this stage to identify knockout criteria or features that users will never accept, as well as must-have elements.

#### 5.4.3.2 Preference Elicitation

After establishing the list of attributes, the next phase prepares the survey design and execution. It starts with designing the questionnaire-based survey to assess combinations from the list of attributes (i.e., profiles). In the context of cloud services, we propose using adaptive, choice-based conjoint analysis (ACBCA), one of the most advanced CA techniques that combines choice-based and adaptive approaches, for estimating the preference structure. The rationale is as follows: First, choice-based CA (CBCA) enables the prediction of adoption intentions by estimating users' preference structures based on their product choices [21]. To do so, CBCA [57] simulates the decision-making process for a product purchase in a competitive marketplace by presenting participants with hypothetical product choices instead of evaluating individual features. Through these choices, participants' individual utility functions are estimated using Hierarchical Bayes methods

[58]. The part-worth utility reflects the strength of respondents' preferences for specific attribute levels and serves as the basis for determining the relative importance of attributes. The importance for each of the features is implicitly derived from the absolute range between the highest and the lowest part-worth utility values of the attribute.

Second, combined with the adaptive approach, respondents have to perform a self-explicated task [59] through evaluating attributes individually and screening product profiles to identify possibility for them to purchase/use or not. The screening of product profiles provides insights into non-compensatory behavior, identifying must-have attribute levels as well as unacceptable options, which are excluded from subsequent choice tasks. ACBCA can easily handle the high number of attributes prevalent in software design and its use supported by our analysis of existing CA studies (see Sect. 5.2.3). Studies that used traditional or CBCA had an average list of six attributes, whereas studies that used adaptive methods evaluated more than 10 attributes.

In terms of stimulus or product profile representation, most studies employ verbal description as concepts or scenarios, and only few present actual products or mock-ups for stimuli representation [28, 29]. For cloud service design, we recommend adopting this latter approach, as it offers greater significance for participants and facilitates a more realistic and accurate evaluation. Two options are available: either presenting full prototypes that combine multiple features or focusing on individual features instead.

For selecting survey participants, it is recommended to use a representative sample of existing and target users of the cloud service. For mass-market services, crowdsourcing platforms such as MTurk or Prolific offer a very convenient way to get data from large sets of users [12]. Once the data is collected, data analysis can be conducted using one of the following approaches: (1) statistical software such as R or SPSS, equipped with a "conjoint"[1] package, or (2) specialized platforms providing comprehensive CA solutions, such as Sawtooth Software or Globalpark Software [33], that administer an online survey and perform the CA.

Optimally, the survey is designed in multiple selection stages to eliminate any selection bias and calibrate the preference formula. For our study we provided four stages: (1) a **self-explicated task** or a **build your own (BYO)** section where respondents are asked to indicate their preferred levels of some of the attributes, (2) **screening** section where participants' decisions are scanned in order to recognize non-compensatory behavior, (3) the **choice tournament** section where respondents evaluate concepts that fit their preference structure, and finally (4) a **calibration** section where respondents are asked to evaluate BYO concept, winning concept from choice tournament and four others for a consistency check.

---

[1] http://keii.ue.wroc.pl/conjoint

### 5.4.3.3 Preference Interpretation

CA supports product managers in analyzing the customers' view on product features, taking different perspectives: (1) customer preferences for attributes and levels based on part-worth utilities, (2) customers' sensitivity to different aspects (e.g., functional aspects, compared to privacy issues or pricing), and (3) cross-elasticity effects and interaction effects of attributes.

Most prominently, having the relative importance of attributes provides a prioritized list of attributes for release planning. To enhance this prioritization scheme, further analysis techniques can support the product manager based on quantitative data:

- **Market segmentation** to develop segments based on groupings generated from sample demographics or specific clustering analysis techniques (e.g., [10]). Cluster-based segmentation identifies groups of customers sharing the same preferences, attitudes, or tradeoffs. The segmentation can be used to tailor targeted offerings and plan releases of product bundles.
- **Willingness to pay** for pricing or attribute tradeoffs. The inclusion of a price attribute can help in simulating realistic decisions by users through comparing different features under a cost constraint. Thus, users will be implicitly performing a cost-benefit analysis, which can help in informing the design through revealing user tradeoffs for certain attributes.
- **Market simulations** to determine those attributes of a product or service which will maximize its share [24]. Simulation "as the use [..] of any artifact (i.e., model, method, instantiation) that imitates the behavior of the system under investigation" [60] was used by few studies in the literature, including Choi et al. [39], Daas et al. [40], and Song et al. [35]. The main purpose is to predict market shares of new products or product modifications based on preference models. This analysis technique can be very interesting as it provides data on how certain attributes (or features) can affect the market shares and thus the business value of the product, thus enabling well-informed decisions of requirements selection for the planned releases of the product. From our field study [51], we suggest different kinds of simulations for competitive analysis: (1) competition analysis, to compare a solution with other competing solutions based on relative similarity of virtual market shares; (2) direct benchmark analysis to obtain a detailed attribute-wise comparison views between two offerings; and also, (3) attribute variation analysis to study the effect of changing attributes on market share predictions.

## 5.5 Demonstration: CA for Personal Cloud Storage Design

To demonstrate the use of the proposed method component, we provide a step-by-step illustration from a study on cloud storage services. We apply the method component to (re-)analyze user requirements for privacy and security features of personal cloud storage in response to increasing data protection regulations and privacy awareness (cf. [61]). While cloud storage is a widely adopted category of cloud services, highly secure cloud storage options have struggled to establish sustainable business models. Applying the method component helps to understand users' attitudes toward the use of secure personal cloud storage, specifically privacy tradeoffs and preferences for enhanced privacy and security features, and helps identify customer segments.

### 5.5.1 Phase 1 "Product Modeling"

In the first phase of the method component, we followed the proposed mixed-method approach to select the relevant attributes and levels: First, we performed a literature review on cloud storage services with a focus on security and privacy aspects resulting in 14 relevant attributes in the initial list. Second, to obtain the user perspective, we ran a focus group with seven experienced and privacy-oriented cloud storage users to identify relevant attributes and eliminate others that were less relevant from the perceptions of the participants. And third, we conducted a market analysis of existing services to examine and validate the attributes and identify levels. Our analysis included 13 products that we selected based on reviews of cloud vendors from comparison websites (e.g., cloudwards.net). The list is composed of the main market players (Google Drive, Dropbox, Microsoft OneDrive, and Amazon Drive), specialized secure cloud storage services (Tresorit, SpiderOak, and SecureSafe), and mid-sized players (Sync, pCloud, Carbonite, SugarSync, ElephantDrive, Box, and Mozy). The final list (see Table 5.5) covered all three requirements types (i.e., functional, non-functional, and economic) and contained seven security and privacy features with their corresponding levels in addition to storage and a summed price attribute pricing.

### 5.5.2 Phase 2 "Preference Elicitation"

In this phase, we constructed the product profiles based on the selected attributes and levels and designed the ACBCA survey to estimate users' utilities through a real-life purchasing scenario. The survey was performed in three sections, as Table 5.6 illustrates: (1) A self-explicated task or a "build your own" where respondents were asked to build the most preferred configuration of cloud storage services. They indicate their preferred levels of attributes given a summed price that they need to keep into consideration. The base price was centered on the storage space and premiums were added on enhanced security and privacy features. Based on the answers, the following sections were adapted. (2) Screening where participants' decisions were scanned regarding possible purchases in order to recognize non-compensatory behavior. In line with the self-explicated task in adaptive studies,

**Table 5.5** List of attributes and levels for personal cloud storage

| Attribute type | Attribute and description | Attribute levels (from basic to enhanced) |
|---|---|---|
| Functional | **Storage space:** Capacity of the file storage | 5 GB, 50 GB, 100 GB, 500 GB, or 1 TB |
| Functional | **Accessibility:** Options of devices supporting the service | (1) Website only, (2) website and desktop application, and (3) website, desktop application, and mobile |
| Functional | **File sharing:** Methods for sharing files with other parties | (1) Link sharing, (2) link sharing with password, and (3) sharing with managed permissions |
| Functional | **File recovery:** Data restore and recovery in case of disasters such as data loss or deletion | (1) Not available, (2) limited to 30 days, (3) limited to 90 days, and (4) unlimited |
| Functional | **File change history:** File versioning and system monitoring depending on the provider's policies | (1) Not available, (2) limited to 10 versions, and (3) full history with "Access and Activity" log |
| Non-functional | **Authentication:** Methods in which credentials are provided for accessing the service | (1) Password only, (2) two-step authentication, and (3) zero-knowledge authentication |
| Non-functional | **Location of cloud servers:** Location of the servers that the service provider deploy to store user data | (1) Worldwide, (2) worldwide (non-USA), (3) countries with high data protection and privacy standards (e.g., Switzerland), and (4) own country |
| Non-functional | **Encryption:** Transformation of the customer data to ciphertext using different encryption algorithms | (1) Server-side encryption and (2) end-to-end encryption (encryption and decryption are done on the client side with a private key) |
| Economic | **Price:** A summed price attribute, which is set based on incremental prices for attributes obtained from a market analysis | Varies between 0$ and 29$/month depending on the selected attribute levels |

respondents were asked on must-have or unacceptable features when their answers showed uniform decisions for certain attributes. We then presented seven screening tasks with three options each. (3) Choice tournament where respondents evaluate concepts presented as verbal descriptions for utility analysis and preference estimation.

For hiring survey participants, we used MTurk, an online crowdsourcing platform that provides a fast, inexpensive, and convenient sampling method and is appropriate for generalizing studies [62]. Aiming for high quality of responses, we restricted the participation in the survey to current cloud storage service users and received 188 responses, from which we included 144 in the analysis. Sawtooth Software was used to complete the survey and analyze the results. With more than 140 responses, ACBCA allowed stabilized estimates given the small sample size compared to the suggested mean in marketing studies. This approach also provides more information from the designed sections, suitable for part-worth estimations [58].

**Table 5.6** ACBCA survey design

## 1) Build your own

| Feature | Select Feature | Cost for Feature |
|---|---|---|
| Storage Space: | ○ 5 GB of cloud storage<br>○ 50 GB of cloud storage (+ $2)<br>○ 100 GB of cloud storage (+ $5)<br>○ 500 GB of cloud storage (+ $8)<br>○ 1 TB of cloud storage (+ $12) | $ 0 |
| Access: | ○ Website only<br>○ Website and desktop application<br>○ Website, desktop application and mobile | $ 0 |
| File Sharing: | ○ Sharing link<br>○ Sharing link with password (+ $1)<br>○ Sharing with managed permissions (+ $2) | $ 0 |
| Authentication: | ○ Password only<br>○ 2-step authentication (+ $2)<br>○ Zero-knowledge authentication (provider has no access to password in unencrypted form) (+ $2) | $ 0 |
| Location of servers: | ○ Own country (+ $2)<br>○ Countries with high data protection and privacy standards (e.g., Switzerland, Iceland, Canada) (+ $2)<br>○ Worldwide (non-US) (+ $1)<br>○ Worldwide | $ 0 |
| Encryption: | ○ Server-side<br>○ End-to-end encryption (encryption and decryption are done on the client-side) (+ $2) | $ 0 |
| Recovery: | ○ Unlimited<br>○ Limited to 90 days<br>○ Limited to 30 days<br>○ Not available | $ 0 |
| File Change History: | ○ Full history with "Access & Activity" log (+ $2)<br>○ Limited to 10 versions (+ $1)<br>○ Not available | $ 0 |
| | **Total (monthly rate)** | $ 0 |

## 2) Screening (non-compensatory behavior)

**Unacceptable Features**

We've noticed that you've avoided services with certain characteristics shown below. Would any of these features be **totally unacceptable**? If so, mark the **one feature that is most unacceptable**, so we can just focus on services that meet your needs.

○ Storage Space: - 100 GB of cloud storage
○ Storage Space: - 1 TB of cloud storage
○ Recovery: - Not available
○ Location of servers: - Worldwide
○ Authentication: - Zero-knowledge authentication (provider has no access to password in unencrypted form)
○ Encryption: - Server-side

○ None of these is totally unacceptable.

**Must Have Features**

We don't want to jump to conclusions, but we've noticed that you've selected cloud storage services with certain characteristics shown below. If any of these is an **absolute requirement**, it would be helpful to know. If so, please check the **one most important feature**, so we can just focus on services that meet your needs.

○ File Change History: - At least: Limited to 10 versions
○ Storage Space: - At most: 50 GB of cloud storage
○ Storage Space: - 50 GB of cloud storage

○ None of these is an absolute requirement.

(continued)

**Table 5.6**   (continued)

### 3) Screening
#### (1 of 7)

| | | | | |
|---|---|---|---|---|
| Storage Space: | 50 GB of cloud storage | 50 GB of cloud storage | 100 GB of cloud storage | 50 GB of cloud storage |
| Access: | Website, desktop application and mobile | Website, desktop application and mobile | Website, desktop application and mobile | Website only |
| File Sharing: | Sharing link | Sharing link with password | Sharing link | Sharing link |
| Authentication: | Password only | Password only | Password only | 2-step authentication |
| Location of servers: | Own country | Worldwide | Countries with high data protection and privacy standards (e.g., Switzerland, Iceland, Canada) | Countries with high data protection and privacy standards (e.g., Switzerland, Iceland, Canada) |
| Encryption: | End-to-end encryption (encryption and decryption are done on the client-side) | End-to-end encryption (encryption and decryption are done on the client-side) | Server-side | End-to-end encryption (encryption and decryption are done on the client-side) |
| Recovery: | Limited to 90 days | Limited to 30 days | Limited to 90 days | Limited to 30 days |
| File Change History: | Full history with "Access & Activity" log | Limited to 10 versions | Limited to 10 versions | Limited to 10 versions |
| Price (Monthly rate): | $7 | $8 | $9 | $12 |
| | ◯ A possibility ◯ Won't work for me | ◯ A possibility ◯ Won't work for me | ◯ A possibility ◯ Won't work for me | ◯ A possibility ◯ Won't work for me |

(continued)

**Table 5.6** (continued)

| 4) Choice tournament (1 of 6) | | | |
|---|---|---|---|
| Storage Space: | 50 GB of cloud storage | 50 GB of cloud storage | 100 GB of cloud storage |
| Access: | Website, desktop application and mobile | Website, desktop application and mobile | Website, desktop application and mobile |
| File Sharing: | Sharing link | Sharing link | Sharing link |
| Authentication: | 2-step authentication | Password only | 2-step authentication |
| Location of servers: | Countries with high data protection and privacy standards (e.g., Switzerland, Iceland, Canada) | Countries with high data protection and privacy standards (e.g., Switzerland, Iceland, Canada) | Countries with high data protection and privacy standards (e.g., Switzerland, Iceland, Canada) |
| Encryption: | End-to-end encryption (encryption and decryption are done on the client-side) | End-to-end encryption (encryption and decryption are done on the client-side) | Server-side |
| Recovery: | Unlimited | Unlimited | Unlimited |
| File Change History: | Full history with "Access & Activity" log | Limited to 10 versions | Full history with "Access & Activity" log |
| Price (Monthly rate): | $10 | $7 | $8 |
| | ○ | ○ | ○ |

## 5.5.3   Phase 3 "Preference Interpretation"

We analyzed the survey data applying the different CA techniques suggested by the method component: relative importance based on part-worth utilities, willingness-to-pay simulation, and segmentation. Based on the part-worth utilities, we could determine the relative importance of attributes and levels (Table 5.7). Our results indicate that price is the most important attribute for personal cloud storage, followed by storage space, which serves as the main functionality of the service, highlighting the price sensitivity of the majority of users. Among security and privacy features, recovery was in the third place, followed by location of servers and access. Features such as file change history and authentication (with less advanced options) were moderately important. File sharing and encryption features were given the least importance by respondents.

Performing a willingness-to-pay simulation provided detailed insights into design tradeoffs, enabling better prioritization of attributes and levels. To assess price sensitivity for security and privacy features, we use a reference product that is a status quo in the market and widely adopted by users (Table 5.8). We then estimate the change in utility ($\Delta$WTP) from the reference product to a compared product with one varied attribute level. This change in utility corresponds to the additional value users assign to the altered attribute. Given the implementation cost of certain attribute levels, users are willing to accept other design alternatives with less secure

**Table 5.7**  User preferences and part-worth utilities

| Attribute | Attribute levels | Average utilities | Standard deviation |
|---|---|---|---|
| Storage space | 5 GB | −6.87 | 104.60 |
| | 50 GB | 24.74 | 64.91 |
| | 100 GB | 5.48 | 27.98 |
| | 500 GB | −5.25 | 60.89 |
| | 1 TB | −18.10 | 91.49 |
| Accessibility | Website only | −30.90 | 23.43 |
| | Website and desktop | 0.89 | 19.95 |
| | Website, desktop, and mobile | 30.01 | 32.03 |
| File sharing | Link | 2.12 | 28.99 |
| | Link with password | 2.59 | 17.39 |
| | Managed permissions | −4.70 | 28.16 |
| Authentication | Password only | 10.12 | 36.93 |
| | Two-step authentication | 3.86 | 28.84 |
| | Zero knowledge | −13.98 | 27.15 |
| Location of servers | Worldwide | 16.26 | 36.68 |
| | Worldwide (non-USA) | −12.19 | 18.39 |
| | Own country | −8.00 | 36.37 |
| | Countries with high privacy | 3.93 | 26.16 |
| Encryption | Server side | 4.20 | 25.07 |
| | End-to-end encryption | −4.20 | 25.07 |
| Recovery | Not available | −28.93 | 27.49 |
| | Limited to 30 days | −7.95 | 21.18 |
| | Limited to 90 days | −8.12 | 24.60 |
| | Unlimited | 45.00 | 39.18 |
| File change history | Not available | −10.36 | 35.82 |
| | Limited to 10 versions | −3.21 | 16.73 |
| | Full history with log | 13.58 | 36.88 |
| Price | 0 $ | 79.27 | 123.88 |
| | 29 $ | −79.27 | 123.88 |

options. However, we also see that users are willing to pay more for products with certain security options, which can enhance the prioritization scheme, as previously explained. The simulation resulted with favorable preferences for more advanced file sharing options (more for sharing link with password), two-step authentication, and end-to-end encryption.

Finally, we determined customer segments based on individual part-worth utilities. The segmentation could be based on demographic and professional background information, which proved to be insignificant in our case. We therefore applied clustering analysis. Using the Convergent Cluster & Ensemble Analysis (CCEA) module in Sawtooth Software, we ran a simulation for $k$-means clustering for the customer segmentation. We performed multiple replications (starting from $k = 1$ to $k = 5$) to obtain the solution with the highest reproducibility score. We found three segments with specific preferences and privacy concerns (Table 5.9). The first

**Table 5.8** Willingness to pay for changing attribute levels (monthly rate)

| Attribute | Base level | Changed attribute level | ΔWTP ($) |
|---|---|---|---|
| Accessibility | Website, desktop, and mobile | Website and desktop | −2.00 |
| | | Website, desktop, and mobile | −2.00 |
| File sharing | Sharing link | Sharing link with password | −0.20 |
| | | Sharing with managed permissions | −1.00 |
| Authentication | Password only | Two-step authentication | −1.00 |
| | | Zero-knowledge authentication | −2.00 |
| Location of servers | Worldwide | Own country | −2.00 |
| | | Countries with high privacy standards | −1.70 |
| | | Worldwide (non-USA) | −2.00 |
| Encryption | Server side | End-to-end encryption | −1.00 |
| Recovery | Unlimited | Limited to 90 days | −2.00 |
| | | Limited to 30 days | −2.00 |
| | | Not available | −2.00 |
| File change history | Full history with "Access and Activity" log | Limited to 10 versions | −1.50 |
| | | Unavailable | −2.00 |

**Table 5.9** Customer segments of cloud storage services

| | Cluster 1 | Cluster 2 | Cluster 3 |
|---|---|---|---|
| # Participants | 38 (26.39%) | 77 (53.47%) | 29 (20.14%) |
| Privacy concerns | Unconcerned users | Privacy-rights advocates | Privacy-concerned users |
| *Preferences* | | | |
| Storage space | 5–50 GB | 100–500 GB | 500 GB–1 TB |
| Accessibility | Website, desktop, and mobile | Website, desktop, and mobile | Website, desktop, and mobile |
| File sharing | Sharing link | Sharing link with password | Managed permissions |
| Authentication | Password only | Two-step | Two-step |
| Location of servers | Worldwide | Own country or countries of high privacy standards | Countries of high privacy standards or worldwide |
| Encryption | Server side | End to end | End to end |
| Recovery | Unlimited | Unlimited | Unlimited |
| File history | Not available | Full history | Full history |
| Price | High | Low | High |

segment represents traditional users of basic personal cloud storage services who do not have specific privacy concerns. These users target other product features than privacy and security (e.g., storage). The second segment represents a majority of users who are concerned about privacy and security, but would not pay for it. They believe privacy is a right. The last segment represents customers who seek security features and are willing to pay for them. They estimate a cost for the reduced privacy risks. Given the divergent user preferences for privacy and security features, our results suggest the implementation of product bundles to meet the requirements of the different segments, especially Cluster 3 with preferences toward advanced security options.

These findings and segmentation results inform cloud service providers about users' privacy preferences and their WTP for privacy-preserving features for creating convenient services with advanced security options. Further simulations of market shares (e.g., with variation analysis) could enhance this analysis and help product managers in assessing the current release features and deciding on future releases based on the data and available resources.

## 5.6    Expert Evaluation of the Method Component

### 5.6.1    Evaluation Settings

For assessing the method in a real-world context, we performed a practice-oriented evaluation with experts [52]. The experts were first asked about their current practices for requirements elicitation and management in the context of mass-market software design, including the methods they use and the challenges they face in integrating "the voice of the customer." We then presented the method component and illustrated its use in two scenarios: (1) cloud platform design, showcasing its use for product planning and roadmapping, and (2) the design of secure cloud storage services, illustrating its role in release planning scenario. The participants were asked to assess the method component against three criteria [52]: usefulness in supporting requirements management activities, ease of use in terms of setup and efforts required for its application, and the technical feasibility in terms of the ease with which the method component will be operated. The experts evaluated six statements using a 5-Likert scale, with the cumulative results presented in Table 5.10. We then discussed main challenges in applying the method component to mass-market software product management.

**Table 5.10** Expert assessment of the method component

| Evaluation criteria | Score |
| --- | --- |
| The method is useful for incorporating the voice of the customer | 4.5 |
| The method is useful for managing roadmaps and requirements | 3.5 |
| The method is useful for release planning | 3.1 |
| The method is easy to use | 3.7 |
| Using this method is feasible in managing roadmaps and requirements | 3 |
| Using this method is feasible in release planning | 3 |

## 5.6.2 Feedback to Method Component

According to the experts, CA is very valuable for gaining insights from a large number of users and offers techniques useful for simulating designs. Specifically, the experts highlighted that CA can complement existing prototyping approaches by presenting product profiles as comprehensive set of features aligned with requirements. This allows validating the product combinations in early stages, before going into development.

However, they also noted that CA is more effective in defining roadmaps than in prioritizing features for product releases. The method component is particularly effective for engaging customers in proof of concept or in a first pilot, contributing to the optimal product profile for a first product release. As for release planning, the experts expressed contradicting views. One product manager emphasized the value of having a price attribute, considering it an innovative approach to evaluate requirements, especially in planning releases. This information, in combination with the relative importance measures, can be instrumental in specifying successful product combinations and prioritizing features. Interestingly, it became apparent that pricing is typically handled separately from requirements management, making it more complex to incorporate this element in the study. The experts also emphasized that applying CA method to all types of requirements is challenging when dealing with a high number of requirements to handle, as it is often the case with agile methods. Agile development demands fast and continuous delivery, making it difficult to apply the method component for each release. Additionally, one expert pointed out that CA might generate multiple combinations of features that work together and asked: "How can we assess that the set of combination is really significant for all users?". This concern is particularly relevant if the survey respondents are not representative of the entire user base, leading to quantitative assessments that may not accurately represent the needs of all users.

Regarding ease of use, the experts generally agreed that the method component is easy to use, thanks to the procedure model presented and the illustrated scenarios. However, one of the recurring challenges discussed is the aspect of reach. While the method allows integrating the voice of a large number of users, selecting appropriate users and potential customers remains a concern. One product manager suggested collaborating with the marketing team can help establish a panel for continuous evaluation and concepts testing. Additionally, we discussed crowdsourcing platforms as a channel for obtaining a large user as an approach to increase the reach and provide input from a larger audience.

Finally, the experts assessed the feasibility of the method component within their software product management activities. While they expressed a general positive view on its usefulness, their collective assessment was neutral regarding its feasibility of the method component in both product roadmapping and release planning. Most of them felt that applying this method in their real-world context requires additional expertise and skills. They also emphasized the need for further understanding how CA complements existing RE methods to ensure seamless integration within software product management. As one expert noted: "We already apply a mixed set of approaches to get user feedback, CA might be useful in getting additional insights about the user preferences, but we need to fully understand its techniques to be able to use it within the product management domain." The experts suggested that the method component should be incorporated into the knowledge base of requirements engineering for mass-market services and applications.

## 5.7　Summary and Conclusion

Cloud computing introduces innovations and delivers novel features and value propositions to a heterogeneous, globally distributed user base. Designing cloud services extends beyond traditional systems development, as it incorporates on-demand service delivery and the creation of viable business models for pay-per-use services. These complexities pose challenges for software product management, necessitating enhanced techniques for requirements elicitation and management.

Market research techniques that are widely used in new product development have to date not been fully embraced in the development of cloud services but can help address these challenges. Following method-engineering principles, we propose a method component that adapts CA from consumer research to the specific context of cloud services, thereby extending existing requirements engineering techniques. CA offers several advantages when applied to cloud service design. First, CA allows users to evaluate product profiles simultaneously and choose the best-fit alternative based on their preference model. Thus, it provides an understanding of the elements or structures widely accepted by users for product success through a data-driven approach that systematically quantifies users' preferences for understanding design tradeoffs and feature selection. Second, obtaining empirical data from a large set of users or potential helps product managers to avoid bias in design decisions through representative samples. The CA method can be applied at different stages of the life cycle. In the initial phases, it facilitates the concept evaluation of new cloud offerings, including the definition of their business models, target customer segments, and pricing strategies. In the subsequent phases, CA supports product management in refining the product design and prioritizing requirements by constructing utility functions of individual and group preferences. It thereby provides valuable input into product roadmaps and release planning.

It is important to note that CA extends beyond the scope of traditional requirements engineering and software product management approaches. CA not only delivers insights into the most relevant features from the user perspective and their relative importance, as well as group preferences; with willingness-to-pay and accept simulations, it can also inform product design and pricing decisions which are independent activities in current practices, but very important in the cloud context. CA also provides an opportunity for simulating design options through various techniques including competition analysis benchmarking and variation analysis. Based on that, product managers, product owners, business analysts, and product analysts can study utility changes with respect to changes in product combinations or implementation options. This is of course taking into account user's concerns as well as technical dependencies and restrictions.

Based on our insights, we provide future avenues for further extensions of the method component. One important enhancement is the development of user preference models (see Sect. 5.4.3.1) comprising the relevant dimensions for cloud products along with a rigorously developed and validated catalogue of attributes and attribute levels for different types of services. Such preference models would promote attribute reuse and accelerate the setup of CA studies.

While this method component has several benefits if applied in cloud product management, there are also limitations that should be taken into account when applying it. Most prominent is the complexity of the study design in terms of time and efforts. Experts have mentioned that the feasibility of the method component is dependent on the skills and knowledge of the product management team. Thus, having step-by-step guidelines for implementing the CA method is necessary in informing their application. Also, instantiations of the method component employing advanced analysis techniques can help in promoting its use. In addition, the acquisition of suitable study participants is seen as challenging due to the lack of relevant panels. Therefore, the setup of CA studies should be facilitated through the suggested crowdsourcing panels or the creation of specialized ones. Future research should focus on addressing these issues to prove the feasibility of using this method component in real scenarios.

**Acknowledgments** The research reported in this manuscript was partly supported by the Swiss National Science Foundation (SNSF) under grant number 159951.

# References

1. Jarke, M., Loucopoulos, P., Lyytinen, K., Mylopoulos, J., & Robinson, W. (2011). The brave new world of design requirements. *Information Systems, 36*(7), 992–1008.
2. Todoran, I., Seyff, N., & Glinz, M. (2013). How cloud providers elicit consumer requirements: An exploratory study of nineteen companies. In *Proceedings of the 21st IEEE International Requirements Engineering Conference (RE)*.
3. Ebert, C. (2007). The impacts of software product management. *Journal of Systems and Software, 80*(6), 850–861.
4. Maglyas, A., Nikula, U., & Smolander, K. (2011). What do we know about software product management?-A systematic mapping study. In *Proceedings of the Fifth International Workshop on Software Product Management (IWSPM)*, IEEE, pp. 26–35.
5. Fabijan, A., Olsson, H. H., 7 Bosch, J. (2015). Customer feedback and data collection techniques in software R&D: A literature review. In *Proceedings of the International Conference of Software Business* (pp. 139–153). Springer.
6. Ebert, C., & Brinkkemper, S. (2014). Software product management–An industry evaluation. *Journal of Systems and Software, 95*, 10–18.
7. Green, P. E., & Srinivasan, V. (1978). Conjoint Analysis in Consumer Research: Issues and Outlook. *Journal of Consumer Research*, 103–123.

8. Baum, K., Meissner, S., Abramova, O., & Krasnova, H. (2019). Do they really care about targeted political ads? Investigation of user privacy concerns and preferences. In *Proceedings of the 2019 European Conference on Information Systems*.
9. Bouwman, H., Haaker, T., & Vos, H. de. (2008). Mobile applications for police officers. In *Proceedings of BLED 2008*, January 1.
10. Koehler, P., Anandasivam, A., Dan, M., & Weinhardt, C. (2010). Customer heterogeneity and tariff biases in cloud computing. In *Proceedings of the 2010 International Conference on Information Systems*, January 1.
11. Mihale-Wilson, C., Zibuschka, J., & Hinz, O. (2017). About user preferences and willingness to pay for a secure and privacy protective ubiquitous personal assistant. In *Proceedings of the 25th European Conference on Information Systems (ECIS)*.
12. Naous, D., & Legner, C. (2021). Leveraging market research techniques in IS: A review and framework of conjoint analysis studies in the IS discipline. *Communications of the Association for Information Systems, 49*(1), 10.
13. Brinkkemper, S. (1996). Method engineering: Engineering of information systems development methods and tools. *Information and Software Technology, 38*(4), 275–280.
14. Van De Weerd, I., Brinkkemper, S., Nieuwenhuis, R., Versendaal, J., & Bijlsma, L. (2006). Towards a reference framework for software product management. In *Proceedings of the 14th IEEE International Conference on Requirements Engineering*, IEEE, pp. 319–322.
15. Dahlstedt, A., Karlsson, L., Persson, A., NattochDag, J., & Regnell, B. (2003). Market-driven requirements engineering processes for software products – A report on current practices. In *Proceedings of the International Workshop on COTS and Product Software, Held in Conjunction with the 11th IEEE International Requirements Engineering Conference*.
16. Cito, J., Leitner, P., Fritz, T., & Gall, H. C. (2015). The making of cloud applications: An empirical study on software development for the cloud. In *Proceedings of the 10th Joint Meeting on Foundations of Software Engineering*.
17. Groen, E. C., Seyff, N., Ali, R., Dalpiaz, F., Doerr, J., Guzman, E., Hosseini, M., Marco, J., Oriol, M., & Perini, A. (2017). The crowd in requirements engineering: The landscape and challenges. *IEEE Software, 34(2*, 44–52.
18. Carlshamre, P., & Regnell, B. (2000). Requirements lifecycle management and release planning in market-driven requirements engineering processes. In *Proceedings of the 11th international workshop on database and expert systems applications* (pp. 961–965). IEEE.
19. Achimugu, P., Selamat, A., Ibrahim, R., & Mahrin, M. N. (2014). A systematic literature review of software requirements prioritization research. *Information and Software Technology, 56*(6), 568–585.
20. Karlsson, J., & Ryan, K. (1997). A cost-value approach for prioritizing requirements. *IEEE Software, 14*(5), 67–74.
21. McFadden, D. (1986). The choice theory approach to market research. *Marketing Science, 5*(4), 275–297.
22. Luce, R. D., & Tukey, J. W. (1964). Simultaneous conjoint measurement: A new type of fundamental measurement. *Journal of Mathematical Psychology, 1*(1), 1–27.
23. Green, P. E., & Rao, V. R. (1971). Conjoint measurement for quantifying judgmental data. *Journal of Marketing Research*, 355–363.
24. Johnson, R. M. (1974). Trade-off analysis of consumer values. *Journal of Marketing Research*, 121–127.
25. Smith, H., Gnanadesikan, R., & Hughes, J. B. (1962). Multivariate analysis of variance (MANOVA). *Biometrics, 18*(1), 22–41.
26. Chen, G., & Tsurumi, H. (2010). Probit and logit model selection. *Communications in Statistics—Theory and Methods, 40*(1), 159–175.
27. Zubey, M. L., Wagner, W., & Otto, J. R. (2002). A conjoint analysis of voice over IP attributes. *Internet Research, 12*(1), 7.
28. Baek, S., Song, Y.-S., & Seo, J. (2004). Exploring Customers' Preferences for Online Games. In *Proceedings of SIGHCI 2004*, January 1.

29. Brodt, T., & Heitmann, M. (2004). Customer centric development of radically new products – A European case. In *Proceedings of the 2004 Americas Conference on Information Systems*, December 31.
30. Kim, Y. (2005). Estimation of consumer preferences on new telecommunications services: IMT-2000 service in Korea. *Information Economics and Policy, 17*(1), 73–84.
31. Mueller-Lankenau, C., & Wehmeyer, K. (2005). Mobile couponing - Measuring consumers, acceptance and preferences with a limit conjoint approach. In *Proceedings of BLED 2005*, December 31.
32. Haaker, T., Vos, H., & Bouwman, H. (2006). Mobile service bundles: The example of navigation services. In *Proceedings of BLED 2006*, January 1.
33. Mann, F., Ahrens, S., Benlian, A., & Hess, T. (2008). Timing is money - evaluating the effects of early availability of feature films via video on demand. In *Proceedings of the 2008 International Conference on Information Systems*, January 1.
34. Krasnova, H., Hildebrand, T., & Guenther, O. (2009). Investigating the value of privacy in online social networks: Conjoint analysis. In *Proceedings of the 2009 International Conference on Information Systems*, p. 173.
35. Song, J., Jang, T., & Sohn, S. Y. (2009). Conjoint analysis for IPTV service. *Expert Systems with Applications, 36*(4), 7860–7864.
36. Doerr, J., Benlian, A., Vetter, J., & Hess, T. (2010). Pricing of Content Services–An Empirical Investigation of Music as a Service. In *Proceedings of the Sixteenth Americas Conference on Information Systems (AMCIS)*, Lima.
37. Ho, K., See-to, E., & Xu, X. (2010). *The impacts of information privacy, monetary reward, and buyers' protection excess on consumers' utility using E-payment gateways: A conjoint analysis.* In *Proceedings of the 2010 Australian Conference on Information Systems*, January 1.
38. Fritz, M., Schlereth, C., & Figge, S. (2011). Empirical evaluation of fair use flat rate strategies for mobile internet. *Business and Information Systems Engineering, 3*(5), 269–277.
39. Choi, J. Y., Shin, J., & Lee, J. (2013). Strategic demand forecasts for the tablet PC market using the Bayesian mixed logit model and market share simulations. *Behaviour and Information Technology, 32*(11), 1177–1190.
40. Daas, D., Keijzer, W., & Bouwman, H. (2014). Optimal bundling and pricing of multi-service bundles from a value-based perspective a software-as-a-service case. In *Proceedings of BLED 2014*, June 1.
41. See-To, E. W. K., & Ho, K. K. W. (2016). A study on the impact of design attributes on e-payment service utility. *Information and Management*.
42. Abramova, O., Krasnova, H., & Tan, C.-W. 2017. How much will you pay? Understanding the value of information cues in the sharing economy, In *Proceedings of the 25th European Conference on Information Systems (ECIS)*, Guimarães, Portugal, June 5–10.
43. Mikusz, M., & Herter, T. (2016). How do consumers evaluate value propositions of connected car services? In *Proceedings of the 2016 Americas Conference on Information Systems*.
44. Schomakers, E.-M., Lidynia, C., & Ziefle, M. (2019). All of me? Users' preferences for privacy-preserving data markets and the importance of anonymity. *Electronic Markets*, 1–17.
45. Wessels, N., Gerlach, J., & Wagner, A. (2019). To sell or not to sell–antecedents of individuals' willingness-to-sell personal information on data-selling platforms. In *Proceedings of the 2019 International Conference on Information Systems*.
46. Zibuschka, J., Nofer, M., Zimmermann, C., & Hinz, O. (2019). Users' preferences concerning privacy properties of assistant systems on the internet of things. In *Proceedings of the 2019 Americas Conference on Information Systems*, Cancun.
47. Burda, D., & Teuteberg, F. (2015). Exploring consumer preferences in cloud archiving – A student's perspective. *Behaviour and Information Technology, 35*(2), 89–105.
48. Naous, D., Giessmann A., & Legner C. (2020). Incorporating the voice of the customer into mass-market software product management. In *Proceedings of the 35th Annual ACM Symposium on Applied Computing*, pp. 1397–1404.

49. Karlsson, F., & Wistrand, K. (2006). Combining method engineering with activity theory: Theoretical grounding of the method component concept. *European Journal of Information Systems, 15*(1), 82–90.
50. Braun, C., Wortmann, F., Hafner, M., & Winter, R. (2005). Method construction - A core approach to organizational engineering. In *Proceedings of the ACM Symposium on Applied Computing*, Santa Fe, New Mexico, pp. 1295–1299.
51. Giessmann, A., & Legner, C. (2013). Designing business models for platform as a service: Towards a design theory. In *Proceedings of the 34th International Conference on Information Systems*, Milan, pp. 1–10.
52. Prat, N., Comyn-Wattiau, I., & Akoka, J. (2015). A taxonomy of evaluation methods for information systems artifacts. *Journal of Management Information Systems, 32*(3), 229–267.
53. Thoring, K., Mueller, R., & Badke-Schaub, P. (2020). Workshops as a research method: Guidelines for designing and evaluating artifacts through workshops. In *Proceedings of the 53rd Hawaii International Conference on System Sciences*.
54. Legner, C., & Löhe, J. (2012). Improving the realization of IT demands: A design theory for end-to-end demand management. In *Proceedings of the 2012 International Conference on Information Systems*.
55. Pohl, K. (1994). The three dimensions of requirements engineering: A framework and its applications. *Information Systems, 19*(3), 243–258.
56. Nuseibeh, B., & Easterbrook, S. (2000). Requirements engineering: A roadmap. In *Proceedings of the Conference on the Future of Software Engineering*, ACM, pp. 35–46.
57. Green, P. E., Krieger, A. M., & Wind, Y. (2001). Thirty years of conjoint analysis: Reflections and prospects. *Interfaces, 31*(3_supplement), S56–S73.
58. Johnson, R., Huber, J., & Bacon, L. (2003). *Adaptive choice-based conjoint*. Sawtooth Software.
59. Johnson, R. M. (1987). Adaptive conjoint analysis. In *Sawtooth Software Conference on Perceptual Mapping, Conjoint Analysis, and Computer Interviewing* (pp. 253–265). Sawtooth Software Ketchum, Sun Valley, ID.
60. Spagnoletti, P., Za, S., & Winter, R. (2013). Exploring foundations for using simulations in IS research. In *Proceedings of the 2013 International Conference on Information Systems*.
61. Naous, D., & Legner, C. (2019). Understanding users' preferences for privacy and security features–A conjoint analysis of cloud storage services. In *Proceedings of the International Conference on Business Information Systems*, Springer, pp. 352–365.
62. Jia, R., Steelman, Z. R., & Reich, B. H. (2017). Using mechanical Turk data in IS research: Risks, rewards, and recommendations. *Communications of the Association for Information Systems, 41*(1), 14.

# Chapter 6
# Managing Generative Products: Different Rules for Software Innovation

**Mohammad Keyhani and Mahdieh Sarbazvatan**

**Abstract** Generative products are significantly influenced by users and their unique ways of utilizing and adapting a product or cloud service to meet their needs. Centralized managed cloud services, such as SaaS solutions, often restrict and predetermine usage patterns, which is contrary to the principles of generative products. However, it is feasible to design generative products within the cloud context. This can be achieved by leveraging existing design patterns and rules, such as APIs, that facilitate generative cloud products. To fully harness the potential of generative products, product management must consider aspects such as patient play, meta problem-solving, hypothesis development, and user tinkering. These considerations impact the release life cycle of cloud products and are illustrated through examples of successful generative products.

**Keywords** Generative products · Cloud services · Cloud products · Product management

## 6.1 Introduction

Once in a while an idea comes along that changes our perspective of the world. In the world of software and technology, the idea of "generativity" theorized by Zittrain [1, 2] and the surrounding package of ideas that have come to be known as Technology Generativity Theory is proving to be a paradigm-changing force. Generativity refers to the capability of a system to produce unprompted change

M. Keyhani (✉) · M. Sarbazvatan
Haskayne School of Business, University of Calgary, Calgary, Canada
e-mail: mkeyhani@ucalgary.ca

© The Author(s), under exclusive license to Springer Nature
Switzerland AG 2025
Y. Hajizadeh et al. (eds.), *Building Cloud Software Products*,
Innovation, Technology, and Knowledge Management,
https://doi.org/10.1007/978-3-031-92184-1_6

endogenously, even beyond the direction and anticipatory capacity of the system's creator(s), through distributed processes involving a multitude of agents (typically "users"). Youngjin Yoo, a world-leading scholar of information systems, has argued that the "age of generativity" is upon us and that it calls for new management practices, as well as new theoretical models and frameworks to guide those practices [3].

In this chapter, our premise is that it is not only broad "technologies" that can be generative, but also specific products developed by specific companies and organizations. We emphasize that not all products are or should be generative, but some products are or could be designed to be more or less generative. There are many good reasons why we would specifically want many products to not have generative characteristics, and we discuss some of these below. But our contention is that (a) it is sometimes desirable to purposefully design for generativity as many of the largest tech successes of the digital age have been fueled by it, and (b) for products that are intended to be generative, and desired to create positive value through their generativity, some of the existing approaches we think of as "best practices" in product management may need to be revisited. We may need to rethink entire mindsets, methods, frameworks, rules of thumb, and guiding principles when we approach entrepreneurship, innovation, product development, and product management around generative products.

Not much has been written on how to go about product management specifically for generative products, and therefore this chapter merely intends to start the conversation. We discuss the meaning and characteristics of generative products, the advantages and disadvantages of generative products, and the shift in mindset that is required to manage generative products. Throughout the chapter, we use anecdotes from a number of generative products on the market, as well as data from a qualitative study we have conducted on the Bubble.io no-code development platform and its ecosystem, which is itself a highly generative product.

### 6.1.1 What Are Generative Products?

Perhaps the most commonly cited definition of generativity is "a system's capacity to produce unanticipated change through unfiltered contributions from broad and varied audiences" ([2], p. 70), which is a variation of Zittrain's earlier definition of generativity as "a technology's overall capacity to produce unprompted change driven by large, varied, and uncoordinated audiences" ([1], p. 1980). The burgeoning literature on technology generativity has offered a multitude of variations and alternative definitions, often clarifying or emphasizing different aspects to generativity. Eck and Uebernickel [4] have analyzed many of the conceptualizations of generativity in the literature and categorize them into those that emphasize the properties of a system that render the system generative vs. those that emphasize the resulting pattern of phenomena that these systems enable.

Those that have emphasized the properties of generative systems have noted various aspects such as their reprogrammability, recombinatory capacity, accessibility, and ability to solicit and implement external contributions from diverse actors. Such properties allow the system to "create" new value beyond what its original creator is capable of or could even have imagined. Wareham et al. [5] state succinctly, "Generativity is the ability of a self-contained system to create, generate, or produce a new output, structure, or behaviour without any input from the originator of the system."

As a result, the pattern caused by generative products is a pattern of emergent self-organizing change and innovation, allowing the product itself and the ecosystem around it to evolve in unanticipated directions in more or less uncontrolled ways. The "unanticipated change" does not necessarily occur within the product itself (although it may), but more generally in the value creation that the product enables. The key source of value in generative products is the ability to mobilize a vast amount of distributed knowledge, creativity, and imagination from external users to create innovations—using the product or within the product itself—beyond what would have been possible if the knowledge and imagination of only the product's creator(s) and their organization constrained the product's usage or evolution.

Most product creators do not want to relinquish *all* control, but it is a matter of degree, and there is typically a trade-off between the level of generativity and the level of control that a product creator can impose [6–9] and consequently the level of security and reliability it can offer its users. In either case, no matter how generative a product is, its evolutionary path is determined and constrained by the initial design, features and capabilities of the product. The level of originality of innovations that are possible by a generative product's users is constrained by the scope of remixing and creativity afforded by the product [8] as well as the toolkits, standards, and guidelines that enable user innovation [10].

### 6.1.2 *Examples of Generative Products*

Zittrain's own examples of "generative technologies" that were the focus of his book were the Internet and the personal computer: "both were generative: they were designed to accept any contribution that followed a basic set of rules (either coded for a particular operating system, or respecting the protocols of the Internet). Both overwhelmed their respective proprietary, non-generative competitors" ([2], p. 3). In general, the concept of generativity is relative rather than binary. It is helpful to think of any product as being on a continuum of generativity, although the position of a product on this continuum is often determined relative to its alternatives that appear in practice. For example, Zittrain considers a hammer to be more generative than a jackhammer, Lego bricks more generative than a prefabricated dollhouse, and a knife more generative than a potato peeler. The smartphone is certainly more generative than the dumbphone, but the Android operating system and Apple's iOS have each been generative in different ways [11].

In the software world, a prime example of a highly generative product is the spreadsheet. Users of spreadsheet software found so many different value-creating uses for it that many consider it to be the first ever "killer app" and the main reason behind the rapid adoption of personal computers [12]. Another example is the WordPress content management system [13], which as of the time of this writing is estimated to be the platform on which more than 30% of the world's websites are built.

Other examples of modern cloud software products that have proved to be highly generative include the Slack.com messaging software; the AirTable.com cloud database software; API connector tools such as Zapier.com and Integromat.com; no-code app development tools such as Bubble.io, Retool.com, and Adalo.com; as well as the new generation of dynamic content management systems such as Notion.so and Coda.io. These are just a few examples of highly generative cloud software products currently available, and most of them fast-growing as of the time of this writing.

As of the time of this writing, a new kind of generative technology called generative AI (where the word "generative" means something different) is taking the world by storm and allowing generative products to become even more so. In the words of Joshua Haas, one of the founders of Bubble.io [14]:

> We're living in a transformational moment—generative AI is changing the way we approach creativity, entrepreneurship, and work in important ways. This parallels the pattern observed in generative products, where emergent self-organizing change and innovation drive evolution. In much the same manner, generative AI harnesses distributed knowledge and creativity, allowing small teams and individuals to leverage technology's potential. The combination of no-code platforms and AI capabilities presents a compelling glimpse into the future of software development, echoing the value proposition of generative products by mobilizing collective intelligence and creativity beyond the boundaries of conventional approaches.

### 6.1.3  What Makes a Product Generative?

Zittrain identifies participation as the key input and innovation as the key output of generativity. So, in essence, the key components of product generativity are to increase the number of people that participate in using, changing, and building with the product and enable them to create and build with the product in such a way that they can exercise their own creativity and innovation rather than be limited by a narrow scope of product use.

How do we increase participation and innovation? Zittrain offers five key characteristics of a generative "system or technology" ([2], p. 71), listed here with examples from generative cloud products:

1. **Leverage:** how extensively it leverages a set of possible tasks ("the more a system can do, the more capable it is of producing change"), for example, Notion. so and Coda.io can be used for something as simple as note-taking or as complex as app building. Bubble.io can be used for simple one-page apps or to build complex enterprise products such as customer relationship management (CRM) systems.

2. **Adaptability:** how well it can be adapted to a range of tasks. How easily the system can be built on or modified to broaden its range of uses, for example, Notion.so was not designed to be a website builder, but its users have effectively figured out how to use it as a website builder with add-on services such as Super.so and HostNotion.co. When generative AI tools like ChatGPT were released, users of Bubble.io were immediately able to build with this new technology through API integrations [15].

3. **Ease of Mastery**: how easily new contributors can master it (understand, adopt, and adapt it); Notion.so and Coda.io are very easy to start with for simple applications and provide learning paths and knowledge bases for people to gradually learn advanced features. Zapier.com allows people to build automations with easy drag and drop tools that previously required professional software scripting. Bubble.io offers a path to building software products that is much simpler than traditional programming.

4. **Accessibility:** how accessible it is to those ready and able to build on it. This includes access to the technology itself as well as access to the information needed to achieve mastery. Notion.so, Coda.io, Zapier.com, Airtable.com, and Bubble.io all have free plans that allow anyone to start using them for a variety of use cases. Moreover, a vast community of users have produced extensive amounts of user-generated learning content and videos to help others learn to use these tools.

5. **Transferability:** how transferable any changes are to others—including (and perhaps especially) nonexperts. Both Notion.so and Coda.io allow their users to copy and import templates and pages from other users. Bubble.io allows this as well and also allows for transfer of ownership of entire apps.

Software products being "digital artifacts" have an exceptionally high potential to be designed for generativity if so desired. This is because the inherent characteristics and features of digital technology are a great fit for generativity. Some authors point out that generativity is a consequence of the combinatory capacity and reprogrammability of digital artifacts [9, 13, 16]. Kallinikos et al. [17] provide a useful listing of the characteristics of digital artifacts, summarized by Eck et al. [18] as follows:

> They distill four immediate characteristics (interactive; editable; reprogrammable; distributed) and three corollary attributes (modular; granular; reflexive) of digital artifacts. Interactivity denotes the possibility to explore a digital artifact, its individual components, and dependencies. Editability relates to the possibility of modifying the artifact while leaving its logical structure unchanged. Reprogrammability reflects the possibility of releasing a digital artifact from its immediate use context, modify its structure, and repurpose it. Distributedness signifies that digital artifacts are not confined to any physical or institutional borders. Modularity refers to the distinct quality of modularized digital artifacts not to be bound to a fixed product architecture, meaning that individual modules of a complex digital artifact can be transferred to completely unrelated use contexts. Granularity stands for the inherent decomposability of digital artifacts, down to their basic binary representation, and for the associated possibility to modify both an insignificant and a substantial part of the artifact on different levels of abstraction. Lastly, the reflexive dynamics of digital artifacts carries the notion that any access, assembly, or otherwise manipulation can only be

performed through making use of other digital artifacts. Consequently, any domain in which digital artifacts enter will invariantly see an increase of digital artifacts over time.

The notion of architectural modularity or "decoupling" is key to most generative products. For example, the decoupling of software and hardware has been key to the generativity of computers: "The essence—and genius—of separating software creation from hardware construction is that the decoupling enables a computer to be acquired for one purpose and then used to perform new and different tasks without requiring the equivalent of a visit to the mechanic's shop" ([2], p. 14).

But no matter what generative features or properties the product itself has, generativity still cannot be achieved if human participation in the use and adaptation of the product is not expanded. A generative product has the features to make this expansion of participation possible, but the solicitation of participation, in general, includes an entirely social and non-technological component. Importantly, generative products require the participation of people outside the product-creating organization in the evolution of the product, because no matter how large an organization is, the amount of knowledge and creativity it can pour into a product is no match for the distributed knowledge and creativity of millions of users across the world and over time.

While the emphasis in discussions of generativity is often on change and adaptability, it is also very important to emphasize that widespread participation and creative contributions to a product are only possible if the product has a well-designed, well-functioning, stable core, around which various innovations can be developed [19]. Without the necessary standardization and stability at the core of a product ecosystem, the system as a whole becomes too unreliable and thus users are not incentivized to "invest" time, effort, and resources in contributing to it.

Furthermore, while the emphasis in discussions of generativity is often on the "uncoordinated" and "unfiltered" nature of contributions, it must also be emphasized that the way in which an organization governs the processes by which external contributions are solicited, incentivized, and disseminated makes a great deal of difference in the ultimate generativity that is achieved by the product and its ecosystem. This governance role has been extensively studied in the literature on software platforms, where it is often referred to as an "orchestrator" role [20, 21].

### 6.1.4  Can Cloud Software Products Be Generative?

In his book, *The Future of the Internet and How to Stop It*, Zittrain, who is himself a scholar of law, is very concerned with the ways in which cloud technology and the trend toward software as a service (SaaS) products may be reducing the generativity of the Internet. He notes that cloud software is centrally controlled and thereby "tethered" such that it gives unprecedented powers to the software provider relative to the previous era of client-side software. The almost dictatorial control and "perfect enforcement" capabilities that cloud-based SaaS architectures give to software producers—and by extension the regulators who have authority over them—can be highly problematic, especially when viewed from a legal perspective.[1]

Zittrain argues that the centralized control of software in cloud architecture reduces the capacity for generative innovations because it takes away the freedom and control of end users over the software. Although he recognizes some benefits of cloud software, he argues that such software is at best only "contingently generative" ([2], p. 129). He clarifies this with the example of Google Maps:

> Because it allows coders access to its map data and functionality, Google's mapping service is generative. But it is also contingent: Google assigns each Web developer a key and reserves the right to revoke that key at any time, for any reason—or to terminate the whole Google Maps service. It is certainly understandable that Google, in choosing to make a generative service out of something in which it has invested heavily, would want to control it. But this puts within the control of Google, and anyone who can regulate Google, all downstream uses of Google Maps—and maps in general, to the extent that Google Maps' popularity means other mapping services will fail or never be built. ([2], p. 124)

While Zittrain's concerns are entirely valid, it is still the case that cloud software products can be intentionally designed for generativity and can end up being more or less generative in practice. It is also the case that some characteristics of cloud software are particularly conducive to generativity. These characteristics include:

- Safety: software hosted on the cloud does not suffer from version incompatibility issues, is typically safe from malware, and is independent of or at least less dependent on problems with the user's hardware or possible human error by the user in installing and maintaining the software.
- Reliability: cloud software enjoys the benefits of professionally managed installation and maintenance, including automatic updates, and independence of "run time" from user hardware, such that software services can continue operating even when a user's hardware is offline.
- Ease of access: accessing cloud software typically requires only a browser, with only barebones hardware requirements, thereby opening access to a broader population of users.
- Cloud-based combinatorial innovation capacity: a key element of generativity involves the ability to combine software with other software. In the cloud this is typically done through application programming interfaces (APIs) that also operate in the cloud, thereby also benefiting from all the above features.

---

[1] As an example of these dictatorial powers, consider the recent case [22] where in September 2020, the Department of Arab and Muslim Ethnicities and Diaspora Studies at the San Francisco State University had planned to hold a virtual seminar where one of the speakers was to be Leila Khaled, a Palestinian activist with a controversial background. Pro-Israel groups pressured the university to cancel the talk, but failing there, they approached Zoom Video Communications, Inc., the company that provided the video conferencing software application on which the talk was to be hosted. Citing federal anti-terrorism laws, Zoom ultimately decided to cancel the event, thereby exercising a power which no private company typically has over university seminars. When the organizers of the talk turned to Facebook as an alternative, they were rejected by the platform. They then turned to YouTube on the day of the seminar, but YouTube shut down the livestream 23 min into the talk.

## 6.2   The Advantages and Disadvantages of Generative Products

Generativity is not always desirable. There are at least three key challenges with generative products: chaos, ambiguity, and time. But these challenges can also act as barriers to competition for those companies that manage to achieve scale with generative products.

For many types of products, it makes more sense to have a specific-use product that cannot be altered by users and does not play the role of an innovation tool. Often in such cases a certain level of reliability and stability is needed that could be compromised by trying to make the product more generative. In such cases the product creator needs to retain full control over the behavior of the product, and in fact cloud software technology provides the ability to retain near-perfect centralized control when needed.

Even when generativity is desirable, the sacrifice of control can have negative consequences. Not all user innovations may be positive and some could be value destroying. This was the case, for example, with the first computer virus that started to infect computers shortly after the technology to connect computers through a network was invented. Such undesired user innovations can ruin the user experience for everyone else.

Another disadvantage of generative products lies in their inherent ambiguity, especially early on in their development before a community of users has had the chance to co-create and discover its main uses. It is often hard to describe to people exactly what a generative product does, and trying to do so could result in imposing one's own imagination on the product and thereby hindering the potential contribution of other people's imaginations to the product's development that are cognitively distant from us. An example is that of SparkFun Electronics which is a company that offers a range of products related to generative hardware platforms such as the Raspberry Pi. After some instances where the company's customers were able to find uses for their product that were out of line for how the company itself had described the product, the company made a purposeful decision to no longer label its products as having limited specific uses [23].

This ambiguity in the definition of the product can of course be problematic in many ways. Perhaps the main challenge lies in communicating the product's value to stakeholders, including investors and customers, but also possibly to yourself and your employees. Back in the 1970s when computers were first marketed for personal use, it was hard to describe to people exactly what the value proposition was until eventually certain "killer apps" such as the spreadsheet (e.g., VisiCalc) were found that convinced many users of the value proposition [12].

It is instructive—and often entertaining—to see how journalists and press releases struggle to talk about a highly generative product. Naturally, articles that are written about generative software products in their early phases will face confusion regarding exactly how to describe the product and what it does. Table 6.1 provides a case in point: five articles written about Coda.io and listed as

**Table 6.1** Examples of how a generative cloud software product (Coda.io) is described in the press

| Metaphor for describing Coda.io | Reference (as found on the Wikipedia entry for Coda.io) |
|---|---|
| A document-based app-builder tool | McCracken, Harry (2019-02-05). "Coda, which wants to turn docs into apps, is now generally available." *Fast Company*. Retrieved 2019-11-19 |
| A new kind of spreadsheet software | Newton, Casey (2017-10-19). "Coda is a next-generation spreadsheet designed to make Excel a thing of the past." *The Verge*. Retrieved 2019-11-19 |
| Rules-based automation platform | "Coda's rules-based Automations feature automates repetitive tasks." *VentureBeat*. 2018-11-16. Retrieved 2019-11-19 |
| A document builder tool ("Minecraft for docs") | Flynn, Kerry. "A startup is taking on Google and Microsoft with a 'Minecraft for docs'." *Mashable*. Retrieved 2019-11-19 |
| A new kind of document editor | "Two Google alums just raised $60M to rethink documents." *TechCrunch*. Retrieved 2019-11-19 |

references in the Wikipedia entry for Coda.io each use a different metaphor to describe the product [24]. Just looking at the first column of Table 6.1, you could hardly guess that they were talking about the same product!

Another disadvantage of generative products is time. It can take quite a while for a generative product to really gain traction. This is because the process of users playing with the product, learning how to work with it, learning to innovate with it, communicating their innovation with others, and learning from others' ideas all take time. Usually a community of hobbyist user-innovators has to develop around the product and eventually clarify the product's value propositions in a way that is accessible to the broader public before a mass market can be persuaded to adopt it.

On the other hand, the time barrier can also act as a barrier to competition for those who successfully achieve scale with a generative product. So can the community. The large communities of users and enthusiasts all engage in activities that create value for the product owner, including knowledge search, discovery, and innovation and also bear some of the burden of financing and risk bearing for those innovations. The user communities also aid in marketing, promotion, and knowledge sharing around the generative product. Users may get involved in a social community around the product and are probably more likely to feel invested in the product because they have a sense of involvement in its development and a sense of ownership over the innovations they create with it.

## 6.3  A New Mindset for Managing Generative Products

Due to the unique characteristics of generative products, the design, development, and management of these products also require a unique approach. Some of what is considered "best practice" in entrepreneurship, innovation, and product management around non-generative products may not be best suited to generative products.

Perhaps the key factor to consider when managing a generative product is the relative incompleteness of knowledge that the product manager is dealing with. Generative products "are built on the notion that they are never fully complete, that they have many uses yet to be conceived of" ([2], p. 43).

In this section we outline some of the ways in which product management requires a different mindset when managing generative products. Specifically, we suggest at least four shifts away from the traditional product mindset are required for generative products. In describing these mindset shifts, we also point out some practical techniques and rules of thumb for managing generative products.

### 6.3.1   From Fail Fast to Patient Play

First, the time challenge with generative products has important implications for product management. Iteration cycles and time to feedback need to be rethought when generativity is a focus. Practices involving feedback collection from users [25], even in their most advanced forms of allowing users to work with minimum viable products (MVPs), must be approached differently.

The idea of "fail fast" [26] fails on both the "fail" and the "fast" for generative products. First, with generative products given their time and ambiguity issues, it is harder to define exactly when failure or success has been achieved, and for a long time the product-creating organization may find that its generative product may experience some signs of moving in the wrong or right direction without being able to clearly demark it as a success or failure. For this reason, a substantial level of patience is required with generative products. Of course, beyond certain thresholds of performance, a course of action can be decided upon. But the thresholds for generative products are somewhat broader and more ambiguous than non-generative products.

With generative products, the product-creating organization typically releases the product into the wild without itself completely knowing yet the full extent of the product's capabilities and applications. The organization then requires the patience to allow users to play with the product and discover new uses for it, discuss those uses with each other, and build on one another's discoveries.

### 6.3.2   From Problem-Solving to Meta Problem-Solving

With generative products the product manager must consider that the aim is to provide a general-purpose tool that can solve certain classes of problems at a meta level rather than to provide a narrow solution to specific problems. They could be called meta-products rather than products. This results in more abstract and vague product descriptions, and visions which are harder to sell as it is harder to explain exactly "what does it do?"

Fewer potential investors or customers will initially "get it" as it will be harder to communicate the value of the product in simple terms. But those that do "get it" realize the immense value of solving problems at a meta level. You are not just solving a single problem but an entire class of problems. These visions are in fact very inspiring to those who "get" it, who are typically more abstract thinkers with more advanced meta-cognitive capabilities [27]. A prime example of this kind of meta-thinker is Alan Turing who was tasked with decrypting intercepted messages in World War II, but instead solved the problem at a meta-level through an algorithmic approach that could adapt to changes in the encryption [28].

### 6.3.3  From Hypothesis Testing to Hypothesis Development

Best practice guidelines regarding the solicitation and collection of feedback and how it is incorporated in the next design iteration assume that the product team (a) knows what kind of people to target as potential users, (b) knows what problems the product is trying to solve for those users, and (c) is able to "get" the answer to whether or not the product is useful to the user rather quickly and cleanly by approaching or observing the user [29]. All of these assumptions may be misguided or at least somewhat shaken with generative products.

With generative products, the emphasis on hypothesis testing shifts to one step earlier in the research process, i.e., hypothesis development. As researchers know, hypothesis testing (best done through quantitative research) is not the only way to acquire knowledge, and in fact in the more early "fuzzy front end" and ambiguous phases of knowledge development, more qualitative and exploratory studies are preferred. Researchers refer to these studies not with the terminology of "hypothesis testing" but with the terminology of "hypothesis development" or "hypothesis generation" [30].

Therefore, the process of testing generative products involves (a) exposing the product to broad populations and large crowds without imposing your own imagination on the boundaries of the target market, (b) allowing users to discover what problem areas the product may be applicable to, and (c) giving the user time and resources to play, experiment, and discover the answer to the question of whether or not the product is useful to them. Instead of "user testers" a generative product in its early phases may be more in need of "problem hunters" that seek to find new problem areas where the product may be able to generate solutions.

### 6.3.4  From Customer Feedback to User Tinkering

Compared to narrow-scope products, with generative products the process of problem discovery continues for longer and has a broader scope. In the lean startup model, problem discovery ends rather quickly, and other steps depend on problem discovery to have been finalized. The aim is to quickly find a rather narrow product-market fit and capitalize on that as soon as possible [25]. With generative products on the other hand, "product-market fit" has a broader meaning and more ambiguous scope and cannot be nailed down early in order to proceed to other things.

Once again, the key is patience. The type of customer feedback data that could validate a customer segment in the search for a viable business model is just not as readily available with generative products as the lean startup model would assume. Instead, the organization must patiently observe and work with users as they tinker with the product, and as they learn to work with it, apply it, and innovate with it. The user tinkering process is a slower process in terms of getting to that elusive "customer validation" mark than the customer feedback process of the lean startup method. For example, in the lean startup approach it is assumed that once the "solution" to a problem is shown to the customer, even in prototype form, the customer will immediately know whether or not they like it or if it is useful to them. "you don't have real data until you see their pupils dilate" ([29], p. 214) is an example of this type of thinking. With the user tinkering approach, however, the user may not immediately have such an "aha!" moment, but may gradually get there on their own after spending some time playing with the product without direction. With generative products, the initial reaction from users could be intrigue and curiosity, rather than immediate delight. In our study of Bubble.io users, we found that users typically reach those "aha" moments only after completing tutorials or spending significant time working with the app to confirm that it can indeed build what they were thinking of building.

Two key tools that need to be provided to users to support and boost their tinkering efforts include modular integrations and knowledge bases. Through various application programming interfaces (APIs) with other tools and even between modular components of the generative product itself, the user is better able to engage in combinatorial innovation by experimenting with various combinations of modules and integrations with other products. Furthermore, detailed and dynamic knowledge bases can help users learn from each other's innovations and best practices and facilitate the cumulative knowledge building process around the generative product. Bubble.io takes full advantage of both of these mechanisms, with its API features and its community forum often being heralded as advantages of their product.

### 6.3.5 Implications for the Cloud Product Release Cycle

Cloud products often go through three stages in their release process: private review, public review, and general availability. The generative product mindset has implications for how this release cycle is managed. First, it must be recognized that in the private review stage, the choice of reviewers is limited by the knowledge constraints and social network of the product creator(s). Therefore, these early reviewers are unlikely to be cognitively distant from the product creators(s) and are consequently unlikely to think of innovative ways to use the product beyond those already imagined by the product creator.

Second, in both the private and public review stage, it must be recognized that clear yes or no answers that can help the company decide on features to include or exclude from the final product may be harder to come by with products that are designed to be generative.

Third, as much of the value of generative products is realized through APIs and interconnections with other products, if these interconnections are not available or functional in the private and public review stages, it may hinder the review process.

Fourth, as in general the value of generative products is realized slowly over time with many dispersed users interacting and tinkering with the product, it must be recognized that private and public review stages are generally unlikely to provide full insights into the generative potential of the product. Therefore, it is recommended that for generative products, the general availability (GA) stage is expedited and feedback mechanisms traditionally reserved for the private and public review stages are incorporated into the GA stage as much as possible.

## 6.4  Concluding Thoughts

While not all products can or should be generative, generative products are a key source of competitive advantage for some of the largest and most successful software and technology companies in the world today. Yet scholars and practitioners alike have paid little attention to the particularities of generative products and how they might differ from other kinds of products.

Generative products are a different kind of beast compared to non-generative narrow-scope products. The unique aspects of generativity should make a difference in how we approach the management of generative products. In essence, product management is an organizational activity and the agency for this activity is typically assumed to be fully residing in the product-creating organization. But generativity starts to mess with this assumption as it results in the product itself taking on some of the agency of organization, especially when it comes to knowledge discovery (e.g., "figuring out what it's good for") and accessing the innovations of users.

Nevertheless, the burden of organization is far from being completely removed from the product-creating organization when managing generative products. Instead, its nature and scope change in interesting ways, and we are just beginning to understand and appreciate exactly what these changes are. This chapter has attempted to provide an initial exploration of the topic, but much work remains to be done.

## References

1. Zittrain, J. (2006). The generative internet. *Harvard Law Review*, 1974–2040.
2. Zittrain, J. (2008). *The future of the internet--and how to stop it*. Yale University Press.
3. Yoo, Y. (2013). The tables have turned: How can the information systems field contribute to technology and innovation management research? *Journal of the Association for Information Systems, 14*(5), 227–236.

4. Eck, A., & Uebernickel, F. (2016). *Untangling generativity: Two perspectives on unanticipated change produced by diverse actors*. Paper presented at the Information systems as a global gateway: 24th European Conference on Information Systems.
5. Wareham, J., Fox, P. B., & Giner, J. L. C. (2014). Technology ecosystem governance. *Organization Science, 25*(4), 1195–1215. https://doi.org/10.1287/orsc.2014.0895
6. Cennamo, C., & Santaló, J. (2019). Generativity tension and value creation in platform ecosystems. *Organization Science, 30*(3), 617–641.
7. Eaton, B. D. (2012). *The dynamics of digital platform innovation: Unfolding the paradox of control and generativity in Apple's iOS*. The London School of Economics and Political Science (LSE).
8. Hill, B. M., & Monroy-Hernández, A. (2013). The remixing dilemma: The trade-off between generativity and originality. *American Behavioral Scientist, 57*(5), 643–663.
9. Tilson, D., Lyytinen, K., & Sørensen, C. (2010). Research commentary—Digital infrastructures: The missing IS research agenda. *Information Systems Research, 21*(4), 748–759.
10. Remneland-Wikhamn, B., Ljungberg, J., Bergquist, M., & Kuschel, J. (2014). Generativity and innovation in smartphone ecosystems. In *Open Innovation Research, Management and Practice* (pp. 267–296). World Scientific.
11. Eaton, B. D., Elaluf-Calderwood, S., Sorensen, C., & Yoo, Y. (2011). *Structural narrative analysis as a means to unfold the paradox of control and generativity that lies within mobile platforms*. Paper presented at the 2011 10th International Conference on Mobile Business.
12. Zynda, M. R. (2013). The first killer app: A history of spreadsheets. *Interactions, 20*(5), 68–72.
13. Um, S. Y., Yoo, Y., Wattal, S., Kulathinal, R. J., & Zhang, B. (2013). *The architecture of generativity in a digital ecosystem: A network biology perspective*. Paper presented at the International Conference on Information Systems, ICIS 2013.
14. Haas, J. (2023). *Why AI + No-Code is the future*. Retrieved from https://forum.bubble.io/t/why-ai-no-code-is-the-future/253708
15. Ahmed, R. (2023). *Pushing the limits of Bubble.io and leveraging the full potential of ChatGPT: A case study*. Retrieved from https://forum.bubble.io/t/pushing-the-limits-of-bubble-io-and-leveraging-the-full-potential-of-chatgpt-a-case-study/268188
16. Eaton, B., Elaluf-Calderwood, S., Sørensen, C., & Yoo, Y. (2015). Distributed tuning of boundary resources. *MIS Quarterly, 39*(1), 217–244.
17. Kallinikos, J., Aaltonen, A., & Marton, A. (2013). The ambivalent ontology of digital artifacts. *MIS Quarterly*, 357–370.
18. Eck, A., Uebernickel, F., & Brenner, W. (2015). *The generative capacity of digital artifacts: A mapping of the field*.
19. Baldwin, C. Y., & Woodard, C. J. (2009). The architecture of platforms: A unified view. In A. Gawer (Ed.), *Platforms, markets and innovation* (Vol. 32, pp. 19–34).
20. Itami, H., & Numagami, T. (1992). Dynamic interaction between strategy and technology. *Strategic Management Journal, 13*(S2), 119–135.
21. Tiwana, A. (2013). *Platform ecosystems: aligning architecture, governance, and strategy*. Newnes.
22. Speri, A., & Biddle, S. (2020). *Zoom censorship of palestine seminars spark fight over academic freedom*. The Intercept. Retrieved from https://theintercept.com/2020/11/14/zoom-censorship-leila-khaled-palestine/
23. Murphy, M. (2014). *Boundary jumping: Understanding the value of modest anarchy in entrepreneurial networks*. Silicon Flatirons Center.
24. Wikipedia Contributors. (2021, January 8). *Coda.io*. Wikipedia, The Free Encyclopedia. Retrieved from https://en.wikipedia.org/w/index.php?title=Coda.io&oldid=999092746
25. Ries, E. (2011). *The lean startup: How today's entrepreneurs use continuous innovation to create radically successful businesses* (1st ed.). Crown Business.
26. Hall, D. (2007). Fail fast, fail cheap. *Business Week, 32*, 19–24.

27. Metcalfe, J., & Shimamura, A. P. (1994). *Metacognition: Knowing about knowing*. MIT Press.
28. Hodges, A. (2012). *Alan Turing: The enigma*. Random House.
29. Blank, S., & Dorf, B. (2020). *The startup owner's manual: The step-by-step guide for building a great company*. Wiley.
30. Hartwick, J., & Barki, H. (1994). Hypothesis testing and hypothesis generating research: An example from the user participation literature. *Information Systems Research, 5*(4), 446–449.

# Chapter 7
# Machine Learning Get Ready to Measure the Value for Supply Chain Management

## Understanding the Value of Machine Learning in the Context of Business Processes

**Ute Riemann and Thomas Ochs**

**Abstract** Machine learning (ML) isn't a solitary endeavour of IT but is having a dramatic impact on the way we can perform business processes. It is one of the quickest expanding areas within the area of artificial intelligence (AI) (Jordan & Mitchell, Science, 349(6245), 255–260, 2015) justified by the high productivity growth promised by these technologies, coupled with the explosive increase of data amounts and the growing availability of low-cost computing power and data storage required to use ML (Court et al., *Big data, analytics, and the future of marketing & sales*. McKinsey & Company Marketing & Sales Paper, March 2015; Jordan & Mitchell, Science, 349(6245), 255–260, 2015; Wess, Mit Künstlicher Intelligenz immer die richtigen Entscheidungen treffen. In P. Buxmann & H. Schmidt (Eds.), Künstliche Intelligenz: Mit Algorithmen zum wirtschaftlichen Erfolg (pp. 143–159). Springer, 2019). ML is so important because it helps using data to a greater value to drive business rule and logic. Already in the 1950s and 1960s the terms AI, ML, pattern recognition and game playing were used in connection with intelligent computers. Methods such as neural networks were also already well known (Minsky, Proceedings of the IRE, 49(1), 8–30, 1961; 20; Samuel, IBM Journal of Research and Development, 3(3), 210–229, 1959). Due to the rapid progress of technology at lower cost, this interest is renewed as big data can now be processed (Jordan & Mitchell, Science, 349(6245), 255–260, 2015; Wess, Mit Künstlicher Intelligenz immer die richtigen Entscheidungen treffen. In P. Buxmann & H. Schmidt (Eds.), Künstliche Intelligenz: Mit Algorithmen zum wirtschaftlichen Erfolg (pp. 143–159). Springer, 2019) and algorithms concerning neural networks and deep learning

U. Riemann (✉)
BT&A EMEA, SAP, Walldorf, Germany
e-mail: ute.riemann@sap.com

T. Ochs
CIO Villeroy & Boch, Mettlach, Germany

© The Author(s), under exclusive license to Springer Nature
Switzerland AG 2025
Y. Hajizadeh et al. (eds.), *Building Cloud Software Products*,
Innovation, Technology, and Knowledge Management,
https://doi.org/10.1007/978-3-031-92184-1_7

111

evolved (Streibich & Zeller, Offene Plattformen als Erfolgsfaktoren für Künstliche Intelligenz. In P. Buxmann & H. Schmidt (Eds.), Künstliche Intelligenz: Mit Algorithmen zum wirtschaftlichen Erfolg (pp. 107–117). Springer, 2019). The initial value of machine learning is that it allows you to continually learn from data and predict the future. With the emergence of digital tools and communications and thus the increase of data volumes, the benefit of ML further enhances—this is of relevance as well in the production and product development where intelligent production machines and smart products constantly produce relevant data (Buxmann & Schmidt, Künstliche Intelligenz: Mit Algorithmen zum wirtschaftlichen Erfolg. Springer Gabler, 2019a; Cheatham et al., McKinsey on Risk - Transforming Risk Efficiency and Effectiveness, 7, 27–34, 2019; Fink, Quick Guide KI-Projekte – einfach machen: Künstliche Intelligenz in Service, Marketing und Sales erfolgreich einführen, Springer Fachmedien Wiesbaden, 2020, S. VI, Mainzer, Künstliche Intelligenz—Wann übernehmen die Maschinen? Springer, 2016; Leukert et al., Das intelligente Unternehmen: Maschinelles Lernen mit SAP zielgerichtet einsetzen. In P. Buxmann & H. Schmidt (Eds.), Künstliche Intelligenz: Mit Algorithmen zum wirtschaftlichen Erfolg (pp. 41–62). Springer, 2019). From the business perspective it is not just the matter of generating huge quantities of data, but also of converting this data into new knowledge and gaining new insights into business processes, which in turn can lead to better decisions (Mainzer, Künstliche Intelligenz—Wann übernehmen die Maschinen? Springer, 2016; Streibich & Zeller, Offene Plattformen als Erfolgsfaktoren für Künstliche Intelligenz. In P. Buxmann & H. Schmidt (Eds.), Künstliche Intelligenz: Mit Algorithmen zum wirtschaftlichen Erfolg (pp. 107–117). Springer, 2019) and led to fundamental changes due to technological innovations (Leukert et al., Das intelligente Unternehmen: Maschinelles Lernen mit SAP zielgerichtet einsetzen. In P. Buxmann & H. Schmidt (Eds.), Künstliche Intelligenz: Mit Algorithmen zum wirtschaftlichen Erfolg (pp. 41–62). Springer, 2019; Preuss, In-Memory-Datenbank SAP HANA. Springer Fachmedien Wiesbaden, 2017; Wuest et al., Production and Manufacturing Research, 4(1), 23–45, 2016) leading to less repetitive and more innovative activities, e.g. within product management (Wellers et al., Why machine learning and why now? [White Paper]. SAP SE, 2017). Machine learning is dominating conversations about how emerging advanced analytics can provide businesses with a competitive advantage to the business. The following article now aims to answer the question what value these powerful set of algorithms and models can be delivered to the process of product management and how the value can be measured to justify the usage of ML technology. Coming from the end-to-end process view and the relevant KPIs, the following article outlines a methodology to quantify and measure the effects of ML while gain insights into patterns and anomalies within data and thus improving processes has.

**Keywords** Machine learning · Supply chain · Application of machine learning · Business case · Key performance indicators · End-to-end processes · Value management

## 7.1 Introduction

There is no debate that existing business leaders are facing new and unanticipated challenges and they all come back to a fundamental truth—the key to success is the data. The question now is how to think about ML in the business process environment and what is the value to offer by ML.

ML has become one of the most important topics within product development that are looking for innovative ways to leverage data assets to help the R&D departments gaining a new level of understanding and agility. We believe that with the appropriate ML mix the business gain the ability to continually predict changes in the business so that they are best able to predict what's next. As data is constantly added, the machine learning models ensure that the solution is constantly updated.

The value is straightforward: If you use the most appropriate and constantly changing data sources in the context of machine learning, you could predict the future.

Overall, intelligent systems are defined as systems that can solve any solvable problem described in a logical notation. In addition, they can be autonomous, perceive their environment, adapt to changes and pursue their own goals [1]. In this context, the degree of intelligence depends on the level of autonomy, complexity of the problem and the efficiency of problem solving [2].

Machine learning is a form of AI that enables a system to learn from data rather than through explicit programming. It is a subset of AI [3–6], and the one method of use for practical software development, robot control, natural language processing and speech recognition and other applications [7]. It uses a variety of algorithms that iteratively learn from data to improve, describe data and predict outcomes [8].

## 7.2 Approaches to Machine Learning

In order to clarify this view of the incomparability of human and AI, there is a proposition to split AI into two different approaches: one measures its success by comparing it to human performance, while the other measures the success of AI against an ideal performance dimension—thinking and acting rationally [1, 9].

Machine learning techniques are required to improve the accuracy of predictive models. Depending on the nature of the business problem being addressed, there are different approaches based on the type and volume of the data such as supervised learning, unsupervised learning and reinforcement learning [6, 7, 10–13].

While focusing on the benefit of ML towards business processes, we will focus on supervised learning in this article as it offers not only a wide range of possible applications [14] serving as a perfect link of ML towards business value analysis [15] but also it promises more reliable outputs due to the successive interaction of individual applications within an integrated system [16] and the identification and verification of the right labels [7, 17]. Supervised learning starts with an established set of data and a discrete (classification) or continuous (regression) data, which are important for data analysis of ML [13, 18–20]. The assignment to the classes is done with a classifier, which represents the model and predicts the classes for input [8, 19]. The target is to find patterns in data that can be applied to an analytics process. The most important supervised learning methods are the fisher discriminant analysis, partial least squares, nearest neighbours, principal component regression, artificial neural networks, support vector machine, Gaussian process regression, decision tree, random forest and so on [21].

## 7.3 The Measuring Framework for Machine Learning

When we aim to measure the value of machine learning towards business processes, we have to understand three fundamentals:

- How can I structure the business processes in a standardized way?
- What needs to be done to measure business processes' efficiency and effectiveness?
- How can I establish a manageable framework to value the machine learning effect?

The measurement of the value of machine learning requires a framework that allows the valuation of machine learning on business processes in a systematic way and to anticipate the impact on the processes due to the use of machine learning.

One cornerstone for this framework is the process categorization of Davenport [22] with the three categories of product development and delivery processes, customer-facing processes and management processes.

For measuring the value of a process—even beyond its company boundaries [23] and thus the impact and relevance of machine learning—we have to apply the concept of a company's process landscape and its end-to-end processes to the framework. As end-to-end processes are defined as value-adding process, which is initiated and ends at the customer without any process interruptions, serving as a consistent structure for the KPI-driven analysis [24], the comprehensive set of processes is described in a corporate process landscape and linked together in a company-specific value chain as a network of connected processes [22, 25, 26] where the performance of one process or activity affects the cost or effectiveness of other processes or activities.

Both, the value chain and the end-to-end process points of view, are essential to understand the value of machine learning as it is more than the costs incurred by the execution of the process activities [27, 24] .

The value chain and process landscape serve as a stable layer of the process architecture [28] and can be structured according to various aggregation levels [28–30].

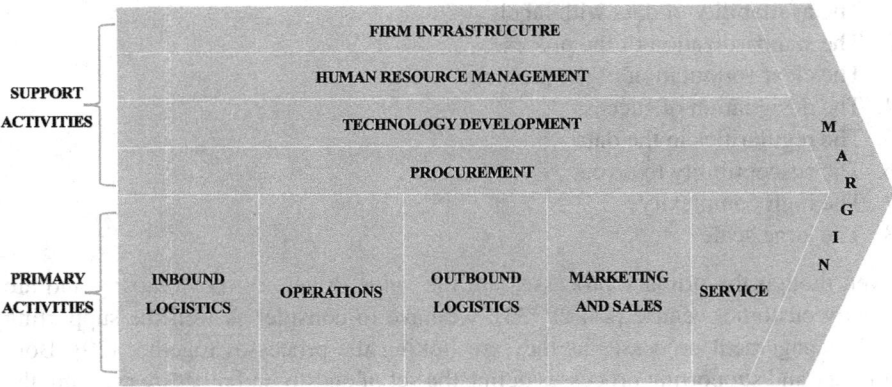

**Fig. 7.1** Value chain (based on Porter)

For the KPI-driven valuation of any process, we need to select the granularity of the business processes [28] where the KPIs become the relevant parameter to identify the value drivers per process and the lever of ML per each process.

While the value chain identifies the importance of a business process [22] and a reference point to consider a competitive advantage (cf. Fig. 7.1) [26], we have to consider additionally the importance and value of any process for a company [26]. Herein, the differentiation of primary and secondary processes [31] needs to be added to our framework to allow the valuation of machine learning for the business [24, 26, 29, 32, 33].

## 7.3.1  Leveraging the Power of Machine Learning

The role of ML in an organization's process will be on making processes faster, simpler, less expensive and more efficient [16, 34, 35]. Nevertheless, there is no universally applicable method of ML; that's why a clear understanding of the conditions for ML of business problems should be expressed [36]. Companies are experiencing a progression in analytics maturity levels ranging from descriptive analytics to predictive analytics to machine learning and cognitive computing even though according to Lee [37] the main requirements of a successful ML are the availability of big data, the computing power and the work of strong AI specialists. To allow a beneficiary and thus measurable usage of ML, we need to make sure that we not only identify the relevant requirements that need to be in place to apply the technology of ML to a business problem, but we need to find a way to quantify the requirements. The following requirements will serve as the basic set that should be given for the support of a business problem and in the local context for business processes [7, 16, 36, 38, 39]:

1. The availability of data with labels
2. The standardization of the process
3. The clear formulation of the problem
4. The designation of success
5. The regularities in the data
6. The susceptibility to errors
7. The high complexity
8. The large scale

Even though the primary processes are the value drivers of the company and are strictly customer-centric [24, 29, 33], we have to consider as well the supporting and management processes as they are linking the processes together [29]. Both primary and supporting processes define the set of end-to-end processes serving the companies' value chain [24, 40]. In the following we will stick to the structure defined by Porter with having the infrastructure processes [27], the human resource processes [24, 31, 41–44], the technology development [40, 42, 45] and procurement [24, 31, 40, 42, 46–48] as the supporting end-to-end processes and logistics [40, 49, 50], operations [24, 27, 32, 51, 52], marketing and sales and services [40, 42, 53] as the end-to-end processes covering mainly the primary activities (Table 7.1).

**Table 7.1** Overview of the end-to-end processes covering the supply chain

| Process (L2) | Area | L3 processes | Process goal |
|---|---|---|---|
| Idea-to-market | R&D | Idea generation Technology development Portfolio decision Commercialization | Fulfil market and customer wishes and give information to the development and sales departments |
| Purchase-to-pay | Procurement and accounts payable | Purchase strategy Supplier agreement Order management Financial settlement | Handle the purchase requirements, the order processing including the payment to suppliers |
| Make-to-stock/order | Production | Manufacturing strategy Production planning Execution Warehousing | Have the right manufacturing strategy for the right products and to produce the exact amount required |
| Order-to-delivery | Distribution | Order management Delivery planning Shipping Billing and Payment | Deliver the exact number of products at the right time and place |
| Demand-to-close | Marketing and sales | Sales/Marketing Planning/Strategy Customer value Value delivery CRM | Correct planning of demand considering production adjustments and the good customer care |

## 7.4   Machine Learning and the Underlying Technologies

### 7.4.1   Definition of Machine Learning as Subset of Artificial Intelligence

The focus of AI was the general approach that was more a kind of creation of a software program, which solves a variety of complex problems and functionally thinks for itself and controls itself with its own thoughts, feelings or strengths, but it wasn't very successful [4, 54].

The ML algorithms, which are interesting here, are part of the narrow AI, because they are created to solve one specific task and nothing beyond that [4]. When we explore machine learning, we focus on the ability to learn and adapt a model based on the data rather than explicit programming [6]. Methods such as neural networks were also already well known ([55]; 20; [56]). AI is a problem-solving tool with a goal-oriented perspective [1, 9]. With the evolution of big data processing capabilities and algorithms such as neuronal networks and deep learning, we see the increase of qualitative outcomes [7, 57, 58].

As a subset of AI [3–6], ML is nowadays the one method of use for practical software development, robot control, natural language processing and speech recognition and other applications [7]. The main aim of ML is to get to know how computers can learn from historical data, and its general procedure covers the phases of the splitting of the data into training and testing subsets and the training of the model on the training set [8, 12, 13, 18, 21, 38, 58–60]. In this context the most important research area is for computer programs to individually learn how to identify complex patterns and based on these make predictions and intelligent decisions [8].

ML is generally differentiated in three different approaches that will be defined in the following [6, 7, 10–13].

There are different approaches to machine learning that are required to improve the accuracy of predictive models—two of them measure the success of AI against an ideal performance dimension—thinking and acting rationally [1], autonomous, perceiving their environment, adapting to changes and pursuing their own goals [1].

The task of ML algorithms in supervised learning is learning a sequence of desired outputs based on labelled training datasets containing pairs of input objects and desired output values in order to produce the correct outputs on a new input with a derived function. For the reinforcement learning the ML algorithms interact with its dynamic environment by generating actions itself in certain situations. These actions affect the condition of the environment, which are receiving feedback, specifically rewards or punishments depending on the consequences. The aim of the algorithms is to learn to act in the way that maximizes the received rewards. Finally, in unsupervised learning the algorithm simply receives inputs, in the form of unlabelled training data without any desired outputs. Meanwhile extracting pattern or hidden structures from the database is also important, but it is still difficult to imagine what the machine could learn without any feedback.

The advantages of using ML are diverse, compared to classical programming and automation. On the one hand, it is possible to make derivations from recurring patterns and experience new incoming data to react flexibly to changes without having to regularly adapt the algorithm and keep it up to date. The actual process from observation to explicit programming to verification is replaced here by training processes of the algorithm [16]. The usage of ML in a company can not only promote human qualities but also improve and push people to their limits. Thus, the successive interaction of individual applications within an integrated system is the basis of the self-learning enterprise today [16]. In this context the focus is particularly on supervised learning, because many developers of AI systems now recognize that, for many applications, it can be far easier and give a better output to train a system by showing it examples of desired input-output behaviour with historical data than to program it manually by anticipating the responses wanted for all inputs [7]. This method is also the one method which is currently being used by companies, especially as there is a wide range of possible applications [14]. It has also far more success than unsupervised learning, in particular because the output is more reliable due to the verification with labels, but maybe in the longer term it will be the other way around [17]. However, for purposes like association, segmentation and dimensionality reduction, unsupervised learning could be the better choice [61]. A big company survey about the implementation of AI and ML has also revealed that most of the companies using ML are searching for the right labels for their datasets that points out that especially supervised learning is important for the company context [62]. Since the concept of applying ML to end-to-end processes presented in this thesis has a strong company linkage, the supervised learning method is analysed in more detail here and the other types will be set aside. Meanwhile it is the simplest and most understandable subcategory of ML and serves therefore as a perfect introduction of ML [15].

## 7.4.2   In-Depth Consideration of Supervised Learning

Supervised learning is one of the three types of ML. Since deep learning is the science of creating and applying deep neural networks as a multi-layered neural network, it is a subset of neural networks [11, 63].

The term data mining often used in the same context as ML is defined as the process of discovering patterns in data and is used after the data model that has been trained and validated and is ready to be used for data mining, such as data clustering, data classification, data visualization, prediction analysis and trend analysis [21, 60]. In this context supervised learning can be applied [8, 64]. Supervised learning typically starts with an established set of data and a certain understanding of how that data is classified. The main function of supervised ML is to learn from a given number of examples and to result in a model of the relationships between pairs of examples to find patterns in data that can be applied to an analytics process. This data has labelled features that define the meaning of data [65]. Regression used for supervised learning helps you understand the correlation between variables. The most commonly considered labelled input or output data in supervised learning appear either in the form of discrete (classification) or continuous (regression) data, which are important for data analysis of ML [8, 13, 18–20]. The assignment to the classes is done with a classifier, which represents the model and predicts the classes for input [8, 19]. The main supervised learning methods are the following, either for classification purposes or regression or for both: the fisher discriminant analysis, partial least squares, nearest neighbours, principal component regression, artificial neural networks, support vector machine, Gaussian process regression, decision tree, random forest and so on [21].

### 7.4.3   Neural Networks and Deep Learning

Neural network models can adjust and learn as data changes. Neural networks are often used when data is unlabelled or unstructured. One of the key use cases for neural networks is computer vision. Deep learning is being leveraged today in a variety of applications. It is a specific method of machine learning that incorporates neural networks in successive layers in order to learn from data in an iterative manner [21, 66]. Deep learning is especially useful when you're trying to learn patterns from unstructured data. Neural networks and deep learning are often used in image recognition, speech and computer vision applications. A neural network consists of three or more layers: an input layer, one or many hidden layers and an output layer [17]. Deep learning is a ML technique that uses hierarchical neural networks to learn from a combination of unsupervised and supervised algorithms [11, 21] where data are ingested through the input layer [66], modified in the hidden layer and where the output layers based on the weights applied these nodes. Using an iterative approach, a neural network continuously adjusts and makes inferences until a specific stopping point is reached [67]. Neural networks are often used for image recognition and computer vision applications.

## 7.5   Leveraging the Power of Machine Learning Towards End-to-End Processes

The business needs to understand and trust data. It is not enough to simply ingest vast amounts of data. Providing accurate machine learning models requires that the source data be accurate and meaningful. In addition, these data sources are meaningful when combined with each other so that the model is accurate and trusted. You must understand the origin of your data sources and whether they make sense when they're combined. In addition to trusting your data, it is also important to perform data cleansing or tidying. Cleaning data means that you transform your data into a form that can be understood by a machine learning algorithm. For example, algorithms use numbers, but data is often in the form of words. You have to turn those words into numbers. In addition, you must make sure those numbers are sensibly derived and internally consistent. You need to decide how you handle missing data and other data irregularities. Data refinement provides the foundation for building analytical models that deliver results you can trust. The process of data refinement will help to ensure that your data is timely, clean and well understood.

Assuming that the focus of ML is to make processes faster, simpler, less expensive and more efficient [16, 34, 35], we need to make sure that there is a consistency between the business and ML problem. As business processes are diverse and individual, there is no universal methodology to apply ML in a beneficiary way to business processes; therefore, a clear and in-depth understanding and qualifying of the business processes is required [36].

When considering the definitional basis of AI and ML, it should not be lost sight of the fact that certain prerequisites have to be considered for the application of ML in a company:

1. Are big datasets including labels available? [7, 10, 13, 36–38]
2. Can the problem be standardized within the process? [8, 16, 36, 38]
3. Can the prediction be clearly formulated? [38, 60]
4. Is there a regular pattern available? [16, 36, 38, 60]
5. Does the issue require ML considering context, effort and benefit in regard to:

   (a) Being error-prone
   (b) Has a high degree of complexity
   (c) Deals with unstructured data

Following these sequences of conditions, the first step to weight the importance of ML for business processes is the conversion into a weighting systematic. The identified eight conditions lead in the simplest way to a weighting of 12.5% per each condition. However, this does not reflect the reality at all since the importance of the prerequisites varies. Assuming that one of several solutions of the inequality system is that (a) is weighted with 20% and (b) and (c) with 17.5% (Table 7.2 formula 2.0). After that there is a weighting left of 45% (cf. Table 7.2 formula 3.0). This must be divided between five conditions and two of these conditions are more important than the other three. Therefore, the two should be weighted higher and the others lower as if they are all weighted the same (Table 7.2 formula 3.1). Furthermore, the two conditions on rank 4 and 5 are seen equally, which are the definable success and the regular pattern (here as d, e). These should be weighted higher than 9% and lower than 17.5%, because of the weighting of (b) and (c). The weighting in the middle is 13.25%, but to simplify it and to have less numbers after the decimal point for the last three weightings, the weightings are chosen with 13.5% for (d) and (e). The three less important and equally weighted conditions on rank 6, 7 and 8 are error-prone (f), complexity (g) and unstructured data (h). The remaining weighting of 18% is divided between those three and the weighting is 6% for each (Table 7.2 formula 4.0 and 4.1).

**Table 7.2** Calculation of weighting system for the conditions

| Formula | Calculation | Description |
|---|---|---|
| 1.0 | $1.00 \div 8 = 0.125 \cong 12.5\%$ | Calculation if each condition had the same weighting, where 1.00 is 100% and all the 8 conditions |
| 2.0 | $0.125 < b = c < a$ <br> $a + b + c > 0.5 \wedge < 1.00$ <br> $a = 0.20 \wedge b, c = 0.175$ | Calculation of the weighting of the three most important conditions ($a$, $b$ and $c$) |
| 3.0 | $1.00$ <br> $- (0.2 \pm 2 \times 0.175) = 0.45 \cong 45\%$ | Calculation of what is left of the weighting for the other conditions |
| 3.1 | $0.45 \div 5 = 0.09 \cong 9\%$ | Calculation if the remaining five conditions were weighted equally |
| 3.2 | $0.09 < d = e < 0.175$ <br> $(0.09 + 0.175) \div$ <br> $2 = 0.1325 \cong 13.25\%$ | Calculation of two more important conditions of the five remaining ones ($d$ and $e$) |
| 4.0 | $0.45 - (2 \times 13.5) = 0.18 \cong 18\%$ | Calculation of what is left for the three last conditions |
| 4.1 | $f = g = h$ <br> $0.18 \div 3 = 0.06 \cong 6\%$ | Calculation of weightings for the three last ones ($f$, $g$ and $h$) |

These prerequisites are the fundamental layer to classify the importance of a business problem in the light of ML meaning that the conditions which are more important than others have a higher weighting than 12.5%.

It is assumed that the different conditions, as described above, are relevant in different ways for the use of ML in the selected processes. Since it is particularly clear in the literature that some conditions are indispensable and should therefore be accompanied by a higher weighting, data availability is such an example. Without data there can't be a ML algorithm; therefore, it is weighted the highest. The justifications of the rank of each condition are also behind the definition of the conditions above. These weightings are then used to make a statement about how well a process is automatable with ML, by calculating a mean value of each process and subprocess (Table 7.3).

Having laid down the fundamentals we can start to apply this logic to the previously defined end-to-end processes to gain an in-depth understanding on the potential and benefit ML may apply to one process. In order to be able to make a better statement about the possible applications of ML in the subprocesses and a comparison between them, the median and mean value of each subprocess shall be made visible with a rating system based on a Likert scale [68, 69]. In order, to give an idea of the exact calculation of the mean value with the weighting system and the better understanding of the reason for the weighting system, an exemplary calculation with the subprocess staffing from Procure-to-Pay (PTP) is provided in Table 7.4.

In Table 7.5 those L3 processes are mentioned with the highest relevance of ML and the clearest application towards a business case with defined KPIs is in place indicating a future business case.

**Table 7.3** Machine learning prerequisites

| ML prerequisites | Importance of ML | Order | Weighting |
|---|---|---|---|
| Big dataset including labels | Most important condition; algorithm could not work without it | 1 | 0.2 |
| Standardized process | Very important for the ML algorithm; otherwise there could not be a clear prediction | 2 | 0.175 |
| Clear prediction formulation | Very important for the ML algorithm; otherwise the goal for the algorithm is unclear and the prediction is difficult | 3 | 0.175 |
| Definable success rate | Important; the supervised algorithm has to know when it predicted something right and the process should show success | 4 | 0.135 |
| Regular patterns visible | Important for the ML algorithm; otherwise no accurate prediction can be made | 5 | 0.135 |
| Error-prone | Moderate; the ML algorithm could also work without this condition | 6 | 0.06 |
| High degree of complexity | Moderate; the ML algorithm could also work without this condition | 7 | 0.06 |
| Unstructured data | Moderate; the ML algorithm could also work without this condition | 8 | 0.06 |

## 7.6 Conclusions

From the benefits it can be deduced that there are significant opportunities associated with the implementation of ML in a company. In particular the direct benefits, the corresponding savings and increases in sales outline promising sources of benefits; in addition, ML promises a lot of indirect benefits.

However, even though this article has not focused on costs and risks, they should be considered while implementing ML [77]. First and foremost, there are risks like the diminishing security and data protection [77, 78], e.g. hidden vulnerabilities that could be exploited, or the ever-increasing amount of data quickly leads to errors such as the inadvertent disclosure of sensitive information that has been anonymized for AI use [77]. Finally, another issue and risk with ML can arise when the models deliver biased results, for example, bias against a group of people; this can happen, for example, if a population is underrepresented in the training data [77, 79].

Nevertheless, since the benefits are undebatable, our recommendation is to start a clear definition of each companies' end-to-end processes and its evaluation in the light of ML. Based on the clear set of supportable processes with ML proven an individual business case, a clear statement about the costs and savings can be set up in advance to allow a proof of the investment. This article is a guideline for the individual cost, savings and risk assessment of a company and makes it clearer which cost and risk factors should be considered.

**Table 7.4** Calculation example of weighted mean value

| ML condition | | | | | | | | | | |
|---|---|---|---|---|---|---|---|---|---|---|
| Subprocess | | | | | | | | | | |
| L2 | L3 | 1 | 2 | 3 | 4 | 5 | 6 | 7 | 8 | Median |
| Weightings | | 0.2 | 0.18 | 0.18 | 0.14 | 0.14 | 0.06 | 0.06 | 0.06 | Σ 1.00 |
| PTP | Order management | ++ | +++ | +++ | +++ | +++ | +++ | +++ | +++ | +++ |
| | | 2 | 3 | 3 | 3 | 3 | 3 | 3 | 3 | 2.8 |
| Calculation example | $0.2 \times (1) + 0.175 \times (2) + 0.175 \times (3) + 0.135 \times (4) + 0.135 \times (5) + 0.06 \times (6) + 0.06 \times (7) + 0.06 \times (8) = x$ | | | | | | | | | |
| Exact calculation for staffing | $0.2 \times 2 + 0.175 \times 3 + 0.175 \times 3 + 0.135 \times 3 + 0.135 \times 3 + 0.06 \times 3 + 0.06 \times 3 + 0.06 \times 3 = 2.8$ | | | | | | | | | |

**Table 7.5** References for ML application potentials

| Process steps | | Mean | |
|---|---|---|---|
| L0 | L1 | value | Explanation |
| ITM (Innovation and Technology Management) | Idea generation | + | • Ideas with the strongest potential are part of an unpredictable process [70] |
| | Technology development | ++ | • Support the development of products and services [71] |
| | Portfolio decision | ++ | • Smarter R&D to access the prototype success and increase the performance in R&D [71] |
| | Commercialization | +++ | • Reduction of time to market with a better demand forecast and a commercialization close to marketing [71] |
| PTP (Procure-to-Pay) | Purchase strategy | + | • Predict inbound logistics and support and operational strategical planning with ML [72] |
| | Supplier agreement | ++ | • Automation with bots to make final selection based on weighted strategies [73] |
| | Order management | +++ | • Simplify operational procurement with bots [40, 73, 16] |
| | Financial settlement | ++ | • Bots can also automate pricing with external partners [73] |
| MTS/MTO (Make-To-Stock/Make-To-Order) | Manufacturing strategy | + | • Limited support of ML possibly due to a disruptive process [74] |
| | Production planning | +++ | • Support forecasting with a reliable data; prediction and an increase of production efficiency [71, 75] |
| | Production execution | +++ | • Replace humans with AI with robots to take over [71, 14, 76] |
| | Logistics | +++ | • Use of ML to forecast demand [71, 14, 76] |
| OTD (On-Time-Delivery) | Order management | +++ | • Support demand forecast ideas for full automation of order processing [71] |
| | Delivery planning | +++ | • Automated good planning with autonomous parcel packing, label applying and transportation [14] |
| | Shipping | ++ | • Intelligent language assistants with speech recognition and learning [73] |
| | Goods reception | ++ | • Measuring lead time automatically in ERP [49] |
| DTC (Direct-To-Customer) | Sales/marketing planning | +++ | • Reliable forecast to better predict sales trends and patterns including stock reduction [71] |
| | Customer value model | +++ | • Use of ML to derive behavioural patterns [16] |
| | Value delivery | ++ | • Digital offerings with online sales; dynamic pricing, personalization [71, 14, 16] |
| | CRM | +++ | • Focus of customer care with digital assistants/chat offers intelligent chatbots based on ML can help [34, 16] |

# References

1. Russell, S. J., Norvig, P., Davis, E., & Edwards, D. (2016). *Artificial intelligence: A modern approach* (3rd ed.). Pearson.
2. Mainzer, K. (2016). *Künstliche Intelligenz—Wann übernehmen die Maschinen?* Springer.
3. Gürtler, O. (2019). Künstliche Intelligenz als Weg zur wahren digitalen Transformation. In P. Buxmann & H. Schmidt (Eds.), *Künstliche Intelligenz: Mit Algorithmen zum wirtschaftlichen Erfolg* (pp. 95–105). Springer.
4. Horowitz, M. C. (2018). Artificial intelligence, international competition, and the balance of power. *Texas National Security Review, 1*(3). https://doi.org/10.15781/T2639KP49
5. Matzer, M. (2016, 31 December). *Big data und deep learning: So spürt Deep Learning Datenmuster auf.* Embedded Software Engineering. Retrieved the 2 February 2020, from https://www.embedded-software-engineering.de/so-spuert-deep-learning-datenmuster-auf-a-584093/
6. Wellers, D., Woods, J., Jendroska, D., & Koch, C. (2017). *Why machine learning and why now?.* [White Paper]. SAP SE.
7. Jordan, M. I., & Mitchell, T. M. (2015). Machine learning: Trends, perspectives, and prospects. *Science, 349*(6245), 255–260. https://doi.org/10.1126/science.aaa8415
8. Han, J., Pei, J., & Kamber, M. (2011). *Data mining: Concepts and techniques* (3rd ed.). Elsevier Science & Technology Books.
9. Ertel, W. (2017). *Introduction to artificial intelligence.* Springer International Publishing.
10. Ghahramani, Z. (2004). Unsupervised learning. In O. Bousquet, U. von Luxburg, & G. Rätsch (Eds.), *Advanced lectures on machine learning* (pp. 72–112). Springer.
11. Kirste, M., & Schürholz, M. (2019). Einleitung: Entwicklungswege zur KI. In V. Wittpahl (Ed.), *Künstliche Intelligenz* (pp. 21–35). Springer.
12. Wuest, T., Weimer, D., Irgens, C., & Thoben, K.-D. (2016). Machine learning in manufacturing: Advantages, challenges, and applications. *Production and Manufacturing Research, 4*(1), 23–45. https://doi.org/10.1080/21693277.2016.1192517
13. Xu, S., Lu, B., Baldea, M., Edgar, T. F., Wojsznis, W., Blevins, T., & Nixon, M. (2015). Data cleaning in the process industries. *Reviews in Chemical Engineering, 31*(5). https://doi.org/10.1515/revce-2015-0022
14. Buxmann, P., & Schmidt, H. (2019b). Grundlagen der Künstlichen Intelligenz und des Maschinellen Lernens. In P. Buxmann & H. Schmidt (Eds.), *Künstliche Intelligenz: Mit Algorithmen zum wirtschaftlichen Erfolg* (pp. 3–19). Springer.
15. Wilson, A. (2019, September 29). *A brief introduction to supervised learning.* Towards Data Science. Retrieved the June 29 2020, from https://towardsdatascience.com/a-brief-introduction-to-supervised-learning-54a3e3932590
16. Leukert, B., Müller, J., & Noga, M. (2019). Das intelligente Unternehmen: Maschinelles Lernen mit SAP zielgerichtet einsetzen. In P. Buxmann & H. Schmidt (Eds.), *Künstliche Intelligenz: Mit Algorithmen zum wirtschaftlichen Erfolg* (pp. 41–62). Springer.
17. LeCun, Y., Bengio, Y., & Hinton, G. (2015). Deep learning. *Nature, 521*(7553), 436–444. https://doi.org/10.1038/nature14539
18. Alpaydin, E. (2019). *Maschinelles Lernen* (2nd ed.). De Gruyter.
19. Kantardzic, M. (2003). *Data mining: Concepts, models, methods, and algorithms.* Wiley-Interscience: IEEE Press.
20. Rasmussen, C. E. (2004). Gaussian processes in machine learning. In O. Bousquet, U. von Luxburg, & G. Rätsch (Eds.), *Advanced lectures on machine learning* (pp. 63–71). Springer.
21. Ge, Z., Song, Z., Ding, S. X., & Huang, B. (2017). Data mining and analytics in the process industry: The role of machine learning. *IEEE Access, 5*, 20590–20616. https://doi.org/10.1109/ACCESS.2017.2756872
22. Davenport, T. H. (1993). *Process innovation: Reengineering work through information technology.* Harvard Business School Press.
23. Hammer, M. (2010). What is business process management? In J. vom Brocke & M. Rosemann (Eds.), *Handbook on business process management 1* (pp. 3–16). Springer.

24. Wagner, C., Sodies, J. G., Meyer, T., & Adam, P. (2019). Die Bedeutung von End-to-End-Prozessen für die Digitalisierung im Finanzbereich. In W. Becker, B. Eierle, A. Fliaster, B. Ivens, A. Leischnig, A. Pflaum, & E. Sucky (Eds.), *Geschäftsmodelle in der digitalen Welt* (pp. 695–711). Springer Fachmedien Wiesbaden.
25. Bergsmann, S. (2012). *End-to-End Geschäftsprozessmanagement: Organisationselement, Integrationsinstrument, Managementansatz.* Springer.
26. Gadatsch, A. (2012). *Grundkurs Geschäftsprozess-Management: Methoden und Werkzeuge für die IT-Praxis; eine Einführung für Studenten und Praktiker* (7th ed.). Springer Vieweg.
27. Porter, M. E. (2014). *Wettbewerbsvorteile: Spitzenleistungen erreichen und behaupten* (8th ed.). Campus Verlag.
28. Van Nuffel, D., & De Backer, M. (2012). Multi-abstraction layered business process modeling. *Computers in Industry, 63*(2), 131–147. https://doi.org/10.1016/j.compind.2011.12.001
29. Harmon, P. (2007). *Business process change: A guide for business managers and BPM and six sigma professionals* (2nd ed.). Elsevier/Morgan Kaufmann Publishers.
30. Ray, J. (2014, October 28). *Business architecture and hierarchical process modeling.* Avio Consulting. Retrieved the 3 October 2020, from https://www.avioconsulting.com/blog/business-architecture-and-hierarchical-process-modeling
31. Porter, M. E. (1998). *The competitive advantage of nations: With a new introduction.* The Free Press.
32. Scheer, A.-W. (1998). *ARIS — Modellierungsmethoden, Metamodelle, Anwendungen.* Springer.
33. Skjott-Larsen, T., & Schary, P. B. (2007). *Managing the global supply chain* (3rd ed.). Copenhagen Business School Press.
34. Hildesheim, W., & Michelsen, D. (2019). Künstliche Intelligenz im Jahr 2018 – Aktueller Stand von branchenübergreifenden KI-Lösungen: Was ist möglich? Was nicht? Beispiele und Empfehlungen. In P. Buxmann & H. Schmidt (Eds.), *Künstliche Intelligenz: Mit Algorithmen zum wirtschaftlichen Erfolg* (pp. 119–142). Springer.
35. Preuss, P. (2017). *In-Memory-Datenbank SAP HANA.* Springer Fachmedien Wiesbaden.
36. Pham, D. T., & Afify, A. A. (2005). Machine-learning techniques and their applications in manufacturing. *Proceedings of the Institution of Mechanical Engineers, Part B: Journal of Engineering Manufacture, 219*(5), 395–412. https://doi.org/10.1243/095440505X32274
37. Lee, K.-F. (2018). *AI superpowers: China, Silicon Valley, and the new world order.* Houghton Mifflin Harcourt.
38. Dahlmeier, D., & Noga, M. (2016). *Enterprise machine learning in a Nutshell* [Presentation]. SAP SE.
39. Weiss, S. M., & Indurkhya, N. (1991). Reduced complexity rule induction. *Proceedings of International Joint Conferences on Artificial Intelligence*, IJCAI, Sydney, 678–684.
40. Gaydoul, R., & Daxböck, C. (2011). Prozessmanagement von End-to-End Prozessen. *Controlling and Management, 55*(S2), 40–46. https://doi.org/10.1365/s12176-012-0332-7
41. Devanna, M. A., Fombrun, C. J., & Tichy, N. M. (1984). A framework for strategic human resource management. In C. J. Fombrun, N. M. Tichy, & M. A. Devanna (Eds.), *Strategic human resource management* (pp. 33–51). Wiley.
42. Porter, M. E. (2008). *Competitive advantage: Creating and sustaining superior performance.* Simon and Schuster.
43. SAP SE. (2016). *Generic Process Map [Presentation].* SAP SE.
44. Strohmeier, S. (2015). Analysen der human resource intelligence und analytics. In S. Strohmeier & F. Piazza (Eds.), *Human resource intelligence und analytics* (pp. 3–47). Springer Fachmedien Wiesbaden.
45. Bandarian, R. (2007). From idea to market in RIPI: An agile frame for NTD Process. *Journal of Technology Management and Innovation, 2*(1), 25–41.
46. Lambert, D. M., & Schwieterman, M. A. (2012). Supplier relationship management as a macro business process. *Supply Chain Management: An International Journal, 17*(3), 337–352. https://doi.org/10.1108/13598541211227153

47. Marjanovic, O., & Seethamraju, R. (2008). Understanding knowledge-intensive, practice-oriented business processes. In *Proceedings of the 41st Annual Hawaii International Conference on System Sciences (HICSS 2008)* (pp. 373–373). https://doi.org/10.1109/HICSS.2008.477
48. Scheer Nederlands. (2017, December 20). *Procure to pay for service items.* Scheer Nederland. Retrieved the 29 May 2020, from https://scheer-nederland.com/bp-bydesign/industry-scenarios-for-sap-business-bydesign/procure-to-pay-for-service-items/
49. Forslund, H., Jonsson, P., & Mattsson, S. (2008). Order-to-delivery process performance in delivery scheduling environments. *International Journal of Productivity and Performance Management, 58*(1), 41–53. https://doi.org/10.1108/17410400910921074
50. Overby, C. S., Tohamy, N., Johnson, C. A., & Meyer, S. (2005). *How RFID improves the order-to-cash process.* Forrester Research Best Practice, May 2005.
51. Gudehus, T., & Kotzab, H. (2012). *Comprehensive logistics.* Springer.
52. Kaminsky, P., & Kaya, O. (2009). Combined make-to-order/make-to-stock supply chains. *IIE Transactions, 41*(2), 103–119. https://doi.org/10.1080/07408170801975065
53. Rainbird, M. (2004). Demand and supply chains: The value catalyst. *International Journal of Physical Distribution and Logistics Management, 34*(3/4), 230–250.
54. Pennachin, C., & Goertzel, B. (2007). Contemporary approaches to artificial general intelligence. In B. Goertzel & C. Pennachin (Eds.), *Artificial general intelligence* (pp. 1–30). Springer. https://doi.org/10.1007/978-3-540-68677-4_1
55. Minsky, M. (1961). Steps toward Artificial Intelligence. *Proceedings of the IRE, 49*(1), 8–30. https://doi.org/10.1109/JRPROC.1961.287775
56. Samuel, A. L. (1959). Some studies in machine learning using the game of checkers. *IBM Journal of Research and Development, 3*(3), 210–229. https://doi.org/10.1147/rd.33.0210
57. Streibich, K.-H., & Zeller, M. (2019). Offene Plattformen als Erfolgsfaktoren für Künstliche Intelligenz. In P. Buxmann & H. Schmidt (Eds.), *Künstliche Intelligenz: Mit Algorithmen zum wirtschaftlichen Erfolg* (pp. 107–117). Springer.
58. Wess, S. (2019). Mit Künstlicher Intelligenz immer die richtigen Entscheidungen treffen. In P. Buxmann & H. Schmidt (Eds.), *Künstliche Intelligenz: Mit Algorithmen zum wirtschaftlichen Erfolg* (pp. 143–159). Springer.
59. Singh, M. (2020, January 31). *Metrics to calculate performance of machine learning model.* Acadgild. Retrieved the 23 June 2020, from https://acadgild.com/blog/metrics-to-calculate-performance-of-machine-learning-model
60. Witten, I. H., & Frank, E. (2005). *Data mining: Practical machine learning tools and techniques* (2nd ed.). Morgan Kaufman.
61. Shaw, R. (2019, June 13). *The 10 best machine learning algorithms for data science beginners.* Dataquest Retrieved the 24 July 2020, from https://www.dataquest.io/blog/top-10-machine-learning-algorithms-for-beginners/
62. Dimensional Research. (2019). *Artificial intelligence and machine learning projects are obstructed by data issues,* Alegion Survey Results.
63. Bileschi, S., Cai, S., Nielsen, E., & Safarian, O. M. C. (2020). *Deep learning with JavaScript.* Manning Publications.
64. Aggarwal, C. C., & Zhai, C. (2012a). An introduction to text mining. In C. C. Aggarwal & C. Zhai (Eds.), *Mining text data* (pp. 1–10). Springer US. https://doi.org/10.1007/978-1-4614-3223-4_1
65. Tipping, M. E. (2004). Bayesian inference: An introduction to principles and practice in machine learning. In O. Bousquet, U. von Luxburg, & G. Rätsch (Eds.), *Advanced lectures on machine learning* (pp. 41–62). Springer.
66. Lapedes, A. S., & Farber, R. M. (1988). How neural nets work. *Neural Information Processing Systems,* 442–456.
67. Goodfellow, I., Bengio, Y., & Courville, A. (2016). *Deep learning.* The MIT Press.
68. Borg, I., & Gabler, S. (2002). Zustimmungsanteile und Mittelwerte von Likert-skalierten Items. *ZUMA Nachrichten, 26*(50), 7–25.

69. Grünwald, R. (2018, November 7). *Likert Skala: Auswertungsmöglichkeiten und Einflusskomponenten*. Novustat. Retrieved the 29 May 2020, from https://novustat.com/statistik-blog/likert-skala-auswertungsmoeglichkeiten.html
70. Lager, T. (2010). *Managing process innovation: From idea generation to implementation* (Vol. 17). Imperial College Press.
71. Bughin, J., Hazan, E., Ramaswamy, S., Chui, M., Allas, T., Dahlström, P., Henke, N., & Trench, M. (2017). *Artificial intelligence the next digital frontier*. McKinsey & Company Discussion Paper, June 2017.
72. Knoll, D., Prüglmeier, M., & Reinhart, G. (2016). Predicting future inbound logistics processes using machine learning. *Procedia CIRP, 52*, 145–150. https://doi.org/10.1016/j.procir.2016.07.078
73. Hilbert, M., Neukart, F., Ringlstetter, C., Seidel, C., & Sichler, B. (2019). KI-Innovation über das autonome Fahren hinaus. In P. Buxmann & H. Schmidt (Eds.), *Künstliche Intelligenz: Mit Algorithmen zum wirtschaftlichen Erfolg* (pp. 173–185). Springer.
74. Chang, K.-H., & Lu, Y.-S. (2010). Queueing analysis on a single-station make-to-stock/make-to-order inventory-production system. *Applied Mathematical Modelling, 34*(4), 978–991. https://doi.org/10.1016/j.apm.2009.07.009
75. Kanawaday, A., & Sane, A. (2017). Machine learning for predictive maintenance of industrial machines using IoT sensor data. In *2017 8th IEEE International Conference on Software Engineering and Service Science (ICSESS)* (pp. 87–90). https://doi.org/10.1109/ICSESS.2017.8342870
76. Manyika, J., Chui, M., Miremadi, M., Bughin, J., George, K., Willmott, P., & Dewhurst, M. (2017). *A future that works: Automation, employment and productivity*, McKinsey & Company Research Paper, January 2017.
77. Cheatham, B., Javanmardian, K., & Samandari, H. (2019). Confronting the risks of artificial intelligence. *McKinsey on Risk - Transforming Risk Efficiency and Effectiveness, 7*, 27–34.
78. Gentsch, P. (2018). *Künstliche Intelligenz für Sales, Marketing und Service: Mit AI und Bots zu einem Algorithmic Business: Konzepte, Technologien und Best Practices*. Springer Gabler.
79. Babel, B., Buehler, K., Pivonka, A., Richardson, B., & Waldron, D. (2019). Derisking machine learning and artificial intelligence. *McKinsey on Risk - Transforming Risk Efficiency and Effectiveness, 7*, 35–48.

**Ute Riemann** gained a master's degree in computer science and an MBA. Ute is head of business transformation in the MEE region for Chemicals and Life Sciences at SAP. Ute is certified as global business transformation manager and lecturer at the Mannheim University of Applied Sciences.

**Thomas Ochs** gained a master's degree and is certified as a global business transformation manager. After starting his business career as an SAP in-house application consultant at international companies such as Robert Bosch and Mannesmann, he is the CIO of the Villeroy & Boch Group since 1999. Thomas is also an Assistant Professor of Computer Science teaching at the Saarland University of Applied Science (Germany).

# Chapter 8
# Systematic Quality Assurance for Blockchain-Based Services

Alexander Poth ⓘ and Andreas Riel

**Abstract** Increasingly many organizations want to profit from the opportunities the blockchain enables to offer services requiring security, trust, traceability, and value transfer in distributed environments. Integrating blockchain-driven development and operation in a company's existing quality assurance framework is a challenge in this endeavor. This article presents a quality as-surance guidance framework for the development and use of Blockchain-based IT-services. This framework can be used in both a top-down (coming from the business process) as well as a bottom-up (coming from the technical building blocks) manner during the service planning and design. In the early phases, a checklist supports analytic quality assurance methods with an evaluation against state-of-the-art blockchain technology. Later on, it helps to identify blockchain-specific focus aspects for testing. A case study performed within a complex enterprise environment involving different business domains is presented for critically evaluating the proposed contributions.

**Keywords** Blockchain · Industrial services · Quality assurance · Risk management · Internet of Things

A. Poth (✉)
Volkswagen AG, Wolfsburg, Germany
e-mail: alexander.poth@volkswagen.de

A. Riel
G-SCOP Laboratory, Grenoble INP - Université Grenoble Alpes, Grenoble, France
e-mail: andreas.riel@grenoble-inp.fr

© The Author(s), under exclusive license to Springer Nature Switzerland AG 2025
Y. Hajizadeh et al. (eds.), *Building Cloud Software Products*,
Innovation, Technology, and Knowledge Management,
https://doi.org/10.1007/978-3-031-92184-1_8

## 8.1 Introduction

Industrial services are increasingly based on blockchain, a decentralized, distributed ledger technology (DLT) that records the provenance of a digital asset as an immutable chain of digital records. Compared to the established centralized, relational database infrastructures, blockchain promises unequaled trust, security, and traceability across the entire industrial value chain. Other than the banking and insurance sector, deployment in manufacturing industry is only very recent, however, rapidly growing (e.g., [1–3]). Technology progress scales the opportunities of the blockchain and accelerates the blockchain-based industrial service and business model trend. Their focus is on production-ready outcomes, which is why scalability, reliability, and security can be considered critical key properties of blockchain-based industrial services (BbS). All these properties are essentially linked to architecture decisions and parameter choices that are made at design time and have to be assured by appropriate quality assurance (QA) methods and processes. Blockchain implementations challenge established industrial quality assurance in that they come with very specific application programming interfaces (APIs) used to implement the business demands. Moreover, their deployment is mostly on top of distributed networks that are external to the enterprise, each having their specific characteristics to fit its business scope. Currently, not many generic approaches to safeguard DLTs are published. Most publications deal with a specific use case which is using a DLT and present a specific way to ensure quality and testing.

Based on these key observations, we aim at addressing the following three research questions in our approach:

1. How can we identify and estimate quality risks of a blockchain-based industrial service? (RQ1)
2. How can we define adequate quality assurance activities to mitigate or reduce quality risks? (RQ2)
3. How can we assure customer confidence in a blockchain-based service at release time? (RQ3)

To answer these questions, we propose a systematic methodical approach integrating a mindset to future development in the DLT domain, as well as their QA and test methods to reflect the technology's fast penetration into different industry domains like Industry 4.0 [4], in particular automotive and mobility [5].

### 8.1.1 Choice and Suitability of Blockchain

Farshidi et al. [6] present decision support for blockchain platform selection. Their approach includes knowledge of blockchain and quality experts to derive the proposed model. Quality characteristics of the ISO 25010 are combined with blockchain features to map the platforms, blockchain features, and quality characteristics. Precht et al. [7] propose a set of criteria beyond blockchain-specific aspects. Their approach includes the ISO 25010 characteristics, enriched by open-source software (OSS) model aspects, as well as level-based maturity model. Koens et al. [8] take a database-oriented view to develop their DLT classification. Based on their classification of a scheme, they propose a questionnaire to support the selection decision, and describe the decision process in an activity chart. This process consists of three main questions: Is a blockchain needed? Which blockchain type is appropriate? Which alternative technologies exist?

Scriber et al. [9] propose a framework whose key elements are immutability, visibility and transparency, trust, identity, distribution, workflow, transaction, historical record, ecosystems vs. internal or installed software, and inefficiency. Wessling et al. [10] model participant interactions for identifying trust areas. Wust et al. [11] identify properties of blockchains and propose a decision flow across these properties: public verifiability, transparency, privacy, integrity, redundancy, and trust anchor. Their decision model leads to the following outcomes: no blockchain, private permissioned blockchain, public permissioned blockchain, and permissionless blockchain. Xu et al. [12] propose a taxonomy of blockchain-based systems for architecture design. They present a set of design decision questions and rate them against the fundamental properties: cost efficiency, performance, and flexibility. The derived process is a flow of questions. Smith [13] consolidates a more generic taxonomy based on dependability, security, and trust. Dependability is refined in availability and maintainability, security in confidentiality and authenticity, and trust in accuracy and reliability. Authenticity and reliability are more complex and need more detailed refinement. Kannengießer et al. [14] identify blockchain technology and DLT characteristics based on a refinement of the DLT in concepts, designs, properties, and characteristics. They derive from this a set of questions for the six characteristics: security, performance, usability, development flexibility, level of anonymity, and institutionalization. They use them for identifying the most appropriate DLT. For specific contexts of usage, they identify trade-offs and include them in their decisions.

To summarize, it is notable that existing published works have derive mostly all blockchain-based system properties from the ISO 25010 standard, or map their proposed properties to the latter. A focus on quality characteristics is visible for functionality, performance, and security. The security property is particularly important for DLT. It is often refined by privacy, confidentiality, authenticity, and trust. However, depending on the scope, other characteristics are emphasized to address the specific demand defined by the scope of the work.

## 8.1.2 Blockchain Development Challenges

### 8.1.2.1 Requirements, Design

Porru et al. [15] identify blockchain-oriented software engineering challenges. This includes data redundancy, check of transaction requirements, recording the transaction sequence, cryptography, and optional scripting for smart contracts [16]. Their work defines the smart contract testing (SCT) and blockchain transaction testing (BTT). Lu et al. [17] propose blockchain design patterns, most notably on-chain and off-chain, data encryption, hash integrity, multiple authorities, dynamic binding, embedded permission, key generation, and file comparison. They evaluate the set of patterns in the context of the quality trancing process, data management, and smart contract design. From both works, we can derive the need for technology-specific QA and testing for DLT, as well as blockchain-specific aspects established for a professional BbS safeguarding.

### 8.1.2.2 Quality Assurance and Testing

Koteska et al. [18] identify blockchain quality challenges related to throughput, latency, bandwidth, scalability, cost, data malleability, authentication, privacy, double spending, security, wasted resources, usability and version including hard forks, and multiple chains. They also propose metrics to address them quantitatively. Ortu et al. [19] compare BbS codes with traditional software based on selected code quality metrics to identify key differences, which in turn have consequences on the QA and testing needs.

Blockchain standards for compliance are still rare. Anjum et al. [20] published a systematic literature analysis identifying and characterizing the most relevant articles and topic clusters. The top five clusters around blockchain are smart contract, cryptocurrency, IoT, security, and privacy. Centobelli et al. [21] elaborate on blockchain standards for trust and compliance based on security and performance principles. The security principles investigated are confidentiality, information availability, integrity, repudiation, provenance, pseudonymity, and selective disclosure. The performance principles are consistency, system availability, failure tolerance, scalability, latency, auditability, liveliness, denial of service resistance, and system complexity.

According to [13], blockchain testing should address dependability, security, and trust. Koul et al. [22] propose approaches to consensus testing with service virtualization, external interaction with data flow testing, functional testing with unit testing, and performance testing with automated tests and security testing. They also suggest an appropriate test environment.

Smart contract testing has to address specific smart contract implementations with their individual functionalities, as shown by Wang et al. [23] for Ethereum during complete smart contract implementation. Liao et al. [24] test smart contracts in a behavior-driven development (BDD) and test-driven development (TDD) style, which is an established approach in software testing. Karinsalo et al. [5] elaborate on testing of smart contracts with specific blockchain test clients. Smart contract security testing is a specific topic of DLT aiming at avoiding loss of cryptocurrency, which may have a high monetary value [25]. The paper suggests that smart contracts have to be built based on patterns allowing systematic testing, depending on the implementation of the blockchain libraries. They propose a local, public test environment, as well as a live system as staging approach. Furthermore, they elaborate on a model-based testing (MBT) approach. Zhou et al. [26] developed an assurance approach for smart contracts to reduce logical risks in the code of smart contracts.

General blockchain security aspects are addressed in [27] by analyzing different security aspects like the surrounding ecosystem, including wallets, as well as methods like the 51% attack (Goldfinger attack [28]). This leads to best practices for higher quality like blockchain-specific approaches, such as wallet management and permissioned chain management, in addition to "classical" methods like code review. Privacy assurance has to deal with de-anonymization [29]. Further aspects to be addressed by QA are confidentiality of transactions and data privacy.

Availability of confirmation is a specific topic of DLT [30]. For example, marking a transaction as finalized together with a timestamp is essential to avoid a later reorganization of the chain (in the worst case a 51% attack). Factors influencing the time of transactions are blockchain-specific parameters like the gas price and limit for Ethereum. However, classical network parameters like delays have an impact, too.

Performance and scaling assurance are addressed in [31] by the evolution of techniques and metrics for performance measures. Furthermore, benchmark approaches for DLT are reviewed as empirical evaluation approach. As analytic approach, modeling is reviewed. However, the established performance parameters with throughput and latency are in scope of the investigation in the context of DLT to identify performance bottlenecks. DLT maturity is addressed in [32] through the proposal of a maturity model for engineering of DLT platforms.

To summarize, there is a need with respect to established approaches, BbS require additional DLT-specific aspects to be addressed by testing, QA, and quality management.

## 8.2  Materials and Methods

This work is based on a grounded field approach, combining results from literature research insights with practical experiences. Since 2018, the authors have been developing their approach to QA for BbS as a generic approach to evaluate DLT from the QA perspective within the Volkswagen Group IT. This approach, which we will name BSea (blockchain-based service evaluation approach) in the following, is an open framework, which has been designed to guide and facilitate agile, autonomous development teams in their choices of integrating the blockchain in the services they develop. At the heart of this framework there is a questionnaire which we initially designed with DLT experts from the Volkswagen Group IT competence team, then analyzed by the Volkswagen blockchain community. This questionnaire addresses relevant aspects of safeguarding DLT with the objective of facilitating the development process. As such, it can be used from early stages to late testing phases for systematic QA of the BbS. To reflect the state of the art, the questionnaire was aligned with results from a profound literature analysis (focused on IEEE Xplore, Springer, and ScienceDirect) whose key results are summarized in the previous section, and integrated into BSea through a methodical alignment. Results were further enriched by relevant findings from published practice-oriented industry media such as gray literature, e.g., non-research publications from practitioners, or white papers.

BSea primarily aims at facilitating project and product teams to safeguard any integrated DLT and BbS. Its application can be bottom-up with a focus on the technical building blocks and top-down driven by the business view. Both use cases are relevant in practice, depending on the evaluation point of time in a BbS's life cycle. In early phases, the business demand can be reflected to help select the most relevant DLT or some other more appropriate technology. Later in the product or service life cycle, the BSea-based evaluation helps identify quality risks and improvement potentials of the BbS.

Finally, we also mapped BSea against the ISO 25010 standard, which represents an established set of product quality characteristics for software. Therefore, this mapping enables the improvement and validation of quality criteria coverage of specific software quality approaches with respect to the generic ones that are recognized as the industry standard.

## 8.3    Results

In order to constitute the BSea questionnaire, we investigated the seven DLT-focused quality topics derived by [11] both in the research and practical context, with the objective of deriving the most relevant questions.

### 8.3.1    Key Concepts

#### 8.3.1.1    Public Verifiability

Several use cases need public verifiability, meaning that a third party can verify a transaction state on a DLT to ensure that the transaction is correctly executed. For example, human resource departments need to verify the actual state of training qualifications easily and regularly [33]. In the IoT domain, public key infrastructure (PKI) for handling public access keys is essential. Here, the performance of the verification process is a significant quality criterion [34]. Furthermore, cloud storage [35] and cloud computing [36] are use cases underlying many other emerging ones and therefore need a high level of adaptability to future demands. All have in common the public verifiability aspect as a quality characteristic of the integrated DLT underlying any BbS. To integrate the DLT adequately, some fundamental questions have to be answered to select the appropriate technology:

1. What is the minimum technology needed for the verification?
2. How is the access to the blockchain data managed for verification?
3. How long does it take to verify transactions (i.e., obtaining the data and computing the algorithms)?

### 8.3.1.2 Transparency, Traceability, Tracking

According to [21], the DLT governance is important for BbS users because they are technologically locked-in with their assets [37]. Depending on the used DLT, the development and strategy for future versions is more or less open and transparent and needs governance and control [38]. Some are managed privately by a consortium, while others are governed by a public community. This impacts participation. Furthermore, particular domains like finance have specific demands to the governance [38]. Based on this organizational level, the implementation of the specific DLT can be reflected against the characteristics of transparency, traceability, and tracking, using the following set of questions:

- Does a business interest to manage/participate in the network of the blockchain exist?
- Could the protocol be enhanced to fit future business process requirements?
- How relevant is the influence on the future development of the blockchain for the business case?

### 8.3.1.3 Privacy, Security

Privacy/security applications are numerous, e.g., the one discussed in [39] with Zerocoin as a cryptographic mixer to hide the link between a Bitcoin and the transaction owner of the spending. Privacy is provided by the blockchain network as state of the art [40]. This leads to a predefined privacy approach with the selection of a specific DLT. Depending on the domain and legal environment, the selection of a DLT is driven by the specific compliance demands. Privacy is also an aspect of regulation compliance, which therefore has a big impact on every business case to be digitalized. Thus, the following questions must be answered:

1. What level of data protection is required?
2. Who is the responsible process (step) owner for compliance and data protection?
3. What data are not allowed in the blockchain to ensure compliance?

### 8.3.1.4 Integrity, Security

Filippi et al. [41] elaborate on novel security challenges based on the DLT. They argue that in the blockchain context, mistrust is a negative attitude towards integrity. Based on the specific implementation of the DLT, the trust and confidence in integrity and security is defined. As integrity is an inherent design aspect of any applied DLT, the DLT's compatibility is a highly relevant derived aspect. Blockchain protocol compatibility spans the following questions:

1. Will the protocol fit future enhancements and capabilities of the business process?

2. Will future enhancements of the protocol be compatible with the business process?
3. Are future process enhancements negotiable?
4. How important is the security and reliability of a blockchain transaction?

### 8.3.1.5 Redundancy

Bagaria et al. [42] model redundancy for blockchains with a strong correlation to throughput as a key performance element. Based on this, a trade-off is required between these two essential characteristics. In addition to that, a certain level of redundancy is intrinsically required for any DLT in order to enable BbS stability [43]. Blockchain redundancy shall be investigated based on the following questions:

1. Is all data stored redundantly?
2. Are different locations used for storing the data?

### 8.3.1.6 Trust, Confidence

According to blockchain advocate Andreas Antonopoulos, blockchain technology enables a "shift from trusting people to trusting math" in that transactional security is achieved via reliance on deterministic computation [41]. The latter affects in particular the computation of the hashing algorithm, especially with regard to the public-private key cryptographic primitives underlying the blockchain, a second factor generating confidence in the economic incentives and game theoretical schemes that govern the network. On the one hand, the consensus algorithm of most blockchain-based networks (e.g., proof-of-work or proof-of-stake) is intended to distribute trust among a large variety of miners, thereby reducing the risk of individual opportunism. On the other hand, because all participating nodes (such as miners and validators) hold a copy of the blockchain, they can always verify that every recorded transaction is valid and legitimate. Hence, anyone interacting with a blockchain may have a high level of confidence that it will operate as planned, even if they do not know (and therefore do not trust) the parties operating or maintaining the network.

Blockchain-based systems are socio-technological assemblages which are made up not only of code but also of a large variety of actors, including miners, validators, programmers, cryptocurrency and token holders, end-users, and, to a lesser extent, regulators. Having confidence in the system ultimately means trusting the whole assemblage of actors associated with that network. The technology displaces trust in the technological artifacts that underpin a blockchain-based system by shifting it towards the network of actors that contribute to operating and maintaining the system. First, a few economic players—such as the largest mining pools and mining farms, as well as the most popular online exchanges and blockchain explorers—have become centralized points of failure and control in the governance of many blockchain networks. Second, core developers and open-source contributors have the power to influence the evolution of the blockchain-based network. They can lobby for or against the introduction of specific features into the technical design of the platform. These decisions may appear to be purely technical in nature. However, they are also political choices, given the implications they have on the identity of the system and potential economic repercussions. Third, cryptocurrency and token holders, as well as users more generally (albeit to a lesser extent), might also have a voice in dictating the type of changes they would like to see in a blockchain-based network. Fourth, regulators might also intervene by either approving or disapproving the use of a blockchain-based system [20, 41].

Trust is therefore a governance aspect that is mostly addressed by the transparency of both the DLT's administration and its governance [44]. Thus, the following questions are in scope for trust:

1. Are the technologies used for a DLT well-known and proved?
2. Is a particular DLT's architecture trustable?
3. Which regulations require the usage of DLT?
4. Which regulations hinder the usage of DLT?

### 8.3.1.7   Scaling

Scaling is limited by the transaction speed of a specific DLT implementation [45, 46]. Another important aspect for scaling is the confirmation time required for transactions and dependencies like post-processing of the BbS. Furthermore, specific blockchain implementations of smart contracts are important for scaling, because depending on the implementation, every node in the network might have to store the code and run the smart contracts [47]. In this setup, the performance of a single node limits transaction scaling. By design, the transaction block size also influences scalability. Based on these characteristics and their interdependencies, it is important to map the transactions to the specific BbS use cases. Consequently, identifying the desired scalability properties requires confident estimations regarding future enhancements and usage of the implemented system in terms of transaction throughput, storage space, as well as the amount and profile of users. The following questions can guide these considerations:

1. How will the number of users grow?
2. How will the number of transactions per second grow?
3. How will the required amount of storage space grow?

## 8.3.2   BSea Framework

Based on the blockchain quality assurance characteristics developed in Sect. 8.4, we aim at proposing a structured, actionable support for industrial product and service development teams for capitalizing on the selected blockchain's specific

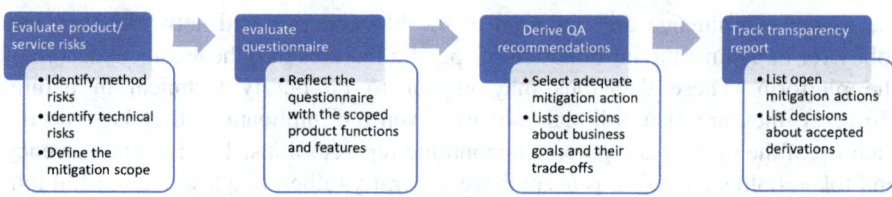

**Fig. 8.1** BSea method steps

capabilities and for making its limitations transparent. As announced previously, we will refer to this support as BSea in the following as a framework which facilities systematic QA of BbS.

BSea shall comprise the following four steps (Fig. 8.1):

1. Product risk evaluation of the product that shall be supported by a blockchain-based approach.
2. Blockchain-based approaches are evaluated to identify best implementation offers which address the product demands and get transparency about the implementation offers' specific risks.
3. QA method recommendations to mitigate specific product risks caused by the blockchain approach.

### 8.3.2.1 Product/Service Quality Risk Evaluation

Product or service teams can make a systematic product quality risk (PQR) evaluation using, e.g., the PQR method [48]. With the systematically derived quality risks and their classification, the relevant functions or features of the product or service can be identified for focusing.

### 8.3.2.2 Evaluate Questionnaire

To address the different levels of a blockchain-based industry service, we defined two abstraction layers as shown in Fig. 8.2. The first layer reflects the business aspects of the BbS. The second layer focuses on the technical solution including its architecture aspects and main building blocks. BSea Layer 2 combines the technical solution and building block views, since in most cases the selected implementation offer requires combining selected building blocks for their implementation. Such cases imply that there is not really a free choice in the BbS-related implementation instantiation.

Table 8.1 addresses the business view abstraction layer, which has been derived from the framework developed in Sect. 8.4. The column ID of Table 8.1 is used for references in the subsequent steps of BSea. The Topic (ISO) column is structured in alignment with the blockchain characteristics investigated in Sect. 8.4. Furthermore,

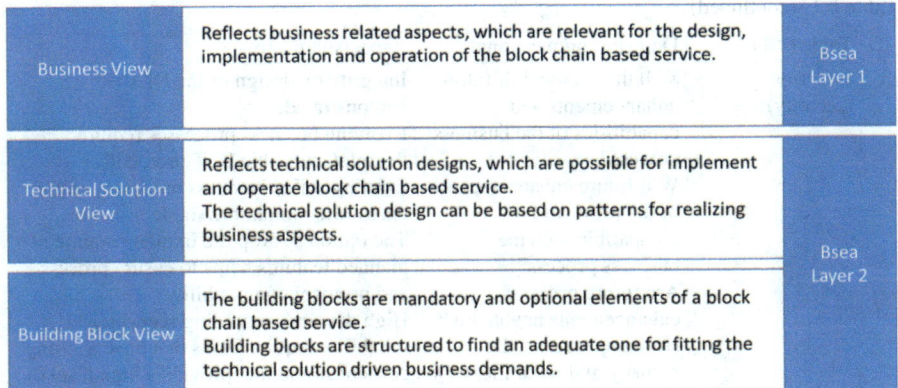

**Fig. 8.2** Abstraction layers of the BSea questionnaire

**Table 8.1** Questionnaire for blockchain-based products/services—business view

| ID | Topic (ISO) | Description/questions | Aspects/indicators |
|----|-------------|----------------------|--------------------|
| 1 | Public verifiability (functional suitability) | What is the minimum technology needed for verification? How is the access to the blockchain data managed for verification? How long does it take to verify transactions (i.e., obtaining the data and computing the algorithms)? | Everybody can access the blockchain transaction log. Everybody has access to the specific verification technology like algorithms. Computing power required for verification is low (everybody can do it) |
| 2 | Transparency, traceability, tracking (functional suitability) | Does a business interest to manage/participate in the network of the blockchain exist? Could the protocol be enhanced to fit future business process requirements? How relevant is the influence on the future development of the blockchain for the business case? | The option to influence future enhancements of the blockchain protocol helps to ensure business process and protocol compatibility |

(continued)

**Table 8.1** (continued)

| ID | Topic (ISO) | Description/questions | Aspects/indicators |
|----|-------------|----------------------|--------------------|
| 3 | Integrity (security) | Will the protocol fit future enhancements and capabilities of the business process? Will future enhancements of the protocol be compatible with the business process? Are future process enhancements negotiable? How important is the security and reliability of a blockchain transaction? | Integrity by design of the DLT is demonstrated. Evolving business processes require flexible/extensible DLT protocols. Existing/stable business processes require backward compatible/stable protocols. The option to drop the implementation of planned features helps to ensure process and protocol compatibility. High demands regarding security and reliability require DLTs that have a strong consensus and that provide a high level of finality. To choose the right DLT, it is necessary to know the point in time when a Tx is almost final. A DLT must be future-proof regarding upcoming attack vectors (quantum computers, algorithms, etc.) |
| 4 | Redundancy (reliability) | Are all data stored redundantly? Are different locations used for storing the data? | Nodes in the DLT are running independently. Nodes of the DLT are in different locations |
| 5 | Trust, confidence (security) | Are the technologies used for a DLT well-known and proofed? Is a particular DLT's architecture trustable? Which regulations require the usage of DLT? Which regulations hinder the usage of DLT? | State-of-the-art approaches for trust are used and transparent. The DLT fits to the required regulations |
| 6 | Privacy (security) | What level of data protection is required? Who is the responsible process (step) owner for compliance and data protection? What data is not allowed in the blockchain to ensure compliance? | GDPR requires DLTs which deal with data deletion in a compliant way. Private/permissioned DLTs may reduce the risks of data leaks/exposure. Public DLTs tend to be more decentralized, thus having a positive impact on immutability. Creating a business process that requires only a small amount of data to be stored on the ledger reduces legal/compliance risks |
| 7 | Scaling (performance efficiency) | How will the number of users grow? How will the number of transactions per second grow? How will the required amount of storage space grow? | High rates of growth regarding transaction throughput, number of users, and storage space consumption require DLTs that already scale or have the potential to scale with future enhancements |

a mapping of the Topic (ISO) column to the ISO 25010 characteristics is made with the terms in parentheses to indicate the anchors for BSea's alignment with the established ISO 25010 standard. Each line of this table addresses a particular topic of Sect. 8.4. Based on this mapping, BSea can be used as a technology-specific refinement of the ISO standard with a quality model for blockchain-based services and IT systems.

The content of column Description/questions has been derived from the insights developed in Sect. 8.4 and represents the essential part of the questionnaire. The column Aspects/indicators provides support for evaluating a real product or service demand against the generic topics and their respective questions. Here, the purpose is to guide engineers rather than to provide them with information that is very specific for particular blockchain technologies. This guidance shall help them think about the important blockchain properties and indicators in their individual contexts. Optionally, such application-specific properties and indicators can be added to BSea, since the latter's design is open for fostering the questionnaire's co-evolution with rapidly emerging DLTs.

Since the business case imposes requirements and constrains to the blockchain technology and vice versa, BSea can be applied in two ways:

1. Top-down: Based on the business demands, the technological building blocks are selected. Following the selected building blocks, the most fitting blockchain implementation is used.
2. Bottom-up: Based on the constraints of the selected blockchain, the business "inherits" limitations from the technology constraints.

Table 8.2 covers the second abstraction layer, i.e., the technical view. It is the central part of BSea, as it provides the basis for the questionnaire used to derive a particular project's, product's, or service's needs with respect to blockchain-based QA. Its content was inspired from both literature and our own experiences. Each line addresses a building block that is used to reflect the relevant product/service functionality or feature. The column Topic collects the technical solution aspects. Ref. to ID establishes the link with the concerned lines of Table 8.1, including the mapping to the ISO 25010 standard. Topic names the related blockchain technology-specific terms. Aspect lists generic implementation patterns and aspects related to the topic. Questions/principle and Indicators are used as in Table 8.1.

### 8.3.2.3   QA Recommendations

Table 8.3 correlates with the aspects of Table 8.2's column 2 (technical view) and recommends some methods or approaches for the aspects which are addressed in the questionnaire. The adequateness of the recommendations depends on the specific business goals and the trade-off between quality risk mitigation effort. It is a case-specific action. This is not a rule-based approach, but rather a practice collection for inspiration to identify QA actions. Most importantly, the selection of mitigation actions has to be adequate for the quality risk mitigation. Adequateness often needs to look beyond the "happy path" of testing. This includes verification of what

**Table 8.2** Questionnaire for blockchain-based products/services—technical view

| Ref. to ID | Topic | Aspect | Questions/principle | Indicators |
|---|---|---|---|---|
| 1,2,3,4,5,7 | Consensus, security, scalability | Byzantine fault tolerance (BFT)/ Sybil attack resistance [49] | The ability to function as desired and correctly reach a sufficient consensus despite malicious components (nodes) of the system failing or propagating incorrect information to other peers. Mechanisms to prevent Sybil attacks are established and thus provide finality | Public, permissionless systems are based on the concept of "spending" economic resources, like<br>– computing power (proof-of-work, PoW) [27]<br>– tokens (proof-of-stake, PoS) [27] |
| 4,7 | Consensus, scalability | Abstract data structure | The technical design of how transactions are recorded across many nodes, so that any involved record cannot be altered retroactively | Blockchain has an optimized BFT design. The data within a block cannot be changed retroactively, which is secured through public key cryptography and linkages to subsequent blocks |
| 1,3,4,5,7 | Consensus | Finality | The affirmation that all well-formed blocks will not be revoked once committed to the blockchain. High finality is realized by the likelihood that a chain is reorganized and causes a rollback of a transaction is approximately 0% | The risk/value estimation is handed over to the reader of the data. In the case of a blockchain, the reader can wait for a certain amount of block confirmations (e.g., for Bitcoin, six block confirmations are recommended). For a low value transaction, zero confirmation can also be sufficient. In other technology implementations, the block confirmations are replaced by confidence values or confirmation rate, dependent on the network architecture |
| 1,3 | Consensus, security | Hashing algorithm | The underlying cryptographic hash function (collision resistance, preimage resistance, second-preimage resistance) used for proof-of-work. The public blockchain used a major and established hash chain. Only relevant in case of PoW | Dependent on Byzantine fault tolerance (BFT). Describes the hashing algorithm used for PoW. Bitcoin uses SHA-256, Ethereum uses Ethash, and IOTA uses Keccak-384 |

| | | | | |
|---|---|---|---|---|
| 3,4,6,7 | Extensibility, scalability | Smart contracts [16] | A set of promises, specified in digital form, including protocols within which the parties perform on these promises. The required business logic can be represented within smart contract capabilities with no or only some limitations | Smart contracts can be distinguished in non-Turing complete and Turing complete. This has severe implications on the complexity of the business logic someone tries to implement. Example: – Ethereum offers Turing-complete smart contracts, which can represent complex business logic. – Bitcoin offers non-Turing-complete smart contracts, which can represent simple business logic |
| 1,2,3,4,5,6,7 | Extensibility, scalability | Sidechains [50, 51], state channels [51] | Sidechain is a functionality to enhance the capability of the existing blockchain. Digital assets (data, tokens, etc.) can be securely used in a separate blockchain and moved back to the main chain. The purpose can be scaling or privacy. Is a high throughput needed, which cannot be achieved with the main chain? Privacy demands are fulfilled by the main chain. The main chain does not limit sidechain demands | A sidechain is a separate blockchain that is connected to its parent blockchain by using a two-way peg. The two-way peg is enabled by Turing-complete smart contracts and offers interchangeability of assets at a predetermined rate between the parent blockchain and the sidechain. State channels are state-altering operations, which can be securely done off-chain, without significantly increasing the risk of any participant |
| 1,4,7 | Scalability | Block confirmation time | The time an additional new block is being founded and added to the end of the blockchain fits to the demands | Time variation depending on load (TPS—transactions per second) or is a constant confirmation time. Strong dependency to finality, immutability, and scalability |
| 1,4,7 | Scalability | Transactions per second (TPS) | The technology capability (max. throughput) fits the demanded amount of transactions per second | Transactions depend on active nodes and scale with it in the complexity of n, log(n), etc. |

(continued)

**Table 8.2** (continued)

| Ref. to ID | Topic | Aspect | Questions/principle | Indicators |
|---|---|---|---|---|
| 1,4,7 | Scalability | Block size | The average size in megabyte (MB) of a block fits into the maximum payload size of a block | Blocks are of constant size or have variation. In case of variation the size scale with n, log(n), etc. |
| 2,5 | Feedback loops, protocol ownership | Decentralized implementation (clients) | The amount (and quality) of different implementation of the same underlying protocol. Is the implementation centralized? What is the maturity of the implementations? How is the progress of the client implementations? | Ethereum and Bitcoin have different client implementations based on the same underlying protocol. Those implementations are community projects based on different programming languages and software patterns. Bitcoin, e.g., Bitcoin Core, Electrum, bitcoind, etc. Ethereum, e.g., Geth, Parity |
| 2,5 | Optimization | Wallet implementations for specific purposes [52] | Strongly correlated to the decentralized implementation aspect with more focus on specific purposes. Are there any implementations for specific purposes like IoT devices, and smartphones? | IOTA Reference Implementation (IRI), IOTA Extensible Interface (IXI) Bitcoin Simplified Payment Verification (SPV) nodes for iOS/Android |
| 2,5 | Feedback loops, protocol ownership | Decentralized protocol | The process of how protocol improvements and thus the future development is decided. What is the process for future protocol enhancements? How big is the impact on the roadmap and the protocol enhancements? | Bitcoin Improvement Proposals (BIP) Ethereum Improvement Proposals (EIP) Token-based decentralized governance mechanisms |
| 2 | Transparency | Development activity | The developer activity is tracked in a version control system. Is the project actively being developed? How many commits in total/weeks/month/year? How many contributors/committers? | Amount of commits Amount of forks Amount of committer |

| | | | | |
|---|---|---|---|---|
| 1,3,4,6 | Security, trust | Privacy | The possibilities of confidential transactions and privacy on chain. Should the data be anonymous? Should the data be pseudonymous? What is the impact of data being publicly accessible? | There are multiple approaches of doing confidential transactions. Most of them are a core component of the blockchain itself. It is crucial to decide early on whether this is important or not. Chain upgrades to increase privacy will most likely be achieved with a hard fork. Confidential transactions Taproot Zero-knowledge proofs |
| 1,2,3,4,5,6 | Security | Immutability | The degree of immutability consists of multiple technical factors. There is no real immutability, but a certainty of a chain reorganization. In other words, a likelihood of which a chain reorganizes. What is the impact of data loss? What is the impact of changed historical data? How fast should a transaction be fixed on-chain? Under which conditions can the blockchain be changed? When can it not? Do those conditions match the problem someone tries to solve? | If a transaction has received a sufficient level of validation, it is counted as immutable. It is important to consider the amount of work (any kind of economic resources) which is needed to rewrite any part of the blockchain. In proof-of-work chains, a majority of 51% hash power (in a longer period of time) is needed to take over the network. In proof-of-stake, a majority of 51% of tokens is needed. Other concepts like the Tangle and its Coordinator have other promises on immutability |
| 3,5 | Consensus, protocol ownership | User-activated hard/soft forks (UAHF/UASF) [53] | The consensus protocol on how to do protocol upgrades/updates and what happened in the past (history of UAHF/ UASF) | Chance to keep or bring in own demands. Is hard or soft fork preferred? Consider upgrade capability, maintainability scope. A prominent example is the SegWit soft fork on Bitcoin (24.08.17) |

(continued)

**Table 8.2** (continued)

| Ref. to ID | Topic | Aspect | Questions/principle | Indicators |
|---|---|---|---|---|
| 3 | Consensus | Technical forks [54] | The process of how chain splits (e.g., competing miners, stakers, etc.) are handled | Strongly correlated to the anonymity of consensus nodes. If consensus nodes are known: chain splits will most likely not occur, or be resolved fairly quickly. If consensus nodes are not known: chain splits will occur regularly when hashing/staking power is distributed on a small subset of participants (e.g., 51%/49%). Cryptoeconomics come into play, since a long-lasting chainsplit is most likely financially unsustainable |
| 1,2,3,4,5 | Trust | Participation | The possibilities of verifying the entire transaction history yourself. What is the level of trust to other participants? Is verifying the data itself needed? Should the entire data history be kept on an own system? | Full nodes have a copy of the blockchain. Every transaction and block that has ever taken place on the blockchain is included. This ensures that the blockchain can neither be controlled by a single entity, nor can it easily be attacked, as there is not one single point of failure. The higher the amount of full nodes, the more decentralized the network (there are also different dimensions of decentralization, e.g., mining pools, persons, token distribution, etc.). In some chains, there are special cases like archival nodes, which also store the entire state history (e.g., see Ethereum). Light node (e.g., Simplified Payment Verification) does not download the entire blockchain, just the headers. Light nodes are connected to full nodes to transmit their transactions and get notifications when a transaction affects them. With light nodes, high trust in full nodes is needed. It also affects the privacy, since the full node gets the transaction, plus notifies when a transaction affects the light node |

**Table 8.3** QA practices for PQR mitigation

| Aspect | QA methods/approaches/checks |
|---|---|
| Consensus | Algorithm and its implementation is analyzed/evaluated; integrate nodes and check data synchronization (private chains), check consensus voting of node (private chain), check fault tolerance of consensus algorithm (private chain), test collisions, and data corruption |
| Security | Analysis of known bugs list (amount, closing time); evaluate adequateness of applied security libraries, frameworks, etc., analyze or make static secure code analysis and penetration tests, peer synchronization validation testing, test data and transaction encryption, check access control synchronization across nodes (private chain) |
| Scalability | Analyze blockchain infrastructure and load statistics, load and performance test of blockchain infrastructure, and own implementation parts (integration aspect, end-to-end transaction testing via wallets), add/remove nodes to check the scaling and sporadic outages (private chains), check relevant metrics like transactions per second (TPS) or confirmation time |
| Extensibility | Assure completeness of available API documentation, identify and assure adequate regression test suite, smart contract testing (aspects: contract to contract, account/wallet integration, network transactions), ICO (initial coin offering) testing (token contracts, security) |
| Optimization | Risk-based testing of the optimized features |
| Feedback loops | Evaluation/analysis of change process (amount, acceptance rate, implementation time). |
| Protocol ownership | Review of code of conduct (CoC) of the protocol; analyze past protocol changes |
| Transparency | Evaluation of licenses, decision logs, run node in the network to "see" how transparency is practiced |
| Trust | Evaluation of used authorization entities (AE), approval of AE "ownership" |

happens if incorrect or unacceptable data is fed into the peer-to-peer network of the BbS. To handle the immutability of a BbS, it is recommended to have a dedicated test network.

#### 8.3.2.4    Transparency Report

Based on the identified risks and the selected QA recommendations, the outcome of the BSea approach is a list of actions rendering transparent the quality improvements that are recommended to achieve a blockchain-based product or service that is state of the art. This implies the regular adaptation of all three BSea tables to reflect the latter.

### 8.3.3    BSea Application

In order to deploy BSea in a large number of independent product and/or service teams, a means of BSea service delivery is required. In order to foster a fast large-scale rollout across several divisions, business units, and departments of the

Volkswagen Group, we decided to provide BSea as a self-service kit (SSK) [55]. With this approach, the product teams can use BSea independently and autonomously within an enterprise setting. The SSK guides the teams through the BSea workflow. The application of BSea in product teams is based on the procedure described in Fig. 8.1. With the identification of the specific product quality risks, the focus for the evaluation with BSea is set. In the next step, the team decides how to use BSea, from the business view or from the technical and building block views. After defining the usage and the working direction, respectively, the team will go through the BSea questionnaire. The two views are processed with the evaluation of the questionnaires. Line by line, the BSea questionnaires guide the team through the reflection of their specific project against the aspects and indicators suggested by the respective tables. The team notes the results as well as suggestions for enhancements and improvements of the BSea artifacts. Depending on the usage and evaluation, the QA actions are derived with the help of Table 8.3. The team should plan at least 2 h for the evaluation. However, depending on the product or service and the team's experience with DLT, the process may need more time to complete.

### 8.3.4    Industry Case Study

#### 8.3.4.1    BSea Evaluation Context

We applied the BSea approach to the evaluation of four blockchain technologies in the project and service context of the Volkswagen Group IT. The services are based on IOTA, Cosmos, Hashgraph, and Ethereum. In the following, we use the research questions cited in the introduction to demonstrate the benefit of the systematic PQR analysis and application of the questionnaires to the product team even in cases where the evaluation was done after development start.

*How can we estimate the quality risks? (RQ1)*

Each product or service is developed to address needs of its customers and generate value. The chance to address the needs typically comes with some specific risks – not all products and services are successful on the market. The PQR approach identifies with De-sign Thinking corresponding service and product specific quality risks. The systematic risk ideation for a specific product or service with the PQR approach is the starting point to define and perform actions to mitigate or reduce the risks. Based on the product vision and the identified product features, the PQR analysis is set up. The following is an extract of the main risks identified by our PQR analysis:

1. PQR1 (inadequate technology selection): leads to insufficient capability of the service
2. PQR2 (inadequate deployment): leads to operating issues about security and trust
3. PQR3 (use case is under extension): leads to changing demands to the blockchain technology

*How can we define adequate quality assurance activities to mitigate or reduce quality risks? (RQ2)*

As BSea is a "tool" which is useful to evaluate DLT it fits to PQR1. The derived action for PQR1 is to make a full application of the BSea approach to different blockchain technologies. This action helps to address PQR3, too. To mitigate PQR2, misuse cases are identified and handled. The handling of PQR1 to PQR3 shows that BSea can help to address quality risks but is not a solution for all potential quality risks such as PQR2 is not direct addressed by BSea. However, BSea gives with the technology reflection an idea which areas could be interesting for misuse cases.

*How can we assure customer confidence in a blockchain-based service at release time? (RQ3)*

Generic metrics for blockchain technologies in the context of application use cases are rare. In our scenario, changes and extensions are reflected on refactoring. Especially refactoring on architectural and blockchain technology levels is an indicator for a "wrong track." For example, having to batch transactions in order to scale them into the performance limitations can be such an indicator. The holistic view of the BSea on DLT gives confidence that relevant aspects are identified and can be handled during development for a mature release. The combination of the PQR and BSea approach helps to identify relevant DLT relat-ed risks and evaluate them to define adequate mitigation actions. The usage of BSea without the PQR approach leads to the risk not to focus the most relevant product or ser-vice specific risk areas. The usage of the PQR approach without the holistic structure and systematic of BSea makes it more difficult to oversee the potential mitigation action areas. Furthermore, BSea is like a knowledge base to reduce efforts to identify potential action areas for mitigation actions.

### 8.3.4.2   BSea Evaluation Case and Survey

The Volkswagen Group can use the BSea method to develop and enhance their blockchain-based products and services. The users' feedback via the internal quality innovation network (QiNET, [56]) enables a continuous discussion and enhancement of BSea. The goal is to offer to all product and service teams a common state-of-the-art approach for QA and testing of BbS. Furthermore, a common quality practice is the basis for reusing BbS without heavy redesign and requalification of "product external" services.

In order to evaluate the applicability of BSea coming from the business perspective, we applied it to two different business domains that are of high importance to us, i.e., digital twin and supply chain transparency. In addition, we considered different DLTs and evaluated their applicability within those business cases.

Within the digital twin domain, we considered Transparent Mileage currently under development. Transparent Mileage aims at showing persistent mileage data of our car fleet in a transparent (particularly to our customers) and immutable way. Thus, the business requirements of Transparent Mileage focus on integrity (because the mileage data must be highly immutable) and scaling (millions of cars and data sets require high transaction throughputs). As soon as we identified our business requirements, we went on and applied our business to technology mapping defined in Table 8.1. As shown in Fig. 8.3, the need for integrity and scalability (see right part of Fig. 8.3) requires 15 of 19 technical building blocks (see left part of Fig. 8.3) in this specific project, respectively, BbS. That is, to implement Transparent Mileage, a DLT must provide those technical building blocks.

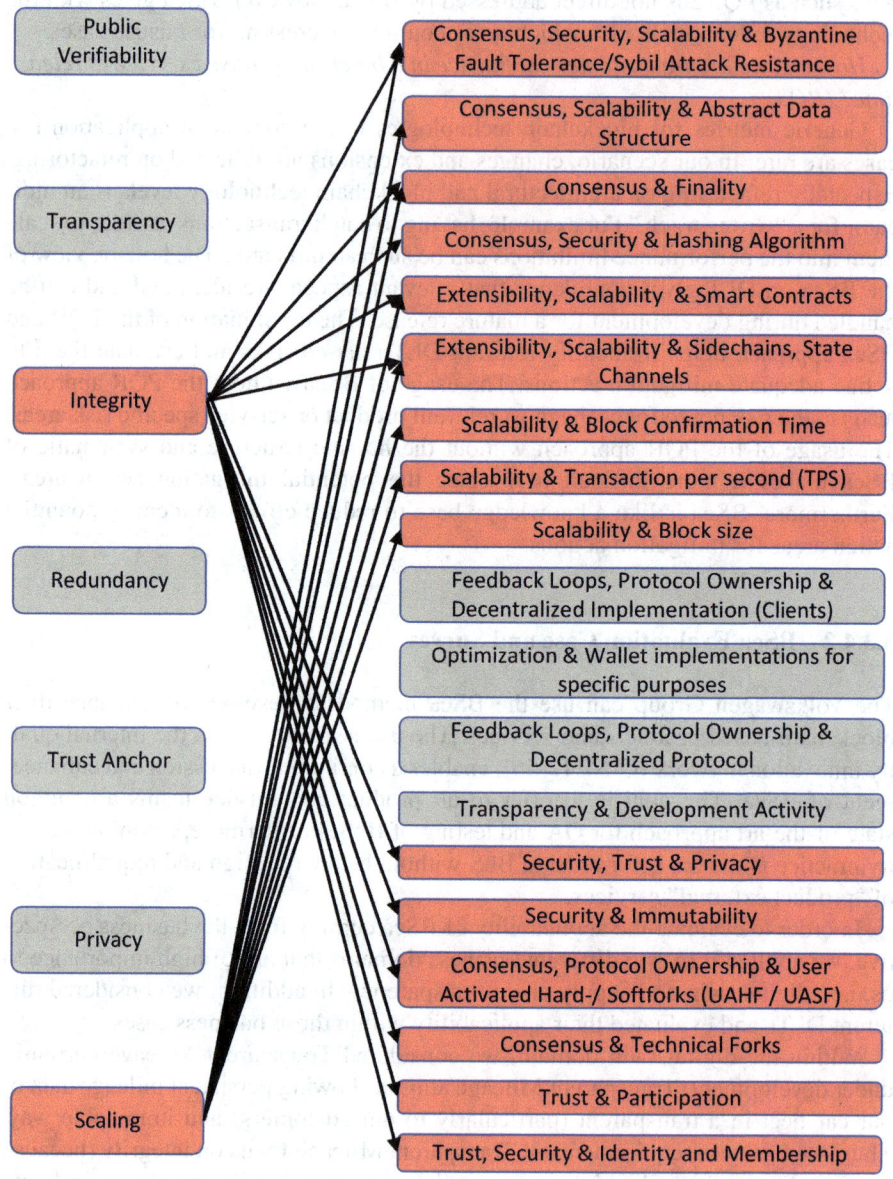

**Fig. 8.3** Business-technology mapping Transparent Mileage

Within the supply chain transparency domain, we evaluated the tracking of cobalt, to ensure that the mining circumstances are transparent and aligned with ecological and ethical values. The crucial business capabilities to be supported are transparency (because the requirements may change significantly in the future) and trust anchor (because the participants of such a supply chain are competitors). Figure 8.4 shows the resulting business to technology mapping. To sum it up, the business need for transparency and trust anchor requires 10 out of 19 technical building blocks to be provided by a DLT.

A closer look at those two businesses to technical building block mappings of our two business cases reveals that the following technical building blocks are of high importance to virtually every business case:

- Extensibility, scalability, sidechains, and state channels
- Consensus, security, scalability, and Byzantine fault tolerance/Sybil attack resistance
- Security and immutability
- Consensus and finality
- Trust and participation

The second part of the evaluation aimed at answering the question if the determined technical building blocks help to identify DLTs that fulfill the requirements of the underlying business case. In our setting, a DLT must cover at least the five technical building blocks above to be applicable to real-world business cases.

We analyzed four representative DLTs (Fig. 8.5, IOTA and Ethereum; Fig. 8.6, Hashgraph and Cosmos) and checked what technical building blocks they cover. The color of the selected DLT in the top left part of the figure corresponds to the color of the building blocks identified for that very DLT on the right side of the figure. Some DLTs imply building blocks than others. Furthermore, in a specific use case like Transparent Mileage, they have to mark the strategic most relevant identified building blocks from Fig. 8.3. The DLT that covers most of the required building blocks fits best to the use case. As a result, only Ethereum would be applicable to our Transparent Mileage (note that Ethereum struggles in terms of transaction throughput, which must be circumvented using sidechains or state channels). In addition, only Ethereum covers all the five technical building blocks that are vital to almost every business case. Hashgraph, IOTA, and Cosmos neither fulfill the business requirements of Transparent Mileage nor the identified five core technical building blocks. In order to be relevant for future applications, those DLTs have to improve significantly with respect to the building blocks required for our use cases.

To evaluate the relevance of BSea, we confronted internal projects and product teams that have applied BSea to at least one project, with the following questions:

- Which insights did the questionnaire-based BSea deliver to the product teams?
- How do different application domains use BSea in their daily work?
- Do the bottom-up and top-down usages of BSea work?
- What is missing to achieve a more effective QA?

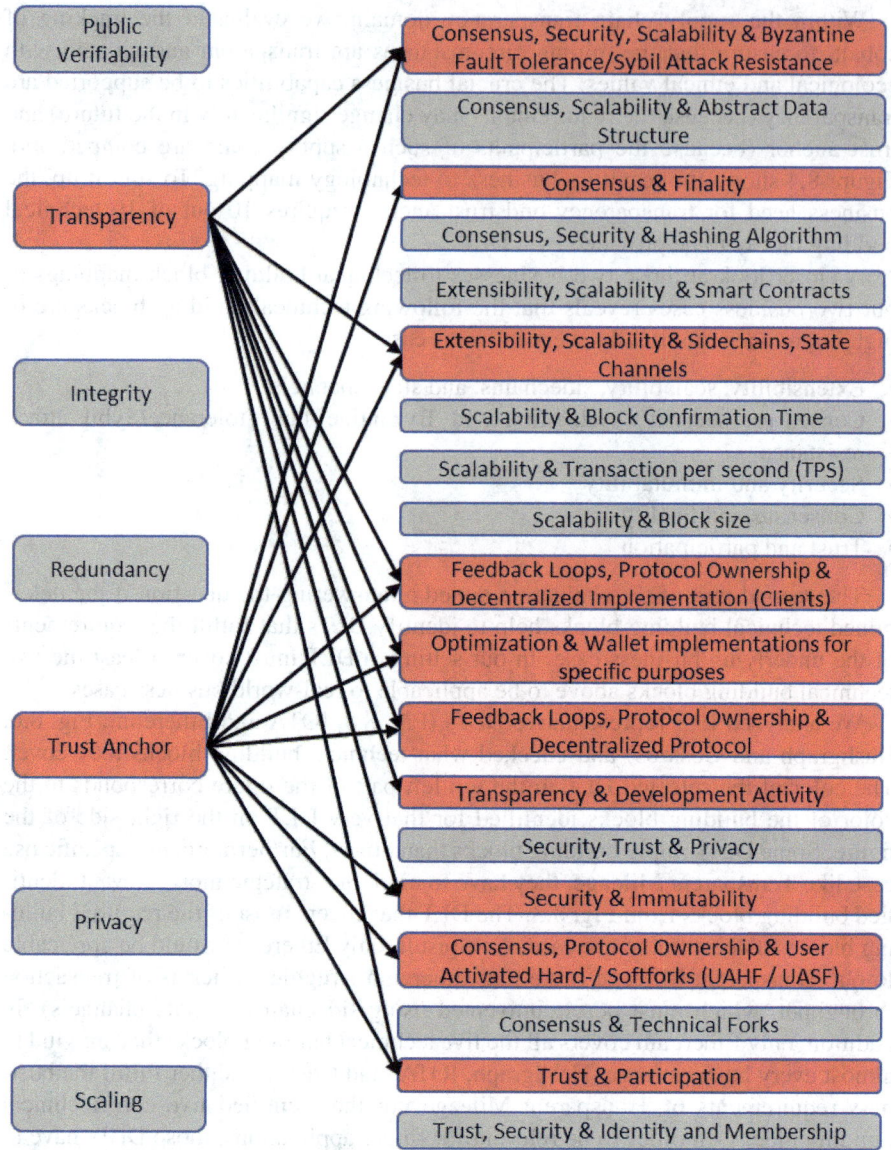

**Fig. 8.4** Business-technology mapping Cobalt Tracking

We present insights from projects of three legal entities of the Volkswagen Group: the passenger cars, the light-duty commercial vehicles, and the financial services. The respective results are:

- Teams argued that they did not systematically address all of the BSea aspects. Especially teams with few blockchain senior experts needed assistance. BSea can help close this assistance gap related to QA aspects.

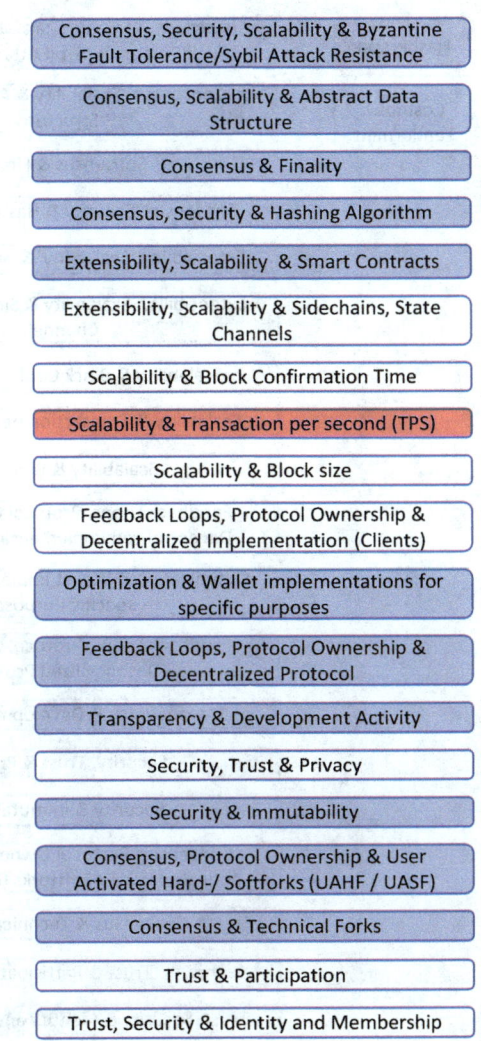

**Fig. 8.5** Technical block fulfillment IOTA, Ethereum

- Different domains were able to apply BSea in the same way. This shows that BSea has obviously reached a sufficient level of genericity, both for its top-down and bottom-up application (Fig. 8.2).
- The usage of BSea in early phases to identify the right blockchain approach is useful—especially for teams with no long blockchain experience to support the self-service mindset of autonomous teams.

Feedback about the BSea questionnaire has led to structural improvements and more precise questions with examples to avoid misunderstanding. This has rendered BSea usable without trained moderators to support the self-service mindset of

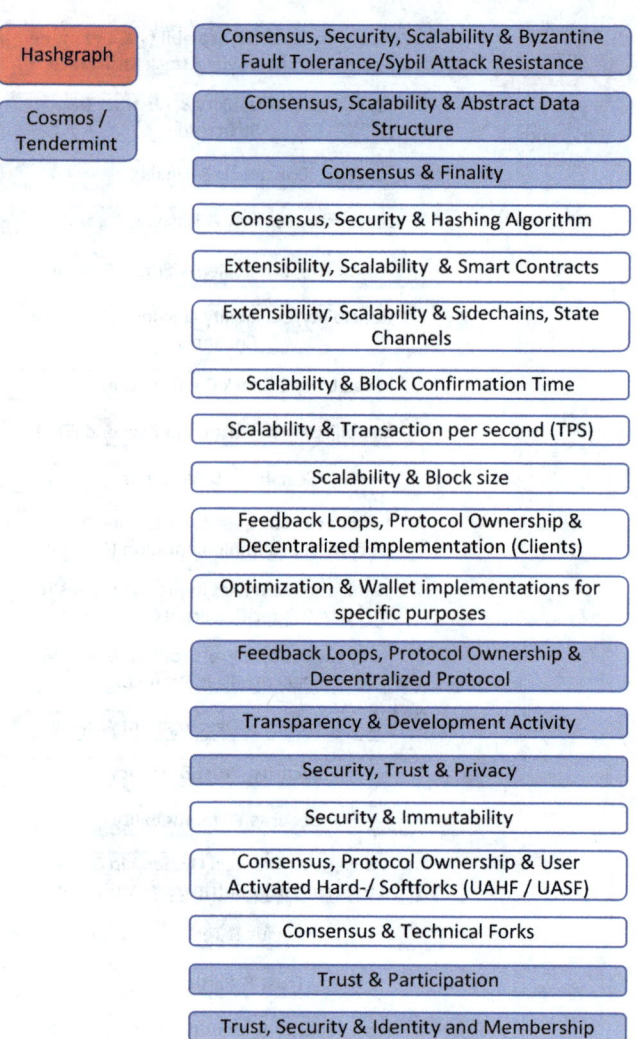

**Fig. 8.6** Technical block fulfillment Hashgraph, Cosmos

autonomous teams. Figure 8.3 shows an example outcome of the application of BSea in a team. The two main aspects identified are scaling and integrity. The aspect of immutability is not so important because the blockchain will be provided by a company itself. In this case, the team worked with Table 8.2, with moderation by the BSea development team.

The different project teams applied BSea in short workshops of 2–3 h each to reflect on the questionnaire. During the BSea application workshop, at least one BSea development team member was present to get insights about the application for ideation about how to enhance the questionnaire to a mature self-service. All the teams collaborated with the Group's competence center for DLT, which gave them sufficient fundamental knowledge to apply BSea adequately without specific blockchain expert support.

Our project validation and feedback loop checks the capability for the general application of the BSea approach and prepares the rollout of BSea. The rollout will quickly establish the base for a broader analysis. The important actualization of BSea by periodic investigation and subsequent integration of the rapidly progressing state of the art will be assured by a dedicated working group.

## 8.4  Discussion

### 8.4.1  Analysis and Findings

The presented BSea activities have proven that the approach is applicable and provides significant benefit in practice. The structured questionnaire revealed aspects that need systematic tracking and mitigation. BSea inspires actions and measures for improving BbS. In particular, BSea leads to transparency about the current state of QA. This leads to active decisions about how much additional qualification of the service is required and useful. Different organizational units have started discussions about common QA and testing practices in the context of BbS. Furthermore, BSea's mapping of DLT characteristic building blocks to the ISO 25010 characteristics is perceived as highly valuable to position DLT-specific QA and testing activities in the organization's QA portfolio.

The presented approach is an instrument helping to pave the way to a systematic QA for blockchain-based products and services. It is neither a generic assessment model nor a QA standard for blockchain-based products and services.

Based on this, BSea's key contributions for practitioners are the following:

- An approach to evaluating existing DLT and blockchain implementation based on building blocks to suit to business demands
- An approach to refining business demands for the quality perspective to select an adequate DLT for implementation
- An evidence that the evolving area around DLT needs continuous observation to update the organization's quality model to be adequate for BbS

Our work provides the following essential research contributions:

- The consolidation of existing work related to DLT and quality models
- A DLT-specific interpretation of the ISO 25010
- A quality guidance framework for DLT that is aligned with the ISO 25010
- The development of an approach (BSea) to apply the quality guidance framework in practice
- A demonstration and evaluation of BSea application in a large industrial setting

### 8.4.2   Limitations

As the DLTs keep evolving rapidly, the proposed guidance framework requires continuous observation of both DLT science and practice in order to align the BSea artifacts with the state of the art which is evolving over time. Furthermore, we evaluated BSea only in the context of the Volkswagen Group so far. Although the BSea artifacts are in no way focused on a particular company or industry sector, this might limit the universal validity of our evaluations. Apart from this, we did not validate all the existing DLTs in our evaluation context.

## 8.5   Conclusions

We proposed a systematic guidance framework for selecting DLTs that are suitable for particular product and service development contexts, as well as for identifying induced requirements for QA and testing. To render this generic framework practicable, we developed the BSea approach that translates the generic framework into questionnaires that guide development teams. We presented and discussed selected particular industrial use cases and evaluated this approach in several departments of the Volkswagen Group.

Our future research and development scope related to BSea will be to extend the questionnaire to address more blockchain approaches and in an even better understandable form. Furthermore, an investigation about typical patterns on blockchain safeguarding will be conducted by collecting results of a wider range of product evaluations based on the structured BSea questionnaires. We also plan investigating metrics for key performance indicators (KPI) related to the effectivity of BSea in different application contexts, in order to foster target-oriented evaluation and improvement.

**Acknowledgments**   We thank Mario Pukall and Yannik Zuehlke for their rich and vital contributions to this article.

## References

1. Mandolla, C., Petruzzelli, A. M., Percoco, G., & Urbinati, A. (2019). Building a digital twin for additive manufacturing through the exploitation of blockchain: A case analysis of the aircraft industry. *Computers in Industry, 109*, 134–152. https://doi.org/10.1016/j.compind.2019.04.011
2. Wang, B., Luo, W., Zhang, A., Tian, Z., & Li, Z. (2020). Blockchain-enabled circular supply chain management: A system architecture for fast fashion. *Computers in Industry, 123*, 103324. https://doi.org/10.1016/j.compind.2020.103324
3. Mattila, J., Seppälä, T., Valkama, P., Hukkinen, T., Främling, K., & Holmström, J. (2021). Blockchain-based deployment of product-centric information systems. *Computers in Industry*, 125. https://doi.org/10.1016/j.compind.2020.103342

4. Bodkhe, U., Tanwar, S., Parekh, K., Khanpara, P., Tyagi, S., Kumar, N., & Alazab, M. (2020). Blockchain for Industry 4.0: A comprehensive review. *IEEE Access, 8*, 79764–79800. https://doi.org/10.1109/ACCESS.2020.2988579
5. Karinsalo, A., & Halunen, K. (2018). Smart contracts for a mobility-as-a-service ecosystem. In *Proceedings – 2018 IEEE 18th International Conference on Software Quality, Reliability, and Security Companion, QRS-C 2018* (pp. 135–138). Institute of Electrical and Electronics Engineers. https://doi.org/10.1109/QRS-C.2018.00036
6. Farshidi, S., Jansen, S., Espana, S., & Verkleij, J. (2020). Decision support for blockchain platform selection: Three industry case studies. *IEEE Transactions on Engineering Management, 67*(4), 1109–1128. https://doi.org/10.1109/TEM.2019.2956897
7. Precht, H., Wunderlich, S., & Gomez, J. M. (2020). Applying software quality criteria to blockchain applications: A criteria. In *Proceedings of the 53rd Hawaii International Conference on System Sciences*; Hawaii International Conference on System Sciences 2020 (pp. 6287–6296).
8. Koens, T., & Poll, E. What blockchain alternative do you need?
9. Scriber, B. A. FEATURE: SOFTWARE ARCHITECTURE. A framework for determining blockchain applicability.
10. Wessling, F., Ehmke, C., Hesenius, M., & Gruhn, V. (2018). How much blockchain do you need?: Towards a concept for building hybrid DApp architectures. In *Proceedings – International Conference on Software Engineering* (pp. 44–47). IEEE Computer Society. https://doi.org/10.1145/3194113.3194121
11. Wust, K., & Gervais, A. (2018). Do you need a blockchain? In *Proceedings – 2018 Crypto Valley Conference on Blockchain Technology, CVCBT 2018* (pp. 45–54). Institute of Electrical and Electronics Engineers. https://doi.org/10.1109/CVCBT.2018.00011
12. Xu, X., Weber, I., Staples, M., Zhu, L., Bosch, J., Bass, L., Pautasso, C., & Rimba, P. (2017). A taxonomy of blockchain-based systems for architecture design. In *Proceedings – 2017 IEEE International Conference on Software Architecture, ICSA 2017* (pp. 243–252). Institute of Electrical and Electronics Engineers. https://doi.org/10.1109/ICSA.2017.33
13. Smith, T. D. (2017). The blockchain litmus test. In J.-Y. Nie (Ed.), *IEEE International Conference on Big Data: proceedings : Dec 11–14, Boston, MA* (pp. 2299–2308). IEEE Computer Society.
14. Kannengießer, N., Lins, S., Dehling, T., & Sunyaev, A. (2020). Trade-offs between distributed ledger technology characteristics. *ACM Computing Surveys, 53*(2). https://doi.org/10.1145/3379463
15. Porru, S., Pinna, A., Marchesi, M., & Tonelli, R. (2017). Blockchain-oriented software engineering: Challenges and new directions. In *Proceedings – 2017 IEEE/ACM 39th International Conference on Software Engineering Companion, ICSE-C 2017* (pp. 169–171). Institute of Electrical and Electronics Engineers. https://doi.org/10.1109/ICSE-C.2017.142
16. Wang, S., Ouyang, L., Yuan, Y., Ni, X., Han, X., & Wang, F. Y. (2019). Blockchain-enabled smart contracts: Architecture, applications, and future trends. *IEEE Transactions on Systems, Man, and Cybernetics: Systems, 49*(11), 2266–2277. https://doi.org/10.1109/TSMC.2019.2895123
17. Lu, Q., Xu, X., Liu, Y., & Zhang, W. (2019). Design pattern as a service for blockchain applications. In *IEEE International Conference on Data Mining Workshops, ICDMW* (Vol. 2018-November, pp. 128–135). IEEE Computer Society. https://doi.org/10.1109/ICDMW.2018.00025
18. Koteska, B., Karafiloski, E., Mishev, A., & Cyril, U. S. *Blockchain implementation quality challenges: A literature review*. http://ceur-ws.org
19. Ortu, M., Orru, M., & Destefanis, G. (2019). On comparing software quality metrics of traditional vs blockchain-oriented software: An empirical study. In *IWBOSE 2019 – 2019 IEEE 2nd International Workshop on Blockchain Oriented Software Engineering* (pp. 32–37). Institute of Electrical and Electronics Engineers. https://doi.org/10.1109/IWBOSE.2019.8666575
20. Anjum, A., Sporny, M., & Sill, A. (2017). Blockchain standards for compliance and trust. *IEEE Cloud Computing, 4*(4), 84–90.

21. Centobelli, P., Cerchione, R., Esposito, E., & Oropallo, E. (2021). Surfing blockchain wave, or drowning? Shaping the future of distributed ledgers and decentralized technologies. *Technological Forecasting and Social Change, 165*, 120463. https://doi.org/10.1016/j.techfore.2020.120463
22. Koul, R. (2018). Blockchain oriented software testing – Challenges and approaches. In *3rd International Conference for Convergence in Technology (I2CT), Pune, India. Apr 06–08* (pp. 1–6). Siddhant College of Engineering Institute of Electrical and Electronics Engineers. Bombay Section. Institute of Electrical and Electronics Engineers.
23. Wang, X., Lo, D., & Shihab, E. (2019). Towards generating cost-effective test-suite for Ethereum smart contract. In *SANER '19: Proceedings of the 2019 IEEE 26th International Conference on Software Analysis, Evolution, and Reengineering, Hangzhou, China, February 24–27* (pp. 549–553). IEEE Computer Society.
24. Liao, C. F., Cheng, C. J., Chen, K., Lai, C. H., Chiu, T., & Wu-Lee, C. (2017). Toward a service platform for developing smart contracts on blockchain in BDD and TDD styles. In *Proceedings - 2017 IEEE 10th International Conference on Service-Oriented Computing and Applications, SOCA 2017* (Vol. 2017-January, pp. 133–140). Institute of Electrical and Electronics Engineers. https://doi.org/10.1109/SOCA.2017.26
25. Destefanis, G., Marchesi, M., Ortu, M., Tonelli, R., Bracciali, A., & Hierons, R. (2018). Smart contracts vulnerabilities: A call for blockchain software engineering? In *2018 IEEE 1st International Workshop on Blockchain Oriented Software Engineering, IWBOSE 2018 – Proceedings* (Vol. 2018-January, pp. 19–25). Institute of Electrical and Electronics Engineers. https://doi.org/10.1109/IWBOSE.2018.8327567
26. Zhou, E., Hua, S., Pi, B., Sun, J., Nomura, Y., Yamashita, K., & Kurihara, H. (2018). Security assurance for smart contract. In *2018 9th IFIP International Conference on New Technologies, Mobility and Security, NTMS 2018 - Proceedings* (Vol. 2018-January, pp. 1–5). Institute of Electrical and Electronics Engineers. https://doi.org/10.1109/NTMS.2018.8328743
27. Keenan, T. P. (2018). Alice in blockchains: Surprising security pitfalls in pow and pos blockchain systems. In *Proceedings - 2017 15th Annual Conference on Privacy, Security and Trust, PST 2017* (pp. 400–402). Institute of Electrical and Electronics Engineers. https://doi.org/10.1109/PST.2017.00057
28. Kroll, J. A., Davey, I. C., & Felten, E. W. (2013). The economics of bitcoin mining, or bitcoin in the presence of adversaries. In *The Twelfth Workshop on the Economics of Information Security (WEIS 2013) Washington, DC* (pp. 1–21).
29. Zhang, R., Xue, R., & Liu, L. (2019). Security and privacy on blockchain. *ACM Computing Surveys, 52*(3). https://doi.org/10.1145/3316481
30. Weber, I., Gramoli, V., Ponomarev, A., Staples, M., Holz, R., Tran, A. B., & Rimba, P. (2017). On availability for blockchain-based systems. In *Proceedings of the IEEE Symposium on Reliable Distributed Systems* (Vol. 2017-September, pp. 64–73). IEEE Computer Society. https://doi.org/10.1109/SRDS.2017.15
31. Fan, C., Ghaemi, S., Khazaei, H., & Musilek, P. (2020). Performance evaluation of blockchain systems: A systematic survey. In *IEEE Access* (pp. 126927–126950). Institute of Electrical and Electronics Engineers. https://doi.org/10.1109/ACCESS.2020.3006078.
32. Thomas, O., & Rose, T. (2020). From a use case categorization scheme towards a maturity model for engineering distributed ledgers. In T. Horst & T. Clohessy (Eds.), *Blockchain and distributed ledger technology use cases: Applications and lessons learned* (pp. 33–50). Springer International. https://doi.org/10.1007/978-3-030-44337-5_2
33. Wickboldt, C., & Kliewer, N. (2019). BLOCKCHAIN FOR WORKSHOP EVENT CERTIFICATES-A PROOF OF CONCEPT IN THE AVIATION INDUSTRY. In *Twenty-Seventh European Conference on Information Systems (ECIS2019); Stockholm-Uppsala, Sweden.*
34. Singla, A., & Bertino, E. (2018). Blockchain-based PKI solutions for IoT. In *Proceedings - 4th IEEE International Conference on Collaboration and Internet Computing, CIC 2018* (pp. 9–15). Institute of Electrical and Electronics Engineers. https://doi.org/10.1109/CIC.2018.00-45

35. Yang, C., Chen, X., & Xiang, Y. (2018). Blockchain-based publicly verifiable data deletion scheme for cloud storage. *Journal of Network and Computer Applications, 103*, 185–193. https://doi.org/10.1016/j.jnca.2017.11.011
36. Dorsala, M. R., Sastry, V. N., & Chapram, S. (2018). Fair protocols for verifiable computations using bitcoin and ethereum. In *IEEE International Conference on Cloud Computing, CLOUD* (Vol. 2018-July, pp. 786–793). IEEE Computer Society. https://doi.org/10.1109/CLOUD.2018.00107
37. Reijers, W., O'brolcháin, F., & Haynes, P. (2016). Governance in blockchain technologies & social contract theories. *LEDGER, 1*, 134–151. https://doi.org/10.5915/LEDGER.2016.62
38. Zachariadis, M., Hileman, G., & Scott, S. V. (2019). Governance and control in distributed ledgers: Understanding the challenges facing blockchain technology in financial services. *Information and Organization, 29*(2), 105–117. https://doi.org/10.1016/j.infoandorg.2019.03.001
39. Bhushan, B., Sinha, P., & Sagayam, K. M. (2020). Untangling blockchain technology: A survey on state of the art, security threats, privacy services, applications and future research directions. *Computers and Electrical Engineering.* https://doi.org/10.1016/j.compeleceng.2020.106897
40. Bordel, B., Alcarria, R., & Robles, T. (2021). Denial of chain: Evaluation and prediction of a novel cyberattack in blockchain-supported systems. *Future Generation Computer Systems, 116*, 426–439. https://doi.org/10.1016/j.future.2020.11.013
41. de Filippi, P., Mannan, M., & Reijers, W. (2020). Blockchain as a confidence machine: The problem of trust & challenges of governance. *Technology in Society, 62.* https://doi.org/10.1016/j.techsoc.2020.101284
42. Bagaria, V., Kannan, S., Tse, D., Fanti, G., & Viswanath, P. (2019). PrisM: Deconstructing the blockchain to approach physical limits. In *Proceedings of the ACM Conference on Computer and Communications Security; Association for Computing Machinery* (pp. 585–602). https://doi.org/10.1145/3319535.3363213
43. Ammous, S. (2016). *Blockchain technology: What is it good for?*
44. Rehman, M. H. U., Salah, K., Damiani, E., & Svetinovic, D. (2020). Trust in blockchain cryptocurrency ecosystem. *IEEE Transactions on Engineering Management, 67*(4), 1196–1212. https://doi.org/10.1109/TEM.2019.2948861
45. Hazari, S. S., & Mahmoud, Q. H. (2019). A parallel proof of work to improve transaction speed and scalability in blockchain systems. In *2019 IEEE 9th Annual Computing and Communication Workshop and Conference, CCWC 2019* (pp. 916–921). Institute of Electrical and Electronics Engineers. https://doi.org/10.1109/CCWC.2019.8666535
46. Walker, M. A., Schmidt, D. C., & Dubey, A. *Testing at scale of IoT blockchain applications.*
47. Scherer, M. (2017). *Performance and scalability of blockchain networks and smart contracts.*
48. Poth, A., & Riel, A. (2020). Quality requirements elicitation by ideation of product quality risks with design thinking. In *Proceedings of the IEEE International Conference on Requirements Engineering* (Vol. 2020-August, pp. 238–249). IEEE Computer Society. https://doi.org/10.1109/RE48521.2020.00034.
49. Vukolić, M. (2016). The quest for scalable blockchain fabric: Proof-of-work vs. BFT replication. In C. Jan & D. Kesdoğan (Eds.), *Open Problems in Network Security* (pp. 112–125). Springer International Publishing.
50. Singh, A., Click, K., Parizi, R. M., Zhang, Q., Dehghantanha, A., & Choo, K. K. R. (2020). Sidechain technologies in blockchain networks: An examination and state-of-the-art review. *Journal of Network and Computer Applications*, 102471. https://doi.org/10.1016/j.jnca.2019.102471
51. Dziembowski, S., Eckey, L., Faust, S., Hesse, J., & Hostakova, K. (2019). Multi-party virtual state channels. In Y. Ishai & V. Rijmen (Eds.), *Advances in cryptology – EUROCRYPT 2019; Lecture Notes in Computer Science* (Vol. 11476, pp. 625–656). Springer International. https://doi.org/10.1007/978-3-030-17653-2

52. Singh, K., Singh, N., & Kushwaha, D. S. (2018). An interoperable and secure E-wallet architecture based on digital ledger technology using blockchain. In *2018 International Conference on Computing, Power and Communication Technologies (GUCON)* (pp. 165–169). https://doi.org/10.1109/GUCON.2018.8674919

53. Till, N., & Hartenstein, H. (2019). Short paper: An empirical analysis of blockchain forks in bitcoin. In G. Ian & T. Moore (Eds.), *Financial cryptography and data security* (pp. 84–92). Springer International.

54. Biais, B., Bisière, C., Bouvard, M., & Casamatta, C. (2019). The blockchain folk theorem. *Review of Financial Studies, 32*(5), 1662–1715. https://doi.org/10.1093/rfs/hhy095

55. Poth, A., Kottke, M., & Riel, A. (2020). The implementation of a digital service approach to fostering team autonomy, distant collaboration, and knowledge scaling in large enterprises. *Human Systems Management, 39*, 573–588. https://doi.org/10.3233/HSM-201049

56. Poth, A., & Heimann, C. (2018). How to innovate software quality assurance and testing in large enterprises? In L. Xabier & I. Santamaria (Eds.), *Systems, software and services process improvement* (pp. 437–442). Springer International.

# Chapter 9
# Make Product and Service Requirements Shippable: From the Cloud Service Vision to a Continuous Value Stream Which Satisfies Current and Future User Needs

**Alexander Poth** (iD)**, Holger Urban, and Andreas Riel**

**Abstract** A cloud service is typically evolved over time to address the growing and changing user group. Furthermore, the used cloud technology itself is evolving and requires continuous adaption of the cloud service to ensure a state-of-the-art service delivery. To develop and deliver the cloud service aligned with these demands, a life-cycle view is useful to focus the relevant service requirements such as functionality, availability, security, etc. for each life-cycle phase adequately. This chapter proposes a life-cycle phase approach to address these requirements. The proposed topics of each life-cycle phase are discussed on a real service instantiation to give practical advices and insights about the application in an enterprise context.

**Keywords** Cloud services · Value stream · Value delivery · Requirements management

## 9.1 Introduction

Any established enterprise comes with an IT in place to run their business. Over years, complex IT systems have been built and consolidated to support specific business processes and services. However, new trends like the cloud technology are

A. Poth (✉) · H. Urban
Volkswagen AG, Wolfsburg, Germany
e-mail: alexander.poth@volkswagen.de; holger.urban@volkswagen.de

A. Riel
G-SCOP Laboratory, Grenoble INP - Université Grenoble Alpes, Grenoble, France
e-mail: andreas.riel@grenoble-inp.fr

© The Author(s), under exclusive license to Springer Nature
Switzerland AG 2025
Y. Hajizadeh et al. (eds.), *Building Cloud Software Products*,
Innovation, Technology, and Knowledge Management,
https://doi.org/10.1007/978-3-031-92184-1_9

adopted into this existing IT landscape. New technologies are a chance to build and deliver new services and capabilities more efficiently by offering improvements for existing parts of the IT landscape, too. This setting leads to an approach called hybrid cloud for at least one phase of the cloud technology adoption process. A hybrid cloud "consists of multiple internal or external providers" [1] to offer services to the customers and users. This hybrid cloud phase typically starts with the buildup of an internal private cloud on the existing company data centers. Step by step, the cloud adoption enables the enterprise the usage of public cloud providers. They can offer services cheaper at scale. However, this leads not by default to the consolidation of one public cloud solution, because many public hyperscalers are integrated into the IT of the enterprise. The phase of hybrid cloud is prolonged significantly as long as the IT strategy does not limit the number of cloud providers to one.

This fact leads to the development of cloud-native enterprise solutions with focus on cloud agnostic. Cloud agnostic ensures portability of enterprise service between different cloud providers. This gives the flexibility to run, for example, on the most economical cloud provider fulfilling the enterprise service requirements. Enterprise service portability is the key quality characteristic [2] to reach this degree of freedom and has to be designed into the service. Cloud native is defined in the service context as operating globally, as well as in a scalable, fault-tolerant, continuously updatable, and secure way by design [3]. It uses as many "benefits" of the underlying cloud capabilities as possible to be fast and cost-efficient. Depending on which capabilities are used, this can lead to a vendor lock-in to the cloud provider which limits the portability significantly. However, the Cloud Native Computing Foundation [4] as part of the Linux Foundation addresses this aspect by providing a generic solution that is deployable on almost all cloud platforms. Depending on the providers, they offer managed service for them. But there are trade-offs which have to be balanced to stay cloud native and agnostic.

This portability requirement is an example for requirements decisions early in the product life-cycle. In an enterprise context, however, the cloud service evolves over time, and this leads to new requirements and changing priorities for existing demands of service capabilities. The life-cycle starts in the seed phase with ideation about the service and the right starting capability. In the first productive phase, a small group of users consumes the service. Then the scaling to different customer and user groups such as brands and legal entities is realized. To serve this, scaling partnerships are established; a completive pricing model is developed. Then a professionalization phase follows that is characterized by the design and offer of trainings with training partners, as well as the pressure to ensure continuous innovation while assuring the quality-of-service delivery. This complex life-cycle journey demands a virtual service team. Furthermore, the development moves to a developer community in which various experts from different legal entities work together to address domain-specific requirements.

This cooperation approach around the service development and delivery within a large enterprise shows that requirements will be raised from internal stakeholders of the service team, the contributors, the partners, the customers (paying), and the users (consuming). Furthermore, the enterprise compliance comes more and more into focus with, for example, privacy regulations (like GDPR), security (like ISO 27001 audits), and tax aspects (like profit shifting in virtual teams based on representatives of different legal entities). To handle all these stakeholders and their requirements, a systematic quality management is needed for the product itself, the services around the product, as well as the procedures and organization allowing to realize these deliveries.

This chapter addresses the complex cloud service life-cycle in an enterprise context and gives an example of the service TaaS (Testing-as-a-Service, [5]) of the Volkswagen Group IT Cloud (GITC) program [6]. TaaS is a scalable test-runtime execution (T-Rex) for functional and nonfunctional testing. The users (developers, testers, etc.) can focus on writing the business relevant tests for safeguarding their IT systems. For each life-cycle phase, the view of the product owner, respectively, the product manager and sponsor from seed to scaling is presented by the authors.

## 9.2   Enterprise Setting and the Hybrid Cloud Strategy

In the past larger companies' heterogeneous IT platforms included specialized hardware, often with long procurement cycles, and required significant manual work to provision new resources. Furthermore, based on our experiences expensive storage solutions were being consumed by applications that doubled in their capacity requirements every 2 years.

Specifically, the infrastructure team needed to unify and automate work streams and platforms across the entire enterprise. New standardized infrastructure was needed to replace existing developer systems yet still connect to legacy applications that maintain important data.

New systems needed to support agile software development as well as website traffic spikes. The search for a new IT platform would kick off a new era for larger enterprises. In early 2015, we started to identify the next-generation infrastructure that would meet all needs in an efficient system that supported speed and innovation.

Furthermore, public cloud options were limited as Germany has some of the strictest information privacy laws, and data residency policies vary greatly across the world. For this reason, it was not uncommon for a first experience to have a private cloud.

To expedite innovative new services, the Volkswagen Group IT needed to reduce the time to provision platform resources from months to hours.

We evaluated proprietary solutions but felt open-source cloud platforms could more quickly incorporate new technologies with their fast innovation cycles. This naturally led to evaluating OpenStack, the leading open-source private cloud platform in 2015.

In mid-2016, we set a milestone by adding the Cloud Foundry Platform-as-a-Service (PaaS) solution to our private cloud. This environment included new CI/CD tool chains that further speeded up development release cycles and improved application quality.

The private cloud was only the first step, of course, and so other public cloud providers were integrated into the company's hybrid cloud portfolio.

The biggest challenge was not which cloud provider delivers the best service, but rather the issue of connectivity to the legacy world. Most of the legacy systems still provide the company-critical data. The main question always is: Is the data being brought to the service or vice versa?

## 9.3 Aspects for Changing and Adopting Requirements

An enterprise product or service offer contains different artifacts based on a complex set of requirements. The current and future demands by customers or users have an impact on three dimensions:

- The *product* or service itself including the associated services enabling a more valuable and convenience usage like trainings, customer-specific adaptation/ integration consulting, and specific coaching.
- The *procedures* to build and serve the deliveries which include core aspects like the automated software delivery pipeline and more indirect processes to ensure the systematic updates of curriculum-based trainings to keep them aligned with the core product or service.
- The *team* developing and delivering the product and services to enhance and develop their skills and technology knowledge to be able to deliver state-of-the-art upcoming releases.

To address these three dimensions adequately, each can be refined into key aspects which have to be handled during the entire product or service life-cycle. The delivered product is a composition of three key aspects:

- Functionality: this is the "face to the user." The part of the product which has to satisfy needs in a comfortable way. However, the users' expectations evolve over time [7]. The functionality requirements of different user groups need to be balanced with the fit of product strategy to avoid contrary enhancement activities.
- Technology: especially in cloud technology with its ongoing transformative effects [8], new and emerging technologies evolve fast [9]. These new options are influencing the existing integrated technologies and open new opportunities for product development. However, it is difficult to select the right options—unforeseen innovations or mergers/acquisitions can impact the product technology stack and enforce significant refactoring efforts.
- Components: the system behind the product is an integration of different components and views [10] which have to be balanced and are leading to requirements during the life-cycle. Cloud agnostic as a strategic goal adds some components, which comes with additional complexity in comparison to cloud-native approaches with cloud vendor lock-in. To manage this, a rigorous architecture of the system components is needed.

These aspects help to deliver a highly available product which can easily be integrated and used by customers and users. The term customer is used as a synonym for user in this article where no differentiation is needed.

The development and service procedures are a composition of four key aspects:

- Agile and lean: the principles of agile and lean supporting fast time to market (TTM) with quick and nimble adaptation to changes [11] have become a necessity for enterprises' [12] action in dynamic markets and technologies. To establish and improve these capabilities is a core objective pursued by building and optimizing procedures and processes.
- Quality: procedures establishing good and best practices. This supports the delivery of every release with the same quality level. Quality addresses the product and its services around, the procedures building and delivering these outcomes and the teamwork quality [13] to enable the "workforce" behind the scene to perform. A holistic quality approach addresses these three pillars to ensure development in an emerging setting.
- Performance: to deliver efficient, and on a high performance level, stable procedures are the base for automation and performance optimization [14]. In a life-cycle view the automation of stable procedures is a strategic investment into faster deliveries.
- Compliance: to ensure compliance to regulations and standards checks and evidences are needed [15]. The deterministic behavior of procedures is an anchor for compliance artifacts and controls [16].

These four aspects are usually addressed in the continuous integration and delivery (CI/CD) chain of the cloud service. Depending on the domain-specific compliance requirements, continuous delivery of deployment is possible [17]. During implementation of CI/CD procedures, quality is a key aspect for sustainable delivery performance [18]. To ensure deterministic quality, a step-by-step automation of value streams is [19] a way to push quality and efficiency. A modular CI/CD chain based on individual pipelines for the different quality, compliance, etc. tasks are the base to adopt the delivery over the different service life-cycle phases. This modular approach makes it easy to change the build and delivery procedure.

The DevOps-delivery team faces more and more responsibility with the evolving service and growing customer and user community. Furthermore, the team grows, too—this implies requirements for new working methods and approaches to ensure high-quality deliveries [20]. Furthermore, each phase has to establish an adequate way to ensure continuous innovation of the product itself, all corresponding services [21], and the needed competencies [22].

Depending on the domain of the product or services around the product itself, this is a faster or slower changing environment which has to be addressed continuously in time and appropriately with evolving requirements which have to be implemented and delivered.

To show all these aspects, the chapter is structured into phases of the life-cycle and deals with the most relevant aspects in this context.

## 9.4    Seed Phase: Product Vision

The seed phase is defined as the time between the idea and the commitment to finance the product to the delivery phases. This enterprise view may differ from typical start-up seed investments [23]. If enterprise-internal investors are committed to a venture, they typically aim for a strategic partnership for a longer period because the role seed venture capitalist does not exist in established enterprises. The product vision has to fit with one or many of the investors' strategic goals (such objectives of an internal program), and a win-win situation is the base for the partnership. This is a crucial point because many enterprise procedures such as the project financing decisions have not been designed to support this kind of "start-up" thinking—a good idea, vision, and business case are not sufficient to survive the typically rigorous enterprise finance-controlling flow. Furthermore, a challenge in enterprises is to get funding from the different stakeholders—think about this analogy: nobody will pay for the construction of a whole pool in order to have a bath once in a while. This makes it difficult to find sponsoring in cross-domain projects and products for early phases if there is no immediately observable benefit. Waiting is a valid option for stakeholders while others make the first high-risk steps.

From the requirements perspective, in this phase everything is about generic nonfunctional requirements which have to be transformed into the product vision and abstract requirements like epics in agile wording [24] (Table 9.1). Then the initial product capability is selected and refined. Based on the product vision and the starting capability, the potential seed sponsors have to be identified. With the commitment of the seed sponsor, the resources for a proof of concept will be committed. With this, some additional requirements will be "set" to ensure alignment with the program context of the sponsor. This is the trigger to build a team of "movers and shakers" to start working on the realization of the product vision. The team starts to work on crucial aspects to mitigate risks early with some proof of concepts. These learnings and insights are used to derive the basic product architecture, technology selections, and the product roadmap. Furthermore, the teams have to understand that users and customers are not the same. In an enterprise, pilot users often do not pay because the commercialization of the service needs time. This "free lunch" helps to iterate and learn about the product and the demands, but does not guarantee that a market will open up (keep in mind: a (cloud) product/service has a market and technology risk). Table 9.1 shows the key aspects of this phase.

To instantiate this phase, the birth of TaaS is presented as an example. In summer 2016, the idea was born to establish cloud technology based on testing to scale and accelerate safeguarding of IT systems within the Volkswagen Group IT. This was in the test and quality assurance (TQA) competence center. After some iterations and refinement of the idea, the sponsoring and context to include the idea was the next big step. As an interesting anchor the running Group IT Cloud (GITC) program with the OpenStack private cloud [26] was identified. The "buy-in" argument was developed: if a private cloud was set up, we would need something cloud native to test all the new cloud services and apps adequately—otherwise we lose speed and opportunities generated by the private cloud approach. The buy-in commitment convinced

**Table 9.1** Key aspects to derive and refine requirements in the seed phase

| Context | Aspect | Description |
|---|---|---|
| Product | Vision | • Have a clear direction for the future development<br>• Establish a way to make implementation options visible, guide decisions, and make progress transparent |
| | Architecture (components and system view) | • Decide whether to use building blocks like FOSS (free and open-source software)<br>• Define the system and software architecture concept like microservices<br>• Select characteristics like cloud agnostic and cloud native<br>• Balance the trade-offs like speed vs. portability<br>• Define derived requirements like the integration with event bus or direct communication |
| | Technology | • Decide level of maturity (how much "beta" is accepted)<br>• Define technology selection approach/guideline<br>• Select technologies suited to the requirements |
| | Capabilities (functional) | • Decide the starting capability of the product<br>• Refine the core features of the capability |
| Procedures | Delivery | • Establish component/module responsibility to ensure delivery<br>• Establish integration responsibility for "delivery owner" |
| | Improvement | • Be aware of the product quality risks (every chance comes with risks) by using approaches like PQR [25]<br>• Build user feedback procedure as early as possible<br>• Interpret bugs and ops issues as feedback and solve them quickly to avoid technical debts |
| Team/orga | Delivery | • Establish communication about "issues" to fix them together<br>• Establish peers and other expert coupling to find good solutions fast |
| | Learning | • Offer time-boxes to evaluate new ideas and approaches<br>• Establish cyclic reflection within the team |

and a set of requirements was inherited from the GITC program and adopted to TaaS. Some example requirements are to be cloud agnostic because in the future hybrid cloud will become more relevant and to be cloud native where possible the service has to be API-based (for easy CI/CD-chain integration) and to be designed "enterprise IT ready."

Based on this setting, the product vision was instantiated into the context of the GITC program. As a first capability of TaaS, the test of load and performance was selected to ensure that the new GITC services and apps were able to scale in a cloud fashion as expected. To answer some technology questions and demonstrate that the vision was realistic, a proof of concept was defined in September 2016 for the internal cloud conference in December of the same year. This conference demonstration was the ticket for sponsoring the next phase. The team decided to develop TaaS based on free and open-source software (FOSS) to build on established and reliable components and ensure the unlimited scaling of the service (i.e., without license limit issues). This decision defined the open-source testing tools as "building blocks." To address the requirements, the idea was to use JMeter [27] with its cluster capability as proof of concept. Furthermore, it was an established testing tool with a high amount of available skilled testers on the market to ensure "customer acceptance." As all in the team were aware that more capabilities were needed in the future such as multi-browser testing and mobile app testing, an extendable microservice architecture was used. As technology to ensure efficient scaling of TaaS as orchestrator, the new technology Kubernetes [28] in combination with the Docker container [29] approach was selected.

To stay on the right track as a team, the product vision was extended with the product vision board. The board established the following attributes: topic, added value, potential of TaaS, feasibility of optimizations, prioritization, and actions. Examples for topics are speed for test execution (minimization), functionality (demand coverage), and costs (benchmark with market). Topics were rated according to added value, potential of TaaS (against status-quo implementation), and feasibility of optimization. Based on the rating, the prioritization led to the implementation of the ideated actions. The motto of the team established in this phase was to work more feedback-driven than specification-driven. However, in this early stage, the team was about to get an idea of the inherent product quality risks. This idea can be systematically elaborated with the product quality risk (PQR) approach. The design thinking-driven approach helps to address quality aspects during product and service design. The initial PQR workshop took place in the first service architecture and design iteration. This was linked to the proof-of-concept phase of the service idea. This early quality risk identification is a chance to mitigate as much as possible of the quality risks with constructive quality actions. Furthermore, the identified quality risks can be reflected during the implementation of the related functions to realize adequate mitigation actions in an effective and efficient way. To interact, the team established refinement sessions for product requirements (stories) and show-and-tell sessions to check the current state of the product (to start ideating). For the teamwork, daily stand-ups and team retrospectives had already been established habits. The team therefore started in a Scrum-oriented sprint mode to meet the deadline of the cloud conference.

## 9.5   Start Deliver Phase: First Customer Project and Users

This phase is defined as the time span in which the product delivery is realized on one particular site to serve the users and customers. Furthermore, the focus is on fast functional and feature development to enrich the customer value. From the functional point of view, this phase establishes a flow from abstract epics to stories via capabilities and features, as well as tasks for implementation to ensure continuous value delivery. From the architecture and system's point of view, a refinement and evolvement are needed to establish a procedure for systematic refactoring in order to ensure a clear and rigorous mapping of the functionality of the product. The technology stack needs to be made transparent, e.g., with a software bill of materials (SBoM). This is also usable to continuously check the consistency and capability of FOSS licenses. For a continuous delivery flow of service-related innovations, a procedure based on ideation is needed. The refinement of the ideas is realized in time-boxed investigation and experimentation. The experimentation sometimes is rather an investigation if existing solutions and building blocks fit into the system and therefore sometimes a "hackspace" to validate assumptions. Then, in the team refinement, the most valuable option is selected for implementation. Where feasible the customer is integrated as early as possible for incremental development of the feature by the feedback. This setting leads to a shipping team with a focus on fast and stable delivery of customer value while remaining open for new ideas and innovations for product evolvement. Table 9.2 shows the key aspects of this phase.

To illustrate this phase, the shipping of the above introduced TaaS is presented as a practical example. In 2017, the focus was to ship the first capability in a simple, lovable, and complete (SLC) product to the customers. This approach avoided the typical minimum viable products (MVP), which can cause a lot of frustration by users and customers because they may notice the missing parts. An enterprise typically does not have as many customers as on the "public market." Furthermore, users in an enterprise may know each other and exchange their experiences with consumed services. Therefore, one has to ensure that their experiences are positive from the very start. One increasingly important experience aspect is the user experience (UX) approach which is difficult to change if later on some fundamental aspects need a significant redesign. In the enterprise context, it is advisable to use an established UX approach based on components like the GroupUI [32] to avoid discussions and trade-off decisions in the team. To ensure a generic positive experience, an active product quality risk management, the PQR approach, is used and cyclically updated. The identified product-specific quality risks are integrated into the template for the Kanban board tickets. The ticket-specific reflection of the PQRs helps to set the small piece into the system context by making the particular risk contribution of a small feature (enhancement as requested on the ticket) transparent. Figure 9.1 shows an example how the PQR aspects are reflected in the context of stories. The story template includes the "PQR footer" to ensure that the PQRs are not forgotten during the refinement and planning. In the ticket refinement, the team can define adequate risk mitigation actions for the system change triggered by the ticket on each level and part of the system if needed. However, in "good" architectures the mitigation actions are typically localized closely to the ticket change/impact areas. Kanban was used for this phase, because it is flow-based to ensure continuous shipping of value. Furthermore, Kanban-professionalized quality workflows such as bugs are feedbacking from the productive stage and have to be documented as bug ticket and prioritized with the other backlog items or done on the fast lane in urgent cases. The overall objective is to fix bugs fast. To avoid bugs systematic testing is established. Beyond unit testing an integration and end-to-end testing

**Table 9.2** Key aspects to derive and refine requirements in the delivery phase

| Context | Aspect | Description |
|---------|--------|-------------|
| Product | Vision | • Ensure focus on the vision with the derived actions |
| | Architecture (components and system view) | • Establish transparency in architecture decisions to avoid later on time-consuming discussion<br>• Systematically identify technical debts and mitigate them to ensure speed and flexibility in the future, too |
| | Technology | • Build the technology stack for the product<br>• Manage the technology stack like the FOSS bill of materials (BoM) to ensure compatibility on all levels<br>• Start observing the market around the technology stack to optimize it |
| | Capabilities (functional) | • Decide the order of the next capabilities of the product<br>• Refine the core features of the upcoming capability |
| Procedures | Delivery | • Where needed and possible offer time-boxed experimentation to find the best solution<br>• Establish a flow with ideation, experimentation, and implementation which handles PQR systematically for each feature and capability<br>• Establish systematic automated testing by refining the trade-offs of fast fixing and proactive avoidance of bugs<br>• Establish an automated build and delivery chain |
| | Improvement | • Build new features with "potential users" where possible to ensure expectations are in line with demands<br>• Fix bugs with prioritization to minimize technical debts and establish a quality culture in the team by showing "quick and dirty" is not a sustainable work product<br>• Build user feedback opportunities like cyclic sounding boards for all users and customers |
| Team/orga | Delivery | • Focus on shipping quality by establishing customer contacts to "devs" to build a failure/bug-sensitive mindset<br>• Establish a devops culture [30] |
| | Learning | • Foster individuals and the team to "safe" time for reflection and looking "beyond" current issues and topics to be open for new and other ideas<br>• Change established procedures where needed in order to smoothly adapt to new situations—apply a transition kit approach [31] |

have to be set up. In the case of TaaS it is easy to use TaaS to test new version of TaaS (and it has the "eat your own dog food" effect). With the growing of the capabilities and features of TaaS, the self-test suite is growing. This test suite evolves over time to a perfect post-deployment self-test of all core capabilities and their features. Depending on the parameters of the self-tests, the test can be performed as a simple functional test or as a performance or load test for TaaS, too. In the first step the API is tested; in later steps one concentrates on the UI workflows of typical use cases. However, Kanban is compatible with the rituals of the seed phase, and the retrospective was adjusted to a monthly event because in Kanban there is no sprint-end to trigger a retrospective.

As a TaaS customers I need a scalable mobile app-testing environment for testing our users' viewports in a more holistic way.
Possible approach: For TaaS the existing selenium grid can be a base with an additional configuration for Appium.
AC:
- Appium is eligible as viewport engine for a test-configuration
- Customer's app is "uploadable" (or as reference to the repo)
- Emulation of "device" is configurable (at least a reference device as default is set in MVP) (user can upload their self-defined device config. file in SLC - see story 329)
- Android images are eligible (at least current version is set as default in MVP) (at least the last 3 vanilla versions are offered in SLC - see story 330)

PQR mapping to story

PQR:
Story has impact on following quality risks:
- result derivation "undetected" (mid – mitigation: test-job workload isolation by environment for stable "results")
- measurement failure frequency (high – new failure sources: device, image and apk – mitigation by cyclic test)
- incorrect test configuration (mid: high variability is risky for misconfigurations – mitigation with rigor UI guidance)
- insufficient cost efficiency (mid - same as other "viewport" emulators and additionally higher virtualization costs)

**Fig. 9.1** Example of a story with the reflection of the PQR in the specific functional context

## 9.6 Scale Phase: More Sites and User Demands

This phase is defined by rolling out the service to multiple sites to serve different demand types of customers in the right place. Furthermore, the functionality evolves with new capabilities and features. At the latest, it is time to ensure alignment with regulatory requirements to enable a compliant service delivery. Compliance is relevant not only for components, since the entire system has to be aligned with the domain-specific compliance requirements. The compliance involves, for example, IT security standards like the ISO 27000 series. The ISO 27000 standard is used to establish an information security management system (ISMS) in an organization or the entire enterprise. One benefit of an organizational-wide implemented standard—in this case the outcome is the ISMS—is that not every project or product/service of this organization has to be validated for standard compliance by the audit. Only a selection of representative samples are proofed by the auditors with a deep dive—this reduces efforts and costs. Furthermore, the privacy approach of the product and service has to be updated to ensure that the scaling aspects are compliant, too. The compliance validation at this point is important because at least now "the pet becomes a cattle." A single local compliance issue can become a global topic after scaling. For example, a security issue or risk on the intranet is not the same as in a multi-deployment environment on the Internet. This leads to a prioritization change because now the holistic system view with compliance demands can gain more "weight" than customer and user voice. To ensure continuous compliance, the build and delivery chain has to incorporate these aspects as quality checks. The value stream delivery from the infrastructure as code (IaC) to the application deployment ensures continuous delivery within the defined quality and compliance actions. One compliance quality action, for example, is to update the FOSS BoM for every release. This active update of the BoM is also an example for active technical debt management as quality requirement. It avoids and mitigates big refactoring and ensures continuous delivery speed in the future. From the process view, it is time to establish core service delivery measures like lead time and deployment frequency and have an eye on mean time to recover (MTTR) in the cases of operational issues and the change fail rate for deployments. The team mindset has to form a "continuous delivery team" with a focus on sustainable high-quality deliveries. Decide what kind of scaling approaches are useful. Not all sites have to be "self-hosted," because cooperations with other organizations or legal entities with more specific domain knowledge within their business in an enterprise setting are valid options to scale, too. Figure 9.2 shows a generic approach to scale in large enterprises.

This scaling phase is typically the time when initial funding is reduced and the product management has to adopt zero-based budgeting [33] for every new year. This is an important change for the entire product and service because billing and strategic monetarization become more important. But the profit/loss is not in balance yet—optimize and share costs in the first step. Hence, it is useful to establish additional partnerships within the enterprise based on the existing success and assets which can complement the potential partners' portfolio. The team has to learn that some big partners can help to scale and to (pre-)finance some activities. Furthermore, the team has to incorporate business aspect into their activities—scaling can leverage some costs, too. Table 9.3 shows the key aspects of this phase.

To instantiate this phase, the multi-site setup of TaaS is presented as an example. In 2018, the "initial sponsoring" ended by refocusing the cloud strategy. However, the demand to serve TaaS outside the private OpenStack cloud was still present. In 2018, this led to the roadmap to scale TaaS to two productive private and two public cloud sites/regions and establish high availability (HA) for the service delivery for all sites. To ensure the service in high quality for the customers, an ISO 27001 audit was planned and compliance according to the new European privacy regulation (GDPR) was initiated. Furthermore, an ISO 20000 alignment for the service

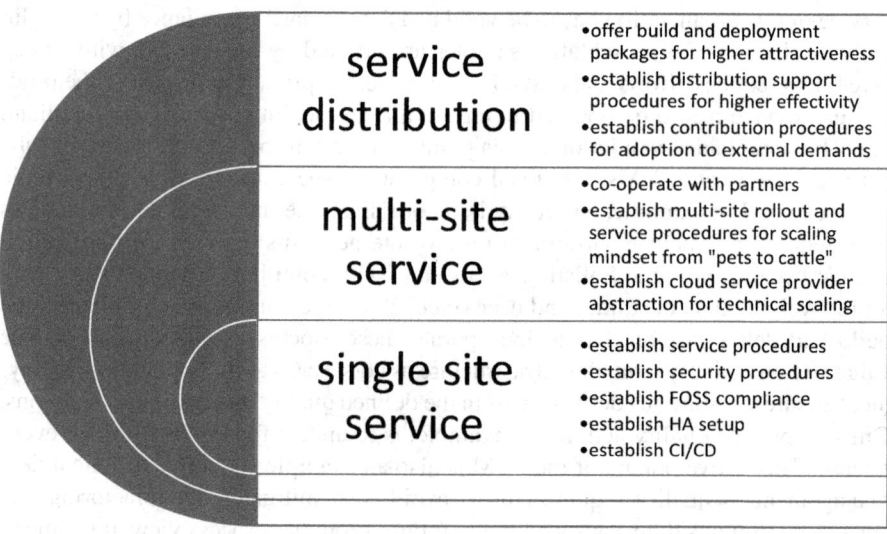

**Fig. 9.2** Schematic visualization of service scaling mindset

**Table 9.3** Key aspects to derive and refine requirements in the scale phase

| Context | Aspect | Description |
|---|---|---|
| Product | Vision | • Ensure focus on the vision with the derived actions |
| | Architecture (components and system view) | • Establish alignment on system level with standards like the ISO 27000<br>• Ensure that the architecture is ready for scaling on different cloud environments<br>• Establish at least all 24*7 relevant system components as high availability (HA) setup |
| | Technology | • Establish an infrastructure as code (IaC) blueprint for scaling facilitation of more sites<br>• Adjust technology stack to facilitate scaling |
| | Capabilities (functional) | • Decide the order of the next capabilities of the product to support the scaling<br>• Refine the core features of the upcoming capability |
| Procedures | Delivery | • Establish an automated delivery chain to serve all sites<br>• Establish rollout procedures |
| | Improvement | • Establish monitoring for the delivery to the sites<br>• Define KPIs for the product and service delivery |
| Team/orga | Delivery | • Partner with scaling and operation experts to facilitate and manage the new complexity dimension<br>• Incorporate the partner into the established devops culture |
| | Learning | • Foster mastery and autonomy of the team to facilitate scaling and distributed working |

operation based on the internal enterprise standards was demanded by a key customer program. To fulfill these process and governance requirements for all sites, the technology stack strategy was refined. The refinement addressed the cloud agnostic approach by avoiding resource allocation for establishing an abstraction layer for the specific cloud provider's API. The approach of Docker and Kubernetes was extended with the emerging Rancher 2.0 to handle the different cloud providers' specific API to scale the high volatile workload in the clusters up and down on demand. The high availability (HA) setup of all relevant service components was realized with the selected technology stack and the three availability zones of all sites. With the scaling, the procedures had to be adopted to ensure that the devops teams were not treating the deployment outcomes as "pets," but rather handled them as "cattle" [34]. For example, the procedures of feature delivery were optimized by a four-step bug template to ensure that not only symptoms were addressed but also root causes. The steps analyzing the root cause develop a solution, check operational effectiveness, and ensure sustainability of the provided solution. Furthermore, the system integration testing before the first production site deployment was extended and a post-deployment test suite established to ensure that the site ran as expected before rolling out a release to the next site. This approach ensured that the same topic was not coming up again and again with new releases or on different sites. This approach rebalanced the effort for quality assurance (QA) with the potential TTM optimization (and a fast fixing if needed). Besides all the efforts, TaaS offered the best effort service level objective (SLO). This approach balances the operational cost with the availability. As TaaS is a development supporting service, the highest availability standards will drive the service offering costs more than value is offered to the users like developers and testers. Transparency is given with the shared responsibly approach. This approach models different quality aspects such as security [35], privacy, and availability. In this case three partners are working together: the cloud provider (depends on the hybrid cloud site), the service provider, and the workload owner (customer as legal "entity"). This approach shows what is delivered by the cloud provider and service partner to the customer/user and what is part of the user, respectively, the workload owner [36]. However, the recovery time from incidents and bugs was brought into focus with the high availability (HA) demand of key customers. The generic metric is the uptime or availability rate of the service in percentage which demands the HA setup to ensure the demanded value. This leads to HA setups with for example redundant microservices. To handle the different user groups from small projects to big programs, a cyclic sounding board was established to get feedbacks and give an outlook on upcoming features. To make the progress of the TaaS development transparent for all users, a weekly blog was established. Furthermore, this blog made the lead time transparent for participants from the sounding board who knew the backlog items. Since a blog is not an effective marketing instrument in an enterprise, an internal "roadshow" was initiated to foster internal business development.

In order to establish a strategic partnership, the integration of TaaS into the developer service DevStack was initiated. Both services benefit from each other. TaaS is visible for all the projects and devstack complements its testing capability. Moreover, the established devstack operations discharged the TaaS devops team from the first and second level tasks. The "TaaS team" started onboarding new colleagues from the devstack operations. To ensure scaling, the team adopted agile methods with standards. The team also fostered mastery and autonomy to manage the new complexity of scaling with the new partners.

## 9.7 Professionalization Phase: Deliver Service for the Core Product

This phase adds optimizations to the product and service for a more convenient and comfortable usage and adaption. This optimization leads to co-services for the core product offer. To identify co-services, the users and customers are an important stakeholder voice, but also a more holistic view and interpretation of the established product vision can open new spheres. Like the strategic orientation to the vision on the enterprise vision or global goals and trends which should be in scope of the customers and users, too. Based on this broadened view, new business models are developed. In the best case, communities are established around these new business models and co-innovation with the user community can be realized. This phase involves the challenge to keep continuous innovation vital by establishing more and more dependencies to partners. Each dependency demands clear flows and procedures, thus limiting fast changes and adaptations. However, not all offers have to be directly monetarized, e.g., ideas and inspirations of smart usage can reduce support efforts. An example are self-service kits, which are offered to users to help them use and integrate the service better and more effectively [37]. Paired with some "good luck," this indirectly creates more consumption and additional business. Furthermore, this phase has a high focus on cost optimization for an efficient delivery. Table 9.4 shows the key aspects of this phase.

To instantiate this phase, the professionalization setup of TaaS is presented as an example. In 2019, the professionalization aligned with ISO 20000 enabled a more reliable delivery and established anchors for extended services. The ISO 20000 establishes an IT service management system (SMS) in an organization. This SMS ensures that all relevant procedures for service delivery are established and applied to the provided services of an organization. One of the first co-services was the ramp-up package. This service supports programs to use and integrate TaaS into their development procedures. The win-win situation was that the programs received TaaS expert knowledge for their setup and the TaaS team got insights into the issues and challenges of integrating SaaS (Software-as-a-Service) solutions into projects and programs. With these insights, the TaaS team started to develop SSKs [38] for different use cases and scenarios beyond the core usage of TaaS like fuzz testing

**Table 9.4**  Key aspects to derive and refine requirements in the professionalization phase

| Context | Aspect | Description |
|---|---|---|
| Product | Vision | • Extend the vision to incorporate potential additional and facilitation services |
| | Architecture (components and system view) | • Alignment/compatibility with/to partner services<br>• Alignment to enterprise strategy<br>• Enhancement to global goals like energy efficiency and sustainability |
| | Technology | • Ensure integration and compatibility to supplemented service technologies |
| | Capabilities (functional) | • Establish facilitation functions and services like self-service-kit (SSK) integration into online help<br>• Establish additional use cases for existing functions (reframing the initial usage scenario) |
| Procedures | Delivery | • Establish holistic delivery approach |
| | Improvement | • Establish measures and dashboards which are incorporating supplemented services<br>• Establish communities around the product and service to trigger innovation, inspiration, and feedback |
| Team/orga | Delivery | • Develop new business models<br>• Partner with for example training providers to address the new additional service dimensions<br>• Incorporate the partner into the established devops culture to ensure that the new services are up-to-date |
| | Learning | • Foster thinking and learning outside the established product to integrate additional services |

[39] or chaos engineering [40] with TaaS. Furthermore, it led to a complete redesign and refactoring of the help and how-to pages of TaaS for a more comfortable and effective usage and information retrieval. In the next step, different training curriculums were designed and offered by the Volkswagen IT Academy (the internal training provider of the Group IT) to deliver professional trainings on various levels for different roles. Based on the open vision, initiatives were triggered to make TaaS more sustainable and aligned with the "goTOzero" [41] initiative of the Volkswagen Group. A rigorous usage of the most energy-efficient CPUs available was realized. Furthermore, an offensive "downsizing" of infrastructure components for deployments and "right-scaling" during runtime was implemented for higher utilization [40]. Both actions combined increased the power efficiency of the service by 25%.

Currently TaaS is capable to run on OpenStack, AWS, and Azure. It operates with at least one site or region and one cluster. The business case calculation for new sites is defined by the fixed costs of the core cluster with the 24*7 nodes, and the dynamic customer workload bill that is refinanced with the site demanding customers. Based on a "typical market price" of TaaS, less than five customers are needed to run an additional cluster (like in a new region of a hyperscaler). In the case of a new cloud provider, the initial adjustments of the templates for the cluster, nodes, etc. are at the top cost position; however, they are assessable and clear. Every additional deployment that is avoided reduces resource allocations, so the objective is to serve new customers at existing sites where possible. However, the costs for operations such as security patching and bug fixing exist in any case, and the development of new features and capabilities will have to be added. In a hybrid cloud setting there will be costs as long as private cloud site needs servicing.

Procedures around the direct product have been established. The focus is on being compliant with the LoD (Level of Done) approach [42] to establish the relevant aspects of the ISO 27000, ISO 20000, and GDPR as base in the leanest way possible. This LoD is extendable to other business domains with their specific regulations like finance or safety. In our example, the partnership with the Volkswagen Financial Services AG will lead to an independent deployment of TaaS. However, a common strategic partnership has been established to develop and maintain TaaS together. This will facilitate a contributing community and a common strategic partnership in the management of the requirements backlog. Additionally, to the cooperation with other legal entities, feedback loops with "reselling" partners of the test factory or the CI/CD-chain team of the Volkswagen Group IT are established to enhance their service delivery based on the usage and integration of TaaS, e.g., the integration of plugins for JMeter. All these stakeholders are invited to the TaaS team rituals like the cyclic "show-and-tell events." Some are part of the (core) team; others are part of the community around TaaS.

On the team level, the agile teamwork quality (aTWQ) approach was introduced to incorporate all team members and develop the team. With the aTWQ approach, systematic transparency regarding teamwork aspects and requirements with improvement actions has been implemented. Additionally, the devops team established "user support and consulting" to get inspirations for new innovations. The team started following tech trends and global markets to be on the leading edge for adoption and opportunities. This has led to close proximity between team members, especially developers, and strong relationships with users and their issues to develop supplementary services around the established product and service offer.

## 9.8 Quality vs. TTM

What is the right quality in a world in which customers expect speed with fast deliveries while having uncertainty in technology decisions a system is built upon? One example is Docker runtime which was the "right" decision in 2016 but with the non-compatibility to the later established Open Container Initiative (OCI) standard Docker was deprecated for Kubernetes based clusters in 2020 [43]. This shows the need for a continuous evaluation of the established and integrated technologies' adequateness for the current and expected demand of the product and services. Furthermore, depending on the product life-cycle phase, some requirements can be mandatory or optional. An example is regression test automation: in early stages it is a feature to deliver faster, whereas in later stages in a continuous flow it is clearly a must to handle all the different deployments on different cloud providers. However, some quality aspects such as FOSS license compliance, privacy, or security have to be built in from the first phase because later integration is difficult, time-consuming, and expensive. These basic concepts have to be part of the system's architecture. Furthermore, license and privacy compliance have legal aspects that have to be established and ensured all the time. The front-loaded conceptions of the ISO 25010 IT security quality characteristic, which also includes functional privacy compliance, allocates resources and therefore impacts TTM. The ISO 25010 standard defines a generic quality model for software products. The standard helps to refine a product-specific quality model based on the predefined quality characteristics like security, reliability, and usability.

Functional suitability as a quality characteristic is a topic which is often linked with privacy and security. Balancing different views takes time and thus affects TTM. In the example of TaaS, IT security is often important for users because the test scripts executed by TaaS are executable specifications. Some product specifications are classified as confidential. Privacy in the case of TaaS is a smaller topic because test data has to be designed in line with privacy compliance requirements.

Functional suitability is also strongly linked to the quality characteristic usability which offers a frame for rigorous usability behavior of workflows. This complex topic can be supported by using the established and accepted UX approach with a component framework which can save a lot of time for a faster TTM. However, each new functionality has to be aligned by design into this UX approach.

The balance of cloud agnostic and cloud native is a trade-off decision of the quality characteristic portability. It allocates resources and costs TTM in the first step, but investment in the quality characteristic portability cannot be avoided if a hybrid cloud approach is a strategic goal. It can be mitigated a little by using an adequate technology stack to hide the "variability" of the different cloud providers, but it comes with complexity, too.

To scale in a safe way, the system has to be built on HA and/or redundant components. This increases infrastructure costs and technical complexity, but ensures more stable and available service delivery. The team can take care of issues in the background as customers take no notice of any disruptions or issue. The preparation of the scaling with the quality characteristic reliability and maintainability allocates resources and impacts TTM.

In each product, mostly all quality characteristics are more or less relevant and an inherent part of the product. It is important to manage them actively and not get manifestations of inherent product quality characteristics "by accident." In this sense, quality is like a shadow: everything has one, and one cannot get rid of it; however, one can actively work and build on the (product's) characteristics and thereby shape the shadow. The art is to balance the characteristics and focus on the right characteristic at a given time. This leads to re-prioritization of backlog items and other decisions that are not easy to handle. A good rule of thumb is to show the product quality risks and technical debts provoked by a decision against a specific quality characteristic in the entire system context of the product. This leads to decisions against the often only user-visible function-driven MVP-driven development which is fast at the beginning, however, slows down quicker than expected, and provokes high refactoring costs at downstream phase of the product life-cycle.

Table 9.5 summarizes the key aspects and their ISO 25010 quality characteristics mapped to the life-cycle phases of a cloud service.

**Table 9.5** Key aspects to prioritize in each phase mapped to ISO 25010 characteristics

| Phase | Aspect (ISO characteristic) | Description |
|---|---|---|
| Seed | Governance of compliance (security) | • Legal compliance like license compliance is set on the first day. Other potentially difficult to change concepts have to be fixed early, too, like privacy and security. With the first customers they become mandatory |
| | Feature delivery (portability) | • Fast shipping of "visible" functionality<br>• Establish core technology stack for shipping<br>• Establish a core architecture for shipping |
| Start delivery | Shipping of new features (usability) | • Ensure constant delivery by avoiding building technical debts<br>• Build on a rigor, holistic, and established UX concept |
| | Feedback-driven (functional suitability) | • Establish a fast bug fixing to show the "early adopters" their feedbacks are implemented<br>• Enhance and extend driven by user feedbacks |
| Scale | Delivery procedures (maintainability) | • Establish procedures for testing and deployment<br>• Establish sustainable bug fixing for all rollouts<br>• Establish monitoring |
| | Reliability is king (reliability) | • Enhance the systems stability and reliability<br>• HA and redundancy core building blocks |
| Professionalize | Co-service creation (compatibility) | • Invent new business model around the established service<br>• Partner with other professionals (gain from their expertise and build own end-to-end competencies) |
| | Cost efficiency (performance efficiency) | • Optimize resources for service delivery<br>• Optimize procedures to stay as lean as possible |

## 9.9   Summary

The life-cycle of a cloud service is based on a fast-evolving technology stack. To be able to develop fast and ship value, a strategy is needed to quickly adopt technology innovations. Furthermore, it is unclear which specific cloud technology and their instantiation will be relevant in the future. This is a challenge because decisions that are currently clear can lead to significant refactoring of the selected technology stack in the future, once another solution dominates the market. This is one reason why not all the services of the initial start phase of the GITC program still exist today. Each service team has defined their ways through the life-cycle, and not everything works well in real life. A few learnings can be identified as a key success factor of the observed TaaS.

For success, product owners (PO) also have to assume the role of product managers (PM) in order to have a holistic view and act like a corporate entrepreneur (i.e., "intrapreneur"). Additionally, they have to be constants in their teams, just like start-up founders. They shall not be actively involved in job rotation processes to be able to learn from failures and continuously evolve the service vision. However, they have to trigger changes in the team to establish working styles and processes that match the current product phase, e.g., starting with Scrum for reaching deadlines and moving to Kanban to ensure stable delivery flows. Similarly, the team's focus shall be continuously redirected to the challenges linked to the constraints and requirements of the current and upcoming phase. Furthermore, there is a continuous change in the head count of the devops team.

Decisions regarding aspects of quality and compliance are of strategic importance, because later on it is very difficult and resource-intensive to integrate security or privacy into a system. To serve the HA demand, the multi-site approach is an adequate setup for a small devops team to ensure 100% functional availability for users also in case of local outages over a longer period of time.

Funding is an issue all the time as long as the product is not self-financing. This "start-up phase" takes years not months, and the devops team of the service has to start with zero budget every January 1. The issue is not to refinance the infrastructure for the ops, but rather the investment in the building of the service. All enterprise finance processes are organized in annual cycles; hence, for a small innovative service it is difficult "to compete" with the big projects and programs. The entire finance planning and allocation procedure is a challenge. To avoid wasting time in these procedures with a lot of organizational overhead, a valid approach can be to start small, while partnering with others and adapt quickly to changes. Furthermore, intrapreneurs need to think big and be resilient to all obstacles in their endurance races...

# References

1. Rimal, B. P., Jukan, A., Katsaros, D., & Goeleven, Y. (2011). Architectural requirements for cloud computing systems: An enterprise cloud approach. *Journal of Grid Computing, 9*(1), 3–26.
2. ISO/IEC 25010:2011 Systems and software engineering — Systems and software Quality Requirements and Evaluation (SQuaRE) — System and software quality models.
3. Gannon, D., Barga, R., & Sundaresan, N. (2017). Cloud-native applications. *IEEE Cloud Computing, 4*(5), 16–21.
4. CNCF internet source. Accessed January 15, 2021, from https://github.com/cncf/toc/blob/master/DEFINITION.md
5. Poth, A., Werner, M., & Lei, X. (2018). How to deliver faster with CI/CD integrated testing services? In *European Conference on Software Process Improvement* (pp. 401–409). Springer.
6. OpenStack Conference internet source. Accessed January 15, 2021, from https://www.youtube.com/watch?v=HL_pzkDnal4
7. Xu, Q. L., Jiao, R. J., Yang, X., Helander, M. G., Khalid, H. M., & Anders, O. (2007). Customer requirement analysis based on an analytical Kano model. In *2007 IEEE International Conference on Industrial Engineering and Engineering Management* (pp. 1287–1291). IEEE.
8. Gill, S. S., Tuli, S., Xu, M., Singh, I., Singh, K. V., Lindsay, D., et al. (2019). Transformative effects of IoT, Blockchain and Artificial Intelligence on cloud computing: Evolution, vision, trends and open challenges. *Internet of Things, 8*, 100118.
9. Adamuthe, A. C., & Thampi, G. T. (2019). Technology forecasting: A case study of computational technologies. *Technological Forecasting and Social Change, 143*, 181–189.
10. Durdik, Z., Klatt, B., Koziolek, H., Krogmann, K., Stammel, J., & Weiss, R. (2012). Sustainability guidelines for long-living software systems. In *2012 28th IEEE International Conference on Software Maintenance (ICSM)* (pp. 517–526). IEEE.
11. Abrahamsson, P., Warsta, J., Siponen, M. T., & Ronkainen, J. (2003). New directions on agile methods: A comparative analysis. In *25th International Conference on Software Engineering, 2003. Proceedings* (pp. 244–254). IEEE.
12. Lowry, P. B., & Wilson, D. (2016). Creating agile organizations through IT: The influence of internal IT service perceptions on IT service quality and IT agility. *The Journal of Strategic Information Systems, 25*(3), 211–226.
13. Poth, A., Kottke, M., & Riel, A. (2020). Agile team work quality in the context of agile transformations–A case study in large-scaling environments. In *European Conference on Software Process Improvement* (pp. 232–243). Springer.
14. Zhang, Y., Vasilescu, B., Wang, H., & Filkov, V. (2018). One size does not fit all: An empirical study of containerized continuous deployment workflows. In *Proceedings of the 2018 26th ACM Joint Meeting on European Software Engineering Conference and Symposium on the Foundations of Software Engineering* (pp. 295–306).
15. Ayala-Rivera, V., & Pasquale, L. (2018). The grace period has ended: An approach to operationalize GDPR requirements. In *2018 IEEE 26th International Requirements Engineering Conference (RE)* (pp. 136–146). IEEE.
16. Arfelt, E., Basin, D., & Debois, S. (2019). Monitoring the GDPR. In *European Symposium on Research in Computer Security* (pp. 681–699). Springer.
17. Poth, A., Jacobsen, J., & Riel, A. (2020). A systematic approach to agile development in highly regulated environments. In *International Conference on Agile Software Development* (pp. 111–119). Springer.
18. Kösling, M., & Poth, A. (2017). Agile development offers the chance to establish automated quality procedures. In *European Conference on Software Process Improvement* (pp. 495–503). Springer.

19. Staron, M., Meding, W., & Baniasad, P. (2019). Information needs for SAFe teams and release train management: A design science research study. In *IWSM-Mensura* (pp. 55–70).
20. Poth, A., Kottke, M., & Riel, A. (2019). Scaling agile–A large enterprise view on delivering and ensuring sustainable transitions. In *Advances in agile and user-centred software engineering* (pp. 1–18). Springer.
21. Poth, A., & Heimann, C. (2018). How to innovate software quality assurance and testing in large enterprises? In *European Conference on Software Process Improvement* (pp. 437–442). Springer.
22. Bozic, N. (2017). Integrated model of innovative competence. *Journal of Creativity and Business Innovation, 3*, 140–169.
23. Rea, R. H. (1989). Factors affecting success and failure of seed capital/start-up negotiations. *Journal of Business Venturing, 4*(2), 149–158.
24. Schön, E. M., Thomaschewski, J., & Escalona, M. J. (2017). Agile requirements engineering: A systematic literature review. *Computer Standards & Interfaces, 49*, 79–91.
25. Poth, A., & Riel, A. (2020). Quality requirements elicitation by ideation of product quality risks with design thinking. In *2020 IEEE 28th International Requirements Engineering Conference (RE)* (pp. 238–249). IEEE.
26. OpenStack Conference internet source. Accessed January 15, 2021, from https://www.youtube.com/watch?v=5m1eE30vApI
27. Apache JMeter source code repository. Accessed January 15, 2021, from https://github.com/apache/jmeter
28. CNCF Kubernetes source code repository. Accessed January 15, 2021, from https://github.com/kubernetes/kubernetes
29. Docker source code repository. Accessed January 15, 2021, from https://github.com/docker
30. Poth, A., Kottke, M., & Riel, A. (2020). Evaluation of agile team work quality. In *International Conference on Agile Software Development* (pp. 101–110). Springer.
31. Poth, A., Kottke, M., & Riel, A. (2019). Scaling agile on large enterprise level–systematic bundling and application of state of the art approaches for lasting agile transitions. In *2019 Federated Conference on Computer Science and Information Systems (FedCSIS)* (pp. 851–860). IEEE.
32. red-dot design award. Accessed January 15, 2021, from https://www.red-dot.org/project/groupui-41315/
33. Callaghan, S., Hawke, K., & Mignerey, C. (2014). *Five myths (and realities) about zero based budgeting* (pp. 1–4). Mckinsey.
34. Oyelami, O. A., Poth, A., Hintsch, J., & Riel, A. (2019). Quality assurance and traceability in containerized continuous delivery process. In *European Conference on Software Process Improvement* (pp. 368–377). Springer.
35. Almorsy, M., Grundy, J., & Müller, I. (2016). *An analysis of the cloud computing security problem.* arXiv preprint arXiv:1609.01107.
36. Cerf, V., & Ryan, P. (2014). Internet governance is our shared responsibility. *ISJLP, 10*, 1.
37. Poth, A., Kottke, M., & Riel, A. (2020). Scaling agile on large enterprise level with self-service kits to support autonomous teams. In *2020 15th Conference on Computer Science and Information Systems (FedCSIS)* (pp. 731–737). IEEE.
38. Poth, A., Kottke, M., & Riel, A. (2020). The implementation of a digital service approach to fostering team autonomy, distant collaboration, and knowledge scaling in large enterprises. *Human Systems Management, 39*(4), 573–588.
39. Basiri, A., Behnam, N., De Rooij, R., Hochstein, L., Kosewski, L., Reynolds, J., & Rosenthal, C. (2016). Chaos engineering. *IEEE Software, 33*(3), 35–41.
40. Klees, G., Ruef, A., Cooper, B., Wei, S., & Hicks, M. (2018). Evaluating fuzz testing. In *Proceedings of the 2018 ACM SIGSAC Conference on Computer and Communications Security* (pp. 2123–2138).

41. Volkswagen AG go2zero strategy. Accessed January 15, 2021, from https://www.volkswa-genag.com/en/news/stories/2019/07/co2-getting-to-zero.html
42. Poth, A., Jacobsen, J., & Riel, A. (2020). Systematic agile development in regulated environ-ments. In *European Conference on Software Process Improvement* (pp. 191–202). Springer.
43. CNCF changelog for source code. Accessed January 15, 2021, from https://github.com/kuber-netes/kubernetes/blob/master/CHANGELOG/CHANGELOG-1.20.md#deprecation

# Chapter 10
# Engineering of Sustainability with Existing Levers in Cloud Services

Alexander Poth [ID], Olsi Rrjolli, and Andreas Riel

**Abstract** The continuous growing usage of cloud resources produces a non-negligible portion of energy consumption of the world. To counteract this trend, an active and resolute acting is needed. This acting starts by focusing on the right respective needed business function to avoid "waste" by design and goes through the development process into the operation of a cloud service. All life-cycle phases have to contribute to the overall energy footprint reduction of the cloud resources consuming service. An approach for sustainability engineering is presented which is based on general available methods and techniques, but often not systematic used to improve service sustainability. The approach focuses mainly on systematic avoidance and reduction of resource allocations for service delivery. The focus of the presented approach is (hybrid) cloud-native services based on microservice-based container workloads. The suggested approach shows on an example cloud service presented as case study the effects of systematic sustainability engineering to make the service more eco-friendly. It presents the typical trade-offs between different quality characteristics to balance them to an overall adequate solution.

**Keywords** IT sustainability · Green IT · IT cloud sustainability · Cloud-native service

A. Poth (✉) · O. Rrjolli
Volkswagen AG, Wolfsburg, Germany
e-mail: alexander.poth@volkswagen.de; olsi.rrjolli@volkswagen.de

A. Riel
G-SCOP Laboratory, Grenoble INP - Université Grenoble Alpes, Grenoble, France
e-mail: andreas.riel@grenoble-inp.fr

© The Author(s), under exclusive license to Springer Nature
Switzerland AG 2025
Y. Hajizadeh et al. (eds.), *Building Cloud Software Products*,
Innovation, Technology, and Knowledge Management,
https://doi.org/10.1007/978-3-031-92184-1_10

## 10.1    Introduction

As long as not all energy is produced in a "green" way, we have to reduce energy consumption to avoid "claiming" of the green energy proportion which cannot be provided to other energy consumers. The growing cloud workloads have to act to reduce their footprints. Bloomberg estimated that about 1% of the world's electricity goes to cloud computing [1]. The resource allocation footprint is a proxy metric for energy consumption allocated to the dedicated cloud resource. Each cloud resource consumes more or less energy. Energy which is not produced "green" comes with a carbon footprint. Some cloud service providers (CSP) have started facilitating workload monitoring about sustainability aspects like the AWS carbon footprint dashboard [2], Azure with its emission impact dashboard [3], or the GCP carbon footprint monitoring [4]. All these approaches help to make past consumptions of workloads transparent; however, the optimizations of the future footprint will be the work for the cloud service workload engineers. One open topic is the real consumption of specific cloud resources provided by the CSPs. Currently, no detailed information about abstract logical infrastructure components are available like load balancers or API gateways. This makes it difficult to evaluate these resources with respect to their footprints in solution development adequately. Furthermore, a close to real-time information is often needed to assess impacts on recent sustainability optimizations. The problem of missing transparency grows with the abstraction of the resources provided by the CSP. An example is to compare running a workload on an instance, within a container service or serverless. Behind all options, servers are running; however, the implemented resource allocation approach differs. No information is given about the carbon footprints of the internal service management of CSPs. Especially some indicators can make consumers suspect about the overall service sustainability, like the pricing model which does not explicitly address sustainability aspects and sets "wrong" optimization focus on the monetary level. For example, the pricing approach of serverless functions, which motivates short function execution runtimes, is difficult. This provokes optimizing workloads from a commercial (consumer) perspective to shorter running function calls. Each call has an overhead to bring up the "serverless" function execution environment—this is a non-negligible part of short-running customer workloads [5]. The typical serverless function service pricing model of CSPs in this case contradicts the overall resource efficiency optimization. However, a machine running serverless functions has a high utilization with all the context switches (e.g., warm start, cold start [6, 7], and work-arounds to improve at least performance [7]). However, the questions are how much energy could be saved by running more truly value-adding end-customer workload with less internal context-switch workload, and how can this be represented in the pricing model of the function execution. It is unknown how big the sustainability lever is as long as the stack is a black box of a CSP. This topic can only be dealt with by the CSPs through an overall sustainable pricing model for the services or by revealing more details about the "internal" service implementation to customers to establish a fact-based sustainability engineering. Missing transparency leads to focusing on workloads which can run in more transparent runtime and execution stacks.

The focus of this research are container-based workloads. This also includes hybrid-cloud services. This brings up the topic about the additional footprint to be able to run a workload on different cloud platforms. This additional footprint comes from missing standardization of services. The more abstract a cloud service, the less standardized the service is. This missing standardization forces to identify the part of common service interfaces and behavior between the non-standardized services. This step back to the common service core between different CSPs comes with additional overheads for the workloads to adopt or build additional needed requirements which are not in the common core.

Based on today's facts established by the big CSPs, the objective is to focus on areas in which cloud service sustainability engineering is effectively possible at least with relative optimizations and proxy metrics. Against this background, the research questions this work tries to answer are the following:

Q1: Which approaches to resource footprint optimization can be applied in established cloud platforms and services running on them?
Q2: Which existing methods and techniques are useful for an optimization of cloud service resource footprints?
Q3: How does the footprint optimization correlate with other quality characteristics (like availability)?
Q4: How to balance different dependability characteristics, especially the contradicting ones like performance and efficiency?

In the context of this work [8, 9] investigated a quality model for cloud services and concepts for sustainable development of cloud services with respect to these Qs. The following section analyzes literature for published works that can help further structure this subject area and inspire the action research-based methodology that the authors have chosen to provide answers.

## 10.2   Literature Analysis

In terms of works structuring the domain, Piraghaj et al. [10] provide a survey and taxonomy of energy-efficient resource management techniques in platform as a service (PaaS) cloud service models. Bharany et al. [11] published another survey and taxonomy of energy-efficient fault tolerance techniques in green cloud computing. Both together provide a good coverage of the domain of energy efficiency in service-oriented cloud environments. Vafamehr et al. [12] present the criteria, assets, and models for energy-aware cloud computing practices and envision a market structure that addresses the impact of the quality and price of energy supply on the quality and cost of cloud computing services.

In the context of microservices, Lloyd et al. [13] provide a comprehensive investigation into the factors which influence microservice performance afforded by serverless computing. They examine hosting implications related to infrastructure elasticity, load balancing, provisioning variation, infrastructure retention, and memory reservation size. Energy consumption is only considered indirectly. De Nardin et al. [14] propose a lightweight proactive elasticity model that provides resource reorganization for a cloud-based microservice application. Its differential approach appears in improving energy consumption by periodically handling the most appropriate amount of resources to execute an application while maintaining or yet improving the performance of CPU-bound applications. Xu et al. [15] propose an integrated approach for managing energy and brownout in container-based clouds. They introduce a brownout-based architecture by deactivating optional containers in applications or microservices temporarily to reduce energy consumption. Khomh et al. [16] examine the impact on energy consumption of six cloud patterns (i.e., Local Database Proxy, Local Sharding-Based Router, the Priority Message Queue, Competing Consumers, Gatekeeper, and Pipes and Filters patterns), with the aim to provide some guidance to developers about the usage of cloud patterns to improve energy efficiency. Saboor et al. [17] address the dynamic provisioning of containers and microservices in cloud computing environment by building rank-based profiles and using those profiles for allocation of web application's microservices along with containers to the cloud data centers. The MicroRanker service is proposed to rank all of the participating microservices and distribute them across different nodes even before the execution of the cloud services. Further, the MicroRanker service is utilized to dynamically update the container placement due to continuous DevOps actions.

In the context of serverless, Patros et al. [18] describe the real power consumption characteristics of serverless, based on execution traces reported in the literature, as well as potential strategies that can be used to reduce the energy overheads of serverless execution. The main levers are serverless platform design and infrastructure, improved characterization of novel IoT- and AI-driven workloads, paired with smarter decision-making at the application-design level, and automated methodologies that assess the sustainability efficacy of such power and energy-aware methods. Denninnart et al. [19] provide a survey study that unfolds the internal mechanics of the serverless computing and, second, explore the scope for efficiency within this paradigm via studying function reuse and approximation approaches. Jia et al. [20] introduce the concept of energy fungibility, which opens up the possibility of reducing energy consumption. They propose a function-level runtime system that manages resource allocation of functions to guarantee the functions' SLA while minimizing energy consumption. Their experimental results show energy consumption reduction of the same function by 21.2% compared to state-of-the-art techniques while guaranteeing the SLA of the functions' 99th percentile latency.

As for energy-efficient resource allocation and software-focused approaches, Katal et al. [21] provide a survey on the status of software solutions that aids in cloud power consumption reduction. Chauhan et al. [22] propose an enhanced cloud framework that takes a holistic view of the cloud environment, also covering software development, and maps energy-saving opportunities to various cloud components. Steigenwald et al. [23] provide software development practices that help reducing energy consumption. Hameed et al. [24] identify open challenges associated with energy-efficient resource allocation. Their study outlines the problem and investigates existing hardware- and software-based techniques available for this purpose. Furthermore, available techniques already presented in the literature are summarized based on the energy-efficient research dimension taxonomy. The advantages and disadvantages of the existing techniques are comprehensively analyzed against the proposed research dimension taxonomy, namely, resource adaption policy, objective function, allocation method, allocation operation, and interoperability. Lee et al. [25] present two energy-conscious task consolidation heuristics, which aim to maximize resource utilization and explicitly consider both active and idle energy consumption. Zhou et al. [26] address the problem of reducing cloud data-center high energy consumption with minimal service level agreement (SLA) violation. In order to adapt well to the dynamic and unpredictable workload commonly running in cloud data centers, the proposed energy-aware algorithm uses an adaptive three-threshold framework for the classification of cloud data-center hosts into four different classes (i.e., less loaded hosts, little loaded hosts, normally loaded hosts, and overloaded hosts). Qu et al. [27] propose a fault-tolerant model for web applications provisioned by spot instances. From an energy-efficiency perspective, this enables a better utilization of available idle resources in the cloud. Kim et al. [28] present an approach to remove hardware overprovisioning implementing task buffers and scheduler, in terms of energy consumption. Task buffers reorder tasks with various priorities and route them to appropriate virtual machines. The scheduler monitors the task buffering and hardware load status and decides the optimal number of active physical and virtual machines. Lin et al. [29] propose a distributed energy consumption measurement system for heterogeneous cloud environments based on a multicomponent power model. We investigate the mathematical relationship between the resource usage of the key components (CPU, memory, and disk) and the system energy consumption and provide a power modeling method for each component. Lin, Shi et al. [30] provide an exhaustive overview, taxonomy, and analysis of power models and power modeling approaches for cloud servers. Lin, Liu et al. [31] propose an energy-efficient dynamic round-robin (DRR) class of algorithms for energy-aware virtual machine scheduling and consolidation. Chen et al. [32] elaborate a linear power model that represents the behavior of a single work node and includes the contribution from individual components, i.e., CPU, memory, and HDD, to the total power consumption of a single work node. Their results could be part of a power characterization module integrated into clusters' monitoring systems. Wu et al. [33] analyze the power signatures of virtual machines in different configurations through experiments and propose a virtual machine power model able to adapt to the reconfiguration of VMs and provide accurate power estimating under CPU-intensive workload.

## 10.3   Method

The research context is the Volkswagen Group IT with a focus on cloud services. The selected example cloud service—Testing as a Service (TaaS)—has a high dynamic workload profile: scaling in/out a three-digit number of virtual machines which serve the demanded workload in a few minutes is not unusual. This example shows that it is important to ensure that an adequate resource allocation for the dynamic workload is established. Adequate service workload delivery has to balance performance, sustainability, and other characteristics.

Based on the insights we gathered from our literature analysis, we decided to take an iterative, learning-focused, and experimental approach to finding answers to our research questions. We considered this to be the most appropriate approach in our environment, which lends itself best to action research. Furthermore, we were seeking to build up knowledge about the key impact factors of serverless configurations on energy consumption in our particular large-scale company group context. We also needed to find ways to experiment with energy consumption impact factors that were achievable through reconfiguration rather than re-implementation of software like scheduler algorithms. This is a requirement found in a regulated and process-constraint company group environment like ours. In particular, dependability parameters, such as availability, reliability, and performance, needed to be guaranteed, since we needed to do our research under real operation conditions.

### 10.3.1 Approach Development

Based on the concept of a digital infrastructure taxonomy [34, 35], the sustainability engineering for cloud services can be defined by the following stack:

User-workload units
Digital products/services units
(Logical) resource provisioning units
(Physical) digital resources units

The (physical) digital resource units are the real infrastructure units in data centers like the server. The physical units are provisioned in the data center, where the art is to realize a high utilization with respect to user workload. On the physical resource unit level, the defined physical metrics for energy based on power ($W = UI$) can be directly measured. The (logical) resource provisioning units are the virtualized infrastructure units, like a virtual machine with a specific amount of RAM and vCPU cores. The utilization objective is still the main optimization aspect, but the measurement of consumption is not directly related to the defined physical measurement units like W. Instead, proxy metrics are needed. For example, proxy metrics are the proportion of the physical resource unit [%] or allocation time [seconds] to define the associated energy proportion. The digital products with their service units are software units like microservices or containers. To run these software units, typically more than one of the resource provisioning units are allocated. The user-workload units are allocating one or more software units.

The generic approach for sustainability engineering for cloud services is to *minimize the resource allocation for the workload execution*. This has two dimensions: (1) *overall runtime* and the (2) *deployed resources*. This does not define how a workload can be scaled or parallelized. It is reasonable to reduce overall runtime by parallel execution, as long as the overhead for parallelization does not have a (significant) negative impact to the integrality of the overall resource allocation for the workload execution compared with other levels of parallelization, considering Amdahl's law [36]. The same applies to scaling and its management overheads. Also, it is adequate to use large resource units to minimize unit-management overheads. This leads to a practical rule of thumb, which consists in shortening the resource allocation time for the workload by keeping the resource footprint for workload and management overheads as small as possible.

In practice, this opens two areas of sustainability optimization: selective hardware allocation and sustainable software behavior. This leads to the following optimization levers for hardware and their corresponding physical digital resource units, as well as logical resource provision units:

- Choose the most adequate infrastructure resource unit for the needed software of the user-workload units. The objective is to downsize the infrastructure resource units to push utilization per unit.
  In practice, this is often limited by CSP defined types of instances like the CPU-RAM relation (like on AWS the m-, c-, or r-instances) and the predefined step size (like on AWS the l-, xl-, 2xl-instances).
- Choose the most energy-efficient resource units. The objective is to optimize, e.g., CPU workloads by selecting the most energy-efficient architecture and implementation. For example, for the x86 architecture the current Intel® implementation is less energy efficient than the implementation of AMD®. Furthermore, the ARM architecture is more energy efficient as the x86 architecture. Additionally, always deploy workloads on the newest available hardware generation to get benefits of the higher performance per resource unit (Moore's law).
  In practice, not all cloud platforms respectively CSPs provide all options. Choose wherever possible providers which offer all architectures like for AWS with the i-, a-, and g-instances. Furthermore, select a CSP with a high and fast adoption rate to move with the technology cycles like for AWS gen 5, 6, or 7 instances.
- Choose storage resource units based on the specific use case which is typically defined by durability, throughput, and I/O. Each data type needs an evaluation of the specific profile for performance and durability while keeping sustainability aspects in mind. Use local storage like block storage for high throughput and I/O where needed, but typically the overall utilization of the hardware over the commission time is lower than in a shared "remote" storage. However, the remote storage comes with an additional overhead for the network and the storage management. Unfortunately, the breakeven point is not transparent (CSPs like AWS do not give all relevant information to optimize workloads with sustainability focus). Furthermore, remote storage can be configured for example as RAID for higher durability. Especially durability is an aspect to choose with focus on the real demand rather than the default offer configuration. For example, object storage often comes with high durability values by default which are realized by

three or more copies. Is the triple resource allocation really needed for the specific use case? Depending on the storage, also the file system can have a huge impact on the allocated physical storage. Choose a file system with copy-on-write options or approaches wherever possible. Furthermore, check if policies for retention time are easy to configure or establish, in order to be able to adjust them to current requirements.

Some CSPs provide additional "parameters" like burstable resources (like AWS t-instances). Especially, this kind of resources are useful for spiky workloads with a low average utilization. This kind of resources can be useful in an initial step for non-optimized setups to learn about behavior to establish actions for systematic resource utilization.

Software unit optimization levers:

- Downsizing of software units to push respectively maximize the amount of executed software units per infrastructure resource unit.
- Optimize code efficiency and performance for sustainability-optimized software units (avoid Wirth's law aka Andy and Bill's law where possible [37]). Not only self-developed code and their algorithm optimization is in scope, but also the wise and selective usage of libraries and other dependencies has a high impact.
- Decouple demands to reduce peaks (avoid Amdahl's law impacts where possible [36]). Try to optimize utilization of allocated resource by establishing a more constant and higher workload to avoid the overheads of elastic scaling or inefficiencies driven delays caused by saturation effects [38].
- Evaluate different availability concepts to address "demand" by minimized resource allocation; some useful concepts without "standby resources" are:
  - Restart checkpoint (reactive)
  - Job migration (reactive)
  - Replication (reactive)
  - Self-healing (active)
  - Preemptive migration (active)
  - System rejuvenation (active)

The strategy is to fit the service-level objective respectively agreement (SLO/SLA) with a minimal set or even better without standby resources. The task is to optimize the service level indicators (SLI), mean time to failure (MTTF) and the outage time (OT) which is mean time to recovery (MTTR) the detected outage, and the time to start the recovery activities with the aspect of sustainable resource allocations to stay in the SLO/SLA availability target. A simplified approach to evaluate the overall availability is:

Availability = (MTTF – OT) / OT

The main objective is to enlarge the MTTF where possible with the listed availability concepts which do not allocate "standby resources." However, some of the concepts come with a short (partial service) outage like restarts.

Another key target is to reduce MTTR where possible and ensure a short deterministic repair time. The second optimization path is to avoid planned downtimes like for maintenance. This results in less and shorter "outages" for customers. To reduce planned downtimes, different established approaches can be used like green/blue deployments [39].

Technically, MTTR can be reduced by using infrastructure as code (IaC) and/or other automated deployment approaches. Then it is easy to measure and optimize the worst-case downtime to set up a new deployment. Also, it is important to detect an outage fast to keep the entire OT short. First a monitoring of the services is needed to detect outages instantly are run the assigned repair procedure. The MTTR is the second relevant part of the OT.

The OT (practical performance indicators: detect and restore time) and the MTTF (practical performance indicators: "historical" frequency of outages) are used to evaluate if the setup without standby resources can fit the SLO/SLA requirements and its corresponding commitments.

In the case that the optimization of OT and MTTF does not fit to SLO/SLA targets, check for the high availability (HA) "concepts" from hot-standby to n/m-relations for overprovisioning of HW to handle outages. A smart setup of the HA approach with a n/m-relation can reduce the 50% "overprovisioning" of hot-standby approaches to a much smaller "overprovisioning." Especially, the mapping to real-world units is important for the deployment and the real "overprovisioning." For example, assume that each unit has a baseload (caused by e.g., the operation system, and the container runtime service) with 1 GB RAM. Furthermore, assume that a workload has 20 services with 1 GB RAM for each service. In this case a non-HA solution needs 21 GB RAM. In real world units typically have 8, 16, or 32 GB RAM. In this case, a 32 GB RAM unit must be used and the overprovisioning is 11 GB RAM. For a setup with a "failover" approach, the needed RAM is 64 GB and the overprovisioning is 22 GB and an additional overhead of 1 GB for the second unit's baseload. An approach with three units leads to a demand of three units with 16 GB RAM to handle an outage of one unit. To enable all units to run within "outage state" with two units, the units together have to reserve 1/3 workload capacity to "take over" the workload of the outage unit (in real operation, each unit needs 1 GB for the baseload, 7 GB for the workload, and 4 GB for "outage reservation" to handle the service units with 1 GB). This leads to an additional overhead of 2 GB and an overprovisioning of 12 GB (plus the "rest" from the service-unit rounding). However, the reserved space for the outage and the overprovisioning of the "outage" unit are usable for non-HA workloads like caches, and the overprovisioning of the other units can be used for service scaling to handle demand variation. What is important is that this example calculation depends on the amount of services and the corresponding RAM size. A change in the service setup needs a check if the overprovisioning can absorb the additional demands; if not a resizing of the units is needed. The relations show that the unit size and the baseload size determine the allocation efficiency—bigger units and smaller baseload are the objective for more "workload" capacity. This relation also implies that a sweet spot exists and too many units have a negative effect with the "growing" baseload-overhead which come with each unit.

Persistence optimization by optimizing the data structures itself, the compression
   for storage and its retention and durability in formats without duplications.
Store only really needed data and optimize data structures to reduce the data size by
   design. Furthermore, choose efficient machine-manageable data structures to
   minimize transformations, copies, etc.
Compress data with adequate algorithms for data usage profile. This includes also
   adequate parameterization of compression algorithm to address read/write relation of the data.
Define for each data type the minimal retention time and the durability to fit the
   SLO/SLA. Finally, store the data in formats with less duplication like choose
   copy-on-write and avoid redundancy like classical RAIDs. Furthermore, decide
   which data can be reproduced in case of an outage or data lost which need for
   example no storage redundancy.
Data transfer optimization is realized by minimizing data transfer where possible by
   design, use caching and choose efficient machine-transferable protocols.

Furthermore, to measure progress, KPIs or at least indicators which are generic
and useful for a continuous improvement approach driven by dedicated sustainability actions are:

- Reduce compute allocation: optimizing allocated computing resources and focus
  on their energy efficiency based on architecture and generation. Push the workload movement to the most energy-efficient compute cores.
  An example action derived from this indicator is active movement to the last
  generation of most energy-efficient computing cores available.
- Reduce persistence allocation: optimizing persistence (storage) allocation size
  drives minimizing data structures and push active durability or redundancy decisions and retention policies for data types.
  An example action derived from this indicator is the active selection of the compression algorithm library and its parameters.
- Reduce RAM allocation: optimizing the RAM footprint helps in avoiding con-
  tinuously growing software units.
  An example action derived from this indicator is to reduce RAM associated to
  microservices to have additional caching space.
- Reduce data transfer: optimizing data transfer helps to minimize streaming and
  other data movements (including storages) to optimize network traffic.
  An example action derived from this indicator is the caching of containers.
- Reduce workload execution time: optimizing the used resource allocation time.
  An example action is to optimize the overhead phase at the beginning (provision-
  ing) or end (decommissioning) of workloads.
- Reduce workload resource allocation: optimizing the allocated resources to exe-
  cute the workload.
  An example action is selecting the best fitting resource units with the highest
  utilization to execute the workload.
- Reduce idle time of allocated resources: optimizing the workload execution to
  avoid waiting/blocking phases.

An example is to reduce the pre-provisioning time of resources until real usage.
- Reduce the mapped (overall) resource consumption to customer/user value units: optimizing the overall energy efficiency with focus on service deliverables to push focusing on the strategic development (future capabilities and features).
- An example action derived from this indicator is the optimization of the specific workload provisioning and decommission time.

The indicators can be measured against an initial baseline. Each improvement action is an additional iteration in the sustainability journey and compared with the baseline or other earlier iteration results to show the progress.

Table 10.1 summarizes the approach based on a taxonomy to structure sustainability engineering with the refinement to levers, building blocks, or actions and related KPIs, measures, and indicators to make the effects transparent. The strategy is to build "offers" based on the lower level that provide the most efficient solutions by choosing the best options for the demand.

## 10.4   Implementation Case Study

Our case study is a cloud service in an enterprise setup. The cloud-native T-Rex Testing as a Service (TaaS) [40] with some specific relevant characteristics like:

- Cloud agnostic to run on private and public clouds
- Determinism to ensure reproducible test executions respective results
- Performance in workload execution to contribute to a shorter time to market
- (Cost) efficiency in workload execution to minimize software quality assurance and its testing costs
- High elasticity to handle the volatile and dynamic test workloads

Derived implementation flow for HW:

Since the initial right-/downsizing of vCPU cores in April 2020 (x-axis in Fig. 10.1) to reduce the footprint of deployed infrastructure to 50% CPU footprint, the amount of microservices has grown by a factor more than 4. With the ongoing optimizations, the footprint of deployed CPU consumption footprint was reduced to approx. 25% compared to the starting point (100%). The optimization comes from moving to more energy-efficient processor platforms like from Intel Xeon to AMD EPYC (Q4/2020) and then to ARM (Q4/2022) [41]. Furthermore, where possible a change to newer processor generations was realized over time like in Q3/2022 to the EPYC gen 3 processor family [42]. Improvements of the energy efficiency often also improve the processor performance—e.g., EPYC gen 2 to 3 with approx. 1/3 more integer performance [43, 44] and a move to ARM like Graviton 3 comes with a more bigger performance gain—for the T-Rex TaaS service demands with the higher amount of microservices to serve, too. This shows that Wirth's law can be "conquered" by rigorous optimization actions that focus on energy consumption footprint. However, the RAM consumption is constant since 2020—optimizations

**Table 10.1** Overview of the sustainable engineering approach for cloud services

| Taxonomy stack | Sustainability lever, building block, action | KPI, measure, indicator |
|---|---|---|
| User-workload units | – Transparency about workload (related) consumption for user<br>– Avoid non-value resource allocations (if not possible map proportion related to value units)<br>– Alignment of workload pricing model with resource allocation<br>– Store data in minimal acceptable durability level<br>– Apply minimal acceptable data retention time<br>– Apply minimal acceptable availability | – Reduce resource allocations per user value units |
| Digital products/ services units | – Optimize algorithms and software components about resource allocation<br>– Choose power-efficient programming languages<br>– Design and build software for power-efficient computer architectures<br>– Downsizing of logical resource unit allocation<br>– Build small, individual, and scalable service units<br>– Decoupling for flattening of workload peaks<br>– Offer data retention time options<br>– Offer data duration options<br>– Establish approach minimizing standby resources for minimal acceptable availability<br>– Reduce data structure size (optimize data at rest and transfer)<br>– Minimize data movements | – Optimize throughput by balancing performance and latency adequately<br>– Reduce workload resource allocation– Reduce workload execution time<br>– Reduce idle time of allocated resources |
| (Logical) resource provisioning units | – Minimize unit size and allocation time by keeping up with the utilization | – Reduce compute allocation<br>– Reduce persistence allocation<br>– Reduce RAM allocation<br>– Reduce data transfer |
| (Physical) digital resources units | – Commission of power-efficient units<br>– Commission of demand-based sizeable units<br>– Durability options for persistence units | – Reduce low utilization |

are used to cache, e.g., container images. The figure focus on the T-Rex TaaS-specific written microservices and neither on other deployed services like the web-server or logging services nor on their operational amount of deployed service instances at runtime. The growing amount of microservices is the base for selective elastic scaling (amount of service instances) with small footprint; however, the

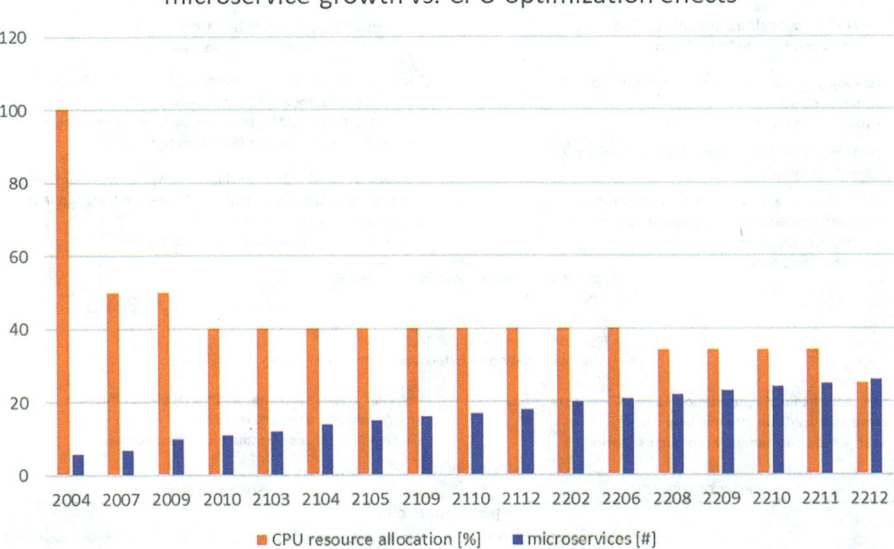

**Fig. 10.1** The effects of service footprint optimizations and CPU resource allocations over time

trade-off between core overhead for running a microservice and the scaling benefits needs to be balanced. Also customer workloads are not in scope; higher service adaptation to the actual usage by customers comes with higher workloads.

Derived implementation flow for SW:

**Performance management**  Better user performance correlates with sustainability optimizations. Because usage of less resource to serve a certain amount of value is per definition higher performance. Furthermore, the "downsizing" of containers contributes to security with less attack surface.

An observation was that the provision of higher values does not always have significant effects. An example is that in the second optimization, the improvement of the I/O and bandwidth of the cache storage does not significantly improve the user performance in the setup of T-Rex. This leads to reducing the bandwidth to the initial value to save at least infrastructure provision costs. Similar results came out of the analysis of lazy loading of containers in 2021. Because important images came prebuild, and the T-Rex DevOps team did not want to rebuild everything, an additional build-time conversion step like the Stargz Snapshotter [45] was required. Both examples show that at some point, engineering efforts and optimization effects come out of balance from an economical sustainability view. However, this point depends on the engineering costs, as well as on scaling effects of the optimization, and is individual for each cloud service. Furthermore, anytime a decision can be made for stopping optimization efforts. In 2022, the new lazy-loading approach with the SOCI Snapshotter [46] was identified. It is currently under observation; however, with the OCI "referrers" dependency, it will still take time to make the move, too.

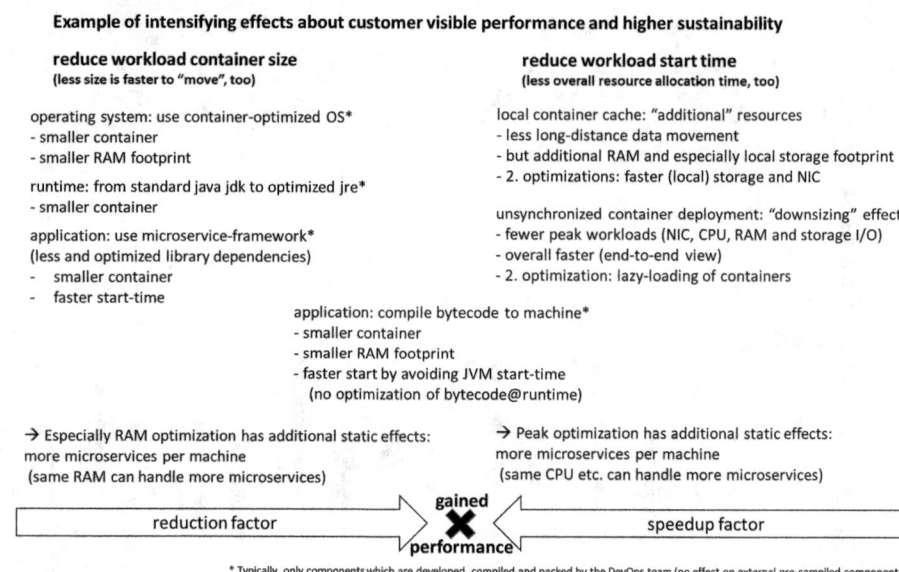

**Example of intensifying effects about customer visible performance and higher sustainability**

**reduce workload container size**
(less size is faster to "move", too)

operating system: use container-optimized OS*
- smaller container
- smaller RAM footprint

runtime: from standard java jdk to optimized jre*
- smaller container

application: use microservice-framework*
(less and optimized library dependencies)
-   smaller container
-   faster start-time

**reduce workload start time**
(less overall resource allocation time, too)

local container cache: "additional" resources
- less long-distance data movement
- but additional RAM and especially local storage footprint
- 2. optimizations: faster (local) storage and NIC

unsynchronized container deployment: "downsizing" effect
- fewer peak workloads (NIC, CPU, RAM and storage I/O)
- overall faster (end-to-end view)
- 2. optimization: lazy-loading of containers

application: compile bytecode to machine*
- smaller container
- smaller RAM footprint
- faster start by avoiding JVM start-time
   (no optimization of bytecode@runtime)

→ Especially RAM optimization has additional static effects:
more microservices per machine
(same RAM can handle more microservices)

→ Peak optimization has additional static effects:
more microservices per machine
(same CPU etc. can handle more microservices)

| reduction factor | gained ✖ performance | speedup factor |

\* Typically, only components which are developed, compiled and packed by the DevOps team (no effect on external pre-compiled components)

**Fig. 10.2** The effects of reductions directly support the speed—sustainability helps to improve performance of user actions. Direct speed optimizations are contributing to sustainability with shorter resource allocation as long as the speed is not generated by adding resources

Figure 10.2 shows an example about throughput optimization by balancing latency and performance efforts. The better throughput correlates with a higher sustainability. A part of performance optimization is to do the work with less—smaller container size leads to more speed during container movement from the registry or cache to the deployment location and faster starting furthermore, it reduces storage respective memory allocation. A part of the latency which is user visible is the workload start time. Optimizing this with selective improvements (examples listed on the figure) leads to a better user experience and less allocation time of resources which improves sustainability. Both aspects are iteratively optimized. The balancing of both throughput aspects leads with the reduction and speedup factor to a better overall user experience with the gained performance (time behavior) and higher utilization of allocated resources under less peaks by allocation of less capacity.

**Availability management** Classical availability approaches with "standby" resources are contradicting to footprint optimizations. However, approaches exist that are not doubling resources for HA. For example, Kubernetes scales odd-numbered master nodes like 3 or 5 and the dynamic worker fleet. But also one big machine has less overhead for managing services than many small machines with own management agents. The case study example T-Rex runs well with smallest instance type which has the best fitting of CPU/RAM ratio for the demanded workload. This is because high utilization of resource unit is possible by fine-grained scaling option. However, for OS and managing agents, approx. 10% of the resource units are "wasted." At the same time, the higher number of units contributes to lower HA overheads. Worst-case HA wastes 50% with a "hot-standby." For example, three units can be used up to 66% to be able to cover the outage of one of the units. The loss of 33% "spare capacity" and 10% for basic overhead are smaller than 50%. The concept works also on scale, e.g., nine units, in this case approx. one unit (~10%) is used for "basic overheads." But, also only ~10% is needed as "spare capacity" for "takeover" cases. Overall, only ~20% is "wasted." Based on Amdahl's law the value comes asymptotic to 10%; it is a theoretical view because it does not cover the "buffer capacity" for peaks/spikes in the workload. Of course, it helps to use bigger units if the value comes "closer" to the 10% by using a double or triple unit size to reduce the overhead value from 10% to 5% or 3%, but an additional buffer capacity is still needed for real-life scenarios. Based on this analysis T-Rex does not use the "hot-standby" HA approach for workload scaling. T-Rex currently runs fine with the three-node approach. An exception is the database which only works in the hot-standby setup for HA (like most relational database systems (RDS)).

Where possible, avoid HA based on standby resources to reduce the redundancy capacity to 0. This is not always possible, but if the SLA/SLO can be reached by other approaches, the SLA should be realized with the resource-optimized footprint. The T-Rex DevOps team analyzed different approaches to realize the demanded availability. An approach that is possible is to optimize for an automatic "disaster recovery" (DR) by infrastructure as code (IaC) an outage time (MTTR) can be assured by the setup time of the DR-IaC script. In the case of T-Rex this is an acceptable approach. One site that has deployed T-Rex uses this approach since 1 year and saves 4/9 resource allocation of the 24*7 footprint in comparison to the resource-optimized HA footprint. The non-HA initiative started in 2021 as a diverse approach to the downsizing and optimization of the established HA setup with over-provisioned resources. One-year operational experience confirms approach to reduce MTTR and avoidance of noticeable outages. To realize the reduced footprint, the following actions are realized:

- IaC for setting up the complete service deployment in approx. 30 min (the DR approach).
- Green/blue deployments via IaC (trains the DevOps-team cyclic and often for the DR "case" and ensures that scripts are working as expected) for releasing, patching, etc. without downtimes for users.
- Restart checkpoints are defined for microservices to avoid noticeable outages of a container workloads.
- Automated job migration activated for the case of "losing" a worker instance to a new commissioned one.

As for storage, the data durability (at the end a kind of redundancy [47]) has to be evaluated for each data type. T-Rex distinguishes between easily reproducible data and data that is difficult to reproduce. Data which is easy to regenerate is not under backup (a kind of duplication and redundancy) or stored with direct redundancy (like RAID or S3).

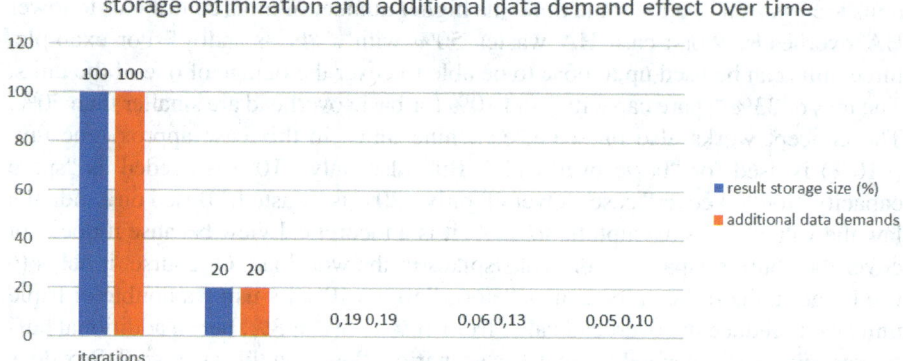

**Fig. 10.3** Iteration effects about result storage size: compression, retention policy, non-redundancy, optimized compression—but changing respective additional data demand has a negative impact

**Persistence management** To reduce the overall amount of storage, data compression is used. Depending on the use case of the data, an adequate compression algorithm has to be selected. Existing algorithms have different compression rates and different execution times. Also, the decompression performance has a high variation [48]. In the case of T-Rex, the compression is done once, while the decompression is done repeatedly. This leads to selecting an algorithm with a good trade-off of data compression rate and decompression performance. T-Rex started with the default zlib and selects zstd as the second compression optimization.

A huge effect can also be realized with data-delete policies. These have to be defined specifically for each stored data type. In the case of T-Rex, the default, e.g., test result retention time from years was reduced to weeks for the data type with the biggest proportion of all data.

Figure 10.3 shows the realized optimization per job result. With the future application of all currently realistic and practicable optimizations, all additional data demands about result-related data like more comprehensive logs, more runtime meta-data etc. will directly lead to growing results and demanded storage. This trend is visible.

**Workload management** Performance and resource utilization/efficiency have to be balanced under sustainability aspects. An example of T-Rex that customers want is fast job execution but also cheap job execution costs. From the technical perspective a fast job start runs on "pre-provisioned" infrastructure significantly faster than to wait for the on-demand provisioning. Pre-provisioned infrastructures is idling until job assignment. From the resource utilization and efficiency view a suboptimal approach. The provision on demand takes time for building everything. From the additional sustainability view the "compromise" is to use in the default case the job infrastructure provisioning on demand, but offers as option a pre-provisioning for dedicated job. So the user can pre-provision the demanded infrastructure for selected tests. Provisioning time is well-known and can be planned by customers and the idle time can be reduced to a short time like seconds. Also the pre-provisioning is metered and shown in the resource consumption dashboard of the users' account.

Also security, efficiency, and performance by infrastructure "reuse" needs to be balanced with a sustainability view. Reuse reduces the provisioning resource allocation efforts and leads to a speedup of the phase to prepare the test-job execution. This performance gains comes with a risk for security because reused resources have, e.g., to be cleaned properly. This cleaning is also a kind of provisioning effort. Furthermore, the reuse really works only if workload can be queued to a batch processing—this reduces individual job delivery performance by the "waiting time." A kind of pre-provisioning of resources waiting for an incoming job is not efficient. From the sustainability perspective a resource is provisioned on demand or reused if a resource is ready for decommissioning. A practical trade-off in this scenario to balance the different views is:

Default job execution is on-demand with a provisioning based on

- Provision on-demand time to avoid significant idle time of resources

  - Leads to high elastic resource allocation

- Avoids reuse of resources for high security and reduction of other side-effect risks impacting determinism
- Requires to optimize resource provision phase to minimize time from test-job demand to test result

  - Leads to minimize containers and other starting relevant parameters

Optional job execution with pre-provisioned resources to optimize time to market.

Optional job execution based on reused/shared resources. Useful for some use-cases such a checks without high requirements about test executions.

To handle, e.g., small regression test-jobs as a dynamic workload in a resource-efficient way, an autoscaler is implemented. In the first step small workloads are group to resource units to have high utilization. In the second step the resource units are scaled to handle the elastic job workloads. The autoscaler ensures that resources are dynamically allocated and decommissioned to handle the demand. To make the autoscaling cloud platform independent, the allocation management is realized via Rancher. Currently the workload is mostly triggered by customers CI/CD chains. These external triggers are independent and can cause spiky workloads if all want their nightly build related regression tests, e.g., at 2:00 a.m. to run. In the next step the trigger can use an optional time range like run the test between 1:30 and 2:30 a.m. to give the execution runtime the option to schedule tests in a kind of "batch" within the customer-defined time range to avoid scaling peaks.

**Measures and learnings** To summarize the instantiation of the measurement indicators for cloud service sustainability, a specific mapping to the cloud service is needed to define the refined measures like *storage for results* for the specific cloud service. The approach of measure relative improvement against the starting point baseline (100%) about CPU, RAM, storage and network is useful to show improvements. Also, the aspects for improvement are useful but need specific selection and instantiation—e.g., what and how to cache? This shows that use case and scenario-specific optimizations and trade-offs can be found with the generic approach. From the presented pool of practices and levers, engineers can choose for their setup and scenarios and initiate a continuous improvement journey. The journey always searches for new opportunities like generic applicable lazy loading for containers to reduce overall workload runtime.

One more thing: sustainability engineering can start with zero budget on an annual view, because by smart selection of actions also cost savings can be realized to "(re-)finance" the engineering efforts and costs. However, step by step, it gets harder to realize enough savings—the effort to implement actions grows in relation to the savings or optimizations realized. This leads to an asymptotic curve of the realized effects (see figures in discussion).

## 10.5   Discussion

A positive learning around availability was that the non-HA deployment of T-Rex runs well for more than a year now. The optimizations about fast recovery was good enough to keep the customers satisfied. With the IaC approach and the green/blue deployments to train the disaster recovery plan, the SLO can be realized without additional standby-based failover resources. However, not all availability demands can be realized with optimized service outage recovery times in combination with reactive actions for smaller outages on cluster level. Alternatives with standby resources directly have negative impact to the footprint. As long as the setup is stable, the standby resources can be provisioned static—the current scenario on another T-Rex setup. It becomes more difficult in the case of dynamic behavior of the microservices, and it is nontrivial to find the best sizing of resource units to minimize "overhead waste" by addressing the dynamic demands. This can become a near future scenario for T-Rex. It is nontrivial because the overhead waste depends on the amount of deployed microservices, deamon sets, etc.; additional investigation about rebalancing the instances for the HA setup is needed to address the dynamic provisioning of an adequate amount of standby resources. The amount of standby resources is depending on current running services and the upcoming changes to ensure the needed standby resources for the demanded availability target in the changed setup. It has to optimize at least two dimensions: (1) the number of instances, and (2) the size of the instances has to change and then the running services have to migrate to the new best-fit HA setup. This is a nontrivial task, especially for non-stateless microservices. Furthermore, it is difficult to predict how long the new best-fit HA setup is relevant before a new "rebalancing" of the resources is needed.

Why not serverless? Serverless is not by design "green" [5], because its cost model motivates "short runtime" which leads to more "context-switch" costs which are coming with overheads. The current price model shows that up to ca. 60% vCPU overheads are calculated for the same revenue per virtual machine (based on 1.5GB Lamba vs c7a.medium EC2) without saving plans (e.g., 29%/a) which make the overhead buffer higher this results in ca. 61% and with saving plan in 43% vCPU utilization as breakeven point. For a corresponding t-instance the vCPU utilization is approx. the half (and fits with the baseline credits of a t2.small which is 20%). For this hypothetical vCPU oriented "price model", a higher utilization than the 20% of the t-instance or 43% for the c-instance shows that a lot of buffer for the context switch is reserved (or is CSP profit); the CSPs have to demonstrate that serverless like Lambda is greener than non-serverless deployments, especially in the case of interpreted code with the runtime start overhead negative scenarios can "occur" for real business value-workloads. A rough concept for a potential AWS serverless architecture of the presented T-Rex service could look like to setup it on the EKS Kubernetes service with Fargate containers for the microservices and usage of the ECR cache service for caching to run the 24*7 services and dedicated EC2 based on-demand customer workload instances. The question is how much more efficient is the serverless approach? Additionally, serverless currently "costs" the cloud agnostic, because every CSP offers its proprietary serverless approach. Without a cloud-agnostic setup, at least the Rancher instance(s) can be "saved." This shows that cloud agnostic comes in this example case with 25% CPU "overhead" and some additional RAM for the, e.g., m6a.large instance(s).

CSPs do not give relevant energy indicators in real time (e.g., AWS months delayed). Furthermore, the setting of all values to "zero" by green energy contracting (e.g., AWS dashboard) does not really help, because it can stop working on "customer" side, if everything is presented by the dashboard as done.

CSPs do not directly correlate pricing and resource footprint. An example for compute resource (instances) allocations in the setup of the T-Rex example and their price is shown in Fig. 10.4. The first improvement iteration with the downsizing of instances "by design" correlates. However, the price of architecture design of the CPU does not correlate with the power efficiency and looks like "political pricing." A more sustainability-oriented pricing approach would help to optimize simultaneously sustainability and costs. Other resources like storage have similar weak correlation behavior between cost and sustainability.

Limitations of the presented work are that the case study does not address all possible scenarios within the analyzed aspects. Furthermore, the work does not address all existing CSP offers. However, the analyzed energy parameters of a cloud service with CPU, RAM, storage, and network are basics in each IT setup and a good starting point. Of course, existing workloads with other energy-intensive resources depending for example on GPUs or tensor cores. The proposed levers and concepts for CPU energy footprint optimization are transferable as long as the GPU or tensor cores are seen as a specialized CPU.

The long-term view about the behavior of the software and hardware correlation of Wirth's law has to be investigated in more real-world cases with active

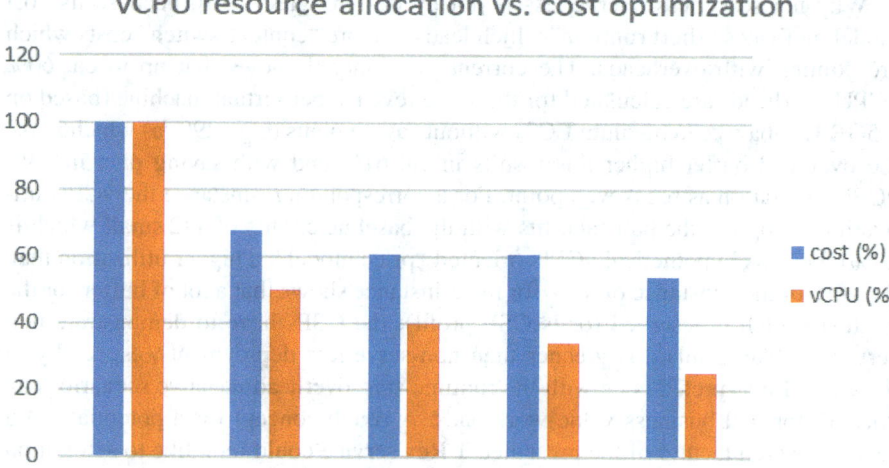

**Fig. 10.4** Sustainability optimization for, e.g., vCPU can have also cost-saving effects

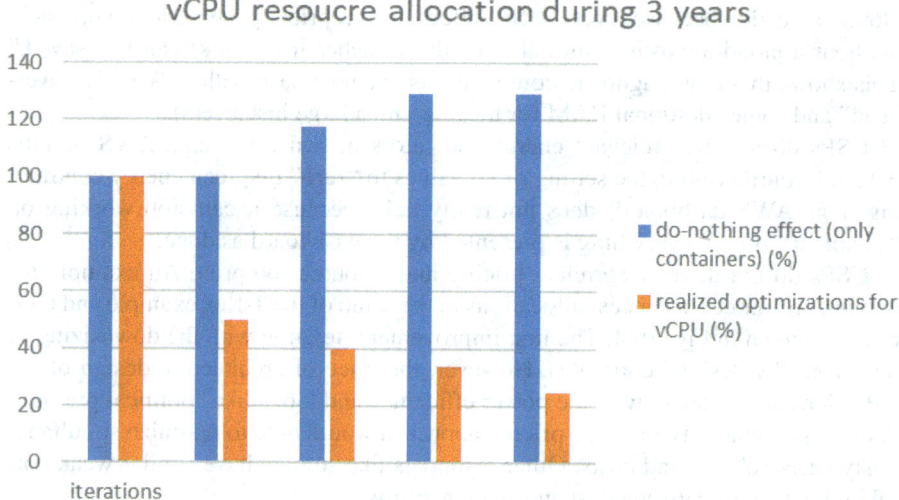

**Fig. 10.5** Instead of growing software and corresponding additional hardware demand (Wirth's law), the sustainability engineering reduces the footprint

sustainability engineering. Figure 10.5 shows the do-nothing effect for the container actions realized in the last 3 years. The real do-nothing effect is higher with all the other actions realized in this time, too. The hypothesis—for a worst-case scenario—assumes that if no further improvements are realized in the future the approx. 100% vCPU footprint against the starting point will be saved (realized by conservation of status quo offset). However, a more realistic scenario, in real life the engineers now have gained in the last 3 years a high awareness about sustainability engineering and the future design decisions, technology selection etc. will show effects on the (software) growing factor. This impacts Wirth's law for the case that the (software) growing factor becomes smaller than Moore's law factor for the hardware.

The best effect to address Wirth's law is avoiding to add new code. This leads with a strategic view into the direction to develop a smart demand management with focusing to do the right things lean from the footprint perspective. The requirement engineering becomes an important role to ensure less software growing by design together with the architecture and design. This approach leads to the establishment of a "sufficiency mindset" by the business (customer) and the demand management which defines the sufficiency within the requirements (respective stories in agile setups).

But in real world the issue is engineering capacity. A trend about the real currency in IT becomes engineering hours and not money. Because so many topics are in the backlog but nobody can do it because the lack of software or cloud engineers is the limiting factor—not the money which is available to finance the implementation of the backlog items and its corresponding demands. So, the real question is how to gain speed with sustainability engineering if no software, cloud, etc. engineers are available to do the work?

## 10.6   Summary and Outlook

An overall summary is that with active sustainability engineering cloud services significantly can be optimized for their energy footprint. Especially, if default settings from CSPs and other standard patterns are used for HA, durability, etc., this insight is important because the hype about cloud usage comes with this overhead on energy footprint as long as no active sustainability engineering is established. The presented deep dives about "white boxing" the cloud service and its sub- or microservices, building blocks, and components are used to optimize the footprint. Furthermore, it is a journey which never terminates—as shown by the presented examples like the evaluation of the new serverless option against established virtual server instances or the selection of the most energy efficient CPU type available for the workload because the cloud is continuously evolving and each new thing should be analyzed because it can be a vehicle to optimize the sustainability. The presented work results and contribution can be summarized in a practical and theoretical contribution.

Contribution to practice:

– Not all cloud services and resources are sufficiently transparent for an effective sustainability engineering. Especially, serverless services have unclear tipping points like about optimizations of shorter runtime of functions calls vs. internal overhead to run a call.

- As long as no direct metrics and values are offered by the CSPs, only relative optimizations of resource allocations are effective approaches. This helps to show trends, but does not exactly show the impact of a sustainability-driven optimization.
- Proxy metrics like utilization or units of cloud resources are needed to "measure" and optimize carbon footprint. Limitations of this approach are to find the trade-offs with the tipping points between different units without a basic calibration as common base. A calibration is useful and needed because often optimization-scenarios effecting different units and have to be compared which only works if they have a common base.

Contribution to theory:

- Generic levers for sustainability engineering are not depending on technology like availability of the service, its data or the compression; however, the realized effects are strongly depending on the used implementation and the used technologies.
- A set of indicators is identified for continuous sustainability engineering for software and IT systems.
- The most effects in sustainability engineering for cloud service are realized in the layer of logical resource allocation and the optimization of software units.
- The focus of potential cloud sustainability research is limited because the transparency approaches of the CSPs is a limiting factor.

The outlook goes in the direction of greener code and architecture as the base for green deployments. In particular, measuring the sustainability impact of changed or added code fragments is important. For developers, it would be useful to have support for architecture and design pattern elicitation to foster sustainable solutions based on greener code. Furthermore, monitoring of indicators and KPIs to measure the "greenness factor" of the service is needed. This starts during development at least on code level and goes to operations to see real deployment footprints [49]. The operational measures help to start an effective continuous improvement cycle [50] to see the effects of the code changes under real workloads. Also interesting would be an account checker on cloud-platform level which indicates potential sustainability issues—similar to security checks which are often included into the governance services of CSPs.

# References

1. Pesce, M. (2021, July). *Cloud Computing's coming energy crisis*. IEEE Spectrum. https://spectrum.ieee.org/cloud-computings-coming-energy-crisis
2. *AWS carbon footprint tool*. Accessed December 2022, from https://aws.amazon.com/about-aws/whats-new/2022/03/aws-launches-customer-carbon-footprint-tool/
3. *Azure emissions impact dashboard*. Accessed December 2022, from https://azure.microsoft.com/en-us/blog/empowering-cloud-sustainability-with-the-microsoft-emissions-impact-dashboard/

4. *Google carbon footprint*. Accessed December 2022, from https://cloud.google.com/carbon-footprint
5. Poth, A., Schubert, N., & Riel, A. (2020, September). Sustainability efficiency challenges of modern it architectures–a quality model for serverless energy footprint. In *European Conference on Software Process Improvement* (pp. 289–301). Springer.
6. Mohan, A., Sane, H., Doshi, K., Edupuganti, S., Nayak, N., & Sukhomlinov, V. (2019). Agile cold starts for scalable serverless. In 11th USENIX Workshop on Hot Topics in Cloud Computing (HotCloud 19).
7. Silva, P., Fireman, D., & Pereira, T. E. (2020). *Prebaking functions to warm the serverless cold start*. Proceedings of the 21st International Middleware Conference.
8. Poth, A., & Iliev, E. (2022). Enhancing the ISO 25010 for evaluating the quality in clouds and cloud services. In *European Conference on Software Process Improvement* (pp. 459–472). Springer.
9. Poth, A., Widok, A. H., Henschel, A., & Eißfeldt, D. (2022). Foster Sustainable Software Engineering (SSE) awareness in large enterprises–a cheat sheet for technical and organizational indicators. In *European Conference on Software Process Improvement* (pp. 60–74). Springer.
10. Piraghaj, S. F., Dastjerdi, A. V., Calheiros, R. N., & Buyya, R. (2017). A survey and taxonomy of energy efficient resource management techniques in platform as a service cloud. In J. Chen, Y. Zhang, & R. Gottschalk (Eds.), *Handbook of research on end-to-end cloud computing architecture design* (pp. 410–454). IGI Global. https://doi.org/10.4018/978-1-5225-0759-8.ch017
11. Bharany, S., Badotra, S., Sharma, S., Rani, S., Alazab, M., Jhaveri, R. H., & Gadekallu, T. R. (2022). Energy efficient fault tolerance techniques in green cloud computing: A systematic survey and taxonomy. *Sustainable Energy Technologies and Assessments, 53*, 102613.
12. Vafamehr, A., & Khodayar, M. E. (2018). Energy-aware cloud computing. *Electricity Journal, 31*(2), 40–49. https://doi.org/10.1016/j.tej.2018.01.009
13. Lloyd, W., Ramesh, S., Chinthalapati, S., Ly, L., & Pallickara, S. (2018). Serverless computing: An investigation of factors influencing microservice performance. In *2018 IEEE International Conference on Cloud Engineering (IC2E)* (pp. 159–169). https://doi.org/10.1109/IC2E.2018.00039
14. de Nardin, I. F., da Righi, R. R., Lopes, T. R., Costa, C., & YoungYeom, H. (2021). On revisiting energy and performance in microservices applications: A cloud elasticity-driven approach. *Parallel Computing, 108*, 102858. https://doi.org/10.1016/j.parco.2021.102858
15. Xu, M., Toosi, A. N., & Buyya, R. (2019). iBrownout: An integrated approach for managing energy and brownout in container-based clouds. *IEEE Transactions on Sustainable Computing, 4*(1), 53–66. https://doi.org/10.1109/TSUSC.2018.2808493
16. Khomh, F., & Abtahizadeh, S. (2018). Understanding the impact of cloud patterns on performance and energy consumption. *Journal of Systems and Software, 141*, 151–170. https://doi.org/10.1016/j.jss.2018.03.063
17. Saboor, A., Mahmood, A. K., Omar, A. H., et al. (2022). Enabling rank-based distribution of microservices among containers for green cloud computing environment. *Peer-to-Peer Networking and Applications, 15*, 77–91. https://doi.org/10.1007/s12083-021-01218-y
18. Patros, P., Spillner, J., Papadopoulos, A. V., Varghese, B., Rana, O., & Dustdar, S. (2021). Toward sustainable serverless computing. *IEEE Internet Computing, 25*(6), 42–50. https://doi.org/10.1109/MIC.2021.3093105
19. Denninnart, C., & Salehi, M. A. (2021). *Efficiency in the serverless cloud computing paradigm: A survey study*. arXiv preprint arXiv:2110.06508.
20. Jia, X., & Zhao, L. (2021). RAEF: Energy-efficient resource allocation through energy fungibility in serverless. In *2021 IEEE 27th International Conference on Parallel and Distributed Systems (ICPADS)* (pp. 434–441). https://doi.org/10.1109/ICPADS53394.2021.00060
21. Katal, A., Dahiya, S., & Choudhury, T. (2022). Energy efficiency in cloud computing data centers: A survey on software technologies. *Cluster Computing*. https://doi-org.sid2nomade-1.grenet.fr/10.1007/s10586-022-03713-0

22. Chauhan, N. S., & Saxena, A. (2013). A green software development life cycle for cloud computing. *IT Professional, 15*(1), 28–34. https://doi.org/10.1109/MITP.2013.6
23. Steigerwald, B., & Agrawal, A. (2011). Developing green software. *Intel White Paper, 9.*
24. Hameed, A., Khoshkbarforoushha, A., Ranjan, R., et al. (2016). A survey and taxonomy on energy efficient resource allocation techniques for cloud computing systems. *Computing, 98,* 751–774. https://doi-org.sid2nomade-1.grenet.fr/10.1007/s00607-014-0407-8
25. Lee, Y. C., & Zomaya, A. Y. (2012). Energy efficient utilization of resources in cloud computing systems. *The Journal of Supercomputing, 60,* 268–280. https://doi-org.sid2nomade-1. grenet.fr/10.1007/s11227-010-0421-3
26. Zhou, Z., Abawajy, J., Chowdhury, M., Hu, Z., Li, K., Cheng, H., et al. (2018). Minimizing SLA violation and power consumption in Cloud data centers using adaptive energy-aware algorithms. *Future Generation Computer Systems, 86,* 836–850.
27. Qu, C., Calheiros, R. N., & Buyya, R. (2016). A reliable and cost-efficient auto-scaling system for web applications using heterogeneous spot instances. *Journal of Network and Computer Applications, 65,* 167–180.
28. Kim, W., & Mvulla, J. (2013). Reducing resource over-provisioning using workload shaping for energy efficient cloud computing. *Applied Mathematics & Information Sciences, 7*(5), 2097.
29. Lin, W., Wang, H., Zhang, Y., Qi, D., Wang, J. Z., & Chang, V. (2018). A cloud server energy consumption measurement system for heterogeneous cloud environments. *Information Sciences, 468,* 47–62.
30. Lin, W., Shi, F., Wu, W., Li, K., Wu, G., & Mohammed, A. A. (2020). A taxonomy and survey of power models and power modeling for cloud servers. *ACM Computing Surveys (CSUR), 53*(5), 1–41.
31. Lin, C.-C., Liu, P., & Wu, J.-J. (2011). Energy-aware virtual machine dynamic provision and scheduling for cloud computing. In *2011 IEEE 4th International Conference on Cloud Computing* (pp. 736–737). https://doi.org/10.1109/CLOUD.2011.94
32. Chen, Q., Grosso, P., Veldt, K., Laat, C., Hofman, R., & Bal, H. (2011). Profiling energy consumption of VMs for green cloud computing. In *2011 IEEE Ninth International Conference on Dependable, Autonomic and Secure Computing* (pp. 768–775). https://doi.org/10.1109/ DASC.2011.131
33. Wu, W., Lin, W., & Peng, Z. (2017). An intelligent power consumption model for virtual machines under CPU-intensive workload in cloud environment. *Soft Computing, 21*(19), 5755–5764.
34. *Digital infrastructure definition.* Accessed December 2022, from https://sdialliance.org/ dictionary/digital-infrastructure/
35. *Digital infrastructure taxonomy.* Accessed December 2022, from https://knowledge.sdial-liance.org/taxonomy
36. Gene, A. (1967). Validity of the single processor approach to achieving large-scale computing capabilities. *AFIPS Conference Proceedings, 30,* 483–485.
37. Wirth, N. (1995). A plea for lean software. *Computer, 28*(2), 64–68. https://doi. org/10.1109/2.348001
38. Rodgers, D. P. (1985, June). Improvements in multiprocessor system design. *ACM SIGARCH Computer Architecture News, 13*(3), 225–231 [p. 226]. ACM. https://doi. org/10.1145/327070.327215. ISBN 0-8186-0634-7. ISSN 0163-5964. S2CID 7083878.
39. Dalbhanjan, P. (2015). *Overview of deployment options on aws.* Amazon Whitepapers.
40. Poth, A., Rrjolli, O., & Riel, A. (2022, December). Integration-and system-testing aligned with cloud-native approaches for DevOps. In *2022 IEEE 22nd International Conference on Software Quality, Reliability, and Security Companion (QRS-C)* (pp. 201–208). IEEE.
41. *Announcing Amazon EC2 C7g instances powered by AWS Graviton3* | Amazon Web Services. Accessed December 2022, from https://youtu.be/JY4EimMEi_A
42. *AMD EPYC energy efficiency.* Accessed December 2022, from https://www.amd.com/en/ campaigns/epyc-energy-efficiency

43. *Benchmark r5a instance*. Accessed December 2022, from https://browser.geekbench.com/v5/cpu/535472
44. *Benchmark r6a instance*. Accessed December 2022, from https://browser.geekbench.com/v5/cpu/16867710
45. *Stargz snapshotter*. Accessed December 2022, from https://github.com/containerd/stargz-snapshotter8
46. *SOCI snapshotter*. Accessed December 2022, from https://github.com/awslabs/soci-snapshotter
47. Daher, Z., & Hajjdiab, H. (2018). Cloud storage comparative analysis amazon simple storage vs. Microsoft azure blob storage. *International Journal of Machine Learning and Computing, 8*(1), 85–89.
48. *Compression algorithms performance evaluation*. Accessed December 2022, from https://indico.cern.ch/event/695984/contributions/2872933/attachments/1590457/2516802/ZSTD_and_ZLIB_Updates_-_January_20186.pdf
49. Poth, A., Eißfeldt, D., Heimann, C., & Waschk, S. (2022, June). Sustainable IT in an agile DevOps setup leads to a shift left in sustainability engineering. In *International Conference on Agile Software Development* (pp. 21–28). Springer Nature Switzerland.
50. Poth, A., & Nunweiler, E. (2022, January). Develop sustainable software with a lean ISO 14001 setup facilitated by the efiS® framework. In *International Conference on Lean and Agile Software Development* (pp. 96–115). Springer.